Oman Reborn

OMAN REBORN

BALANCING TRADITION AND MODERNIZATION

Linda Pappas Funsch

First published in 2015 by PALGRAVE MACMILLAN® in the United States—a division of St. Martin's Press LLC, 175 Fifth Avenue, New York, NY 10010.

Where this book is distributed in the UK, Europe and the rest of the world, this is by Palgrave Macmillan, a division of Macmillan Publishers Limited, registered in England, company number 785998, of Houndmills, Basingstoke, Hampshire RG21 6XS.

Palgrave Macmillan is the global academic imprint of the above companies and has companies and representatives throughout the world.

Palgrave® and Macmillan® are registered trademarks in the United States, the United Kingdom, Europe and other countries.

ISBN: 978-1-137-50200-1

Library of Congress Cataloging-in-Publication Data

Funsch, Linda Pappas, 1947–
    Oman reborn : balancing tradition and modernization / Linda Pappas Funsch.
        pages cm
    Includes bibliographical references.
    ISBN 978-1-137-50200-1 (hardcover)
    1. Oman—History. I. Title.
    DS247.O68F86 2015
    953.53—dc23

                                                          2015005028

A catalogue record of the book is available from the British Library.

Design by Amnet.

First edition: September 2015

10 9 8 7 6 5 4 3 2

Printed in the United States of America.

For David

Contents

List of Illustrations

PREFACE

Little known in the West—or in the East, North, and South—and poorly understood—even in its own region—the Sultanate of Oman is arguably one of the few "good news" stories to emerge from the Middle East in the contemporary era. Largely ignored by a mainstream media that gravitates toward sensation and scandal, Oman remains a hidden gem—a land of ancient lore, natural beauty, and remarkable achievement—that promises to surprise, enchant, and delight.

Located along the southeastern coast of the Arabian Peninsula along one of the world's most important geostrategic and economic trade routes, Oman boasts stunning landscapes and breathtaking vistas, forbidding deserts and lush oases, dramatic mountain ranges and spectacular fjords. The diversity of the country's geographical features is mirrored to a great extent in its cultural landscape. Omani society is a mosaic of racial, linguistic, and religious traditions, a welcome departure from the all-too-familiar narrative of religious intolerance and wanton violence that routinely characterizes other realms of the oft-beleaguered region in which Oman is situated. "Comfortable in their own skin" and gifted with a sense of their collective "self," Omanis are renowned for navigating effortlessly within a culture of diversity. This sense of self is nowhere more apparent than in the hospitality Omanis show to visitors, whatever their faith or culture.

The prevailing acceptance of and respect for the *other* have been cultivated in large part by two major factors: an adherence to an Islamic tradition that is neither Sunni nor Shi'a—one that is somewhat elusive, surprisingly perhaps, to Muslims *as well as* to non-Muslims—and, a legacy of maritime trade and adventures to distant corners of the globe that has cultivated within the Omani national psyche a certain cosmopolitanism, including a pronounced affinity for harmonious interaction with peoples of disparate traditions.

One of the oldest independent countries in the Arab and Muslim world, Oman differs from many of its neighbors in the Middle East. Although its freedom was briefly compromised by Portuguese occupation in the sixteenth and seventeenth centuries, its sovereignty was restored and has continued without interruption to this day. Oman reemerged as a formidable maritime power, establishing its influence and hegemony over vast swaths of valuable distant lands. It is this legacy of independence and sovereignty that unites

Omanis today and, to a great extent, informs their relations with other nations.

Oman not only stands apart from many of its neighbors, but it is unique among postimperial countries in many ways. Its dramatic reemergence in the modern era has been undertaken, consciously and methodically, with a keen eye and an unwavering vision, mindful of its rich and distinctive history and culture. Oman neither adopts modernization and Westernization wholesale nor rejects their components outright. Rather, the standard markers of modernization and Westernization are evaluated individually; each is weighed and measured in terms of its own merits and in the context of a clear and deliberate national agenda.

The twentieth-century Omani narrative is the stuff of legend. It is a story of tribes, desert nomads, and seafarers who, having struggled for many centuries amid harsh conditions, emerged from virtual obscurity and economic deprivation in the third quarter of the twentieth century to form a cohesive, modern, yet culturally authentic, nation-state.

The transformation of Oman, impressive in so many ways, is no accident. As the country has steadily reassumed its place in the global arena in less than two generations, its guiding force has been and continues to be Qaboos bin Said, the sultan of Oman, who has presided over his country's transition, transforming it into a paradigm of modernization and development.

Renowned as an "island of stability" in a turbulent ocean, Oman thrives today as a country of moderate and realistic policies, inspired by a respected head of state with a long-term strategic vision. While the sultanate has enjoyed a history of amicable relations with the United States and Great Britain for more than two centuries and counting, in today's tumultuous, and often chaotic, arena of international affairs it stands as an effective interlocutor and mediator between regional and global adversaries. As contemporary airwaves and cyberspace are dominated by unrelenting torrents of hyperbole—replete with threatening ultimatums, sanctions, and presumed "red lines"—Oman's leadership adheres to an independent and measured foreign policy, acting frequently by design, and preferably out of the limelight, to bridge diplomatic chasms in the interest of peace.

My personal association with Oman is longstanding, beginning in the very early years of an era that its citizens refer to as the modern renaissance (*al-nahda*). Little did I realize on my first visit four decades ago that I would be an eyewitness to pivotal moments in that country's rebirth.

I first visited Oman in 1974 while serving as a project specialist with the Ford Foundation's regional headquarters in Beirut, Lebanon. At the time, I was working with an international team on the design, funding, and monitoring of a research study intended to identify and prioritize areas of critical concern in the fields of maternal and child health, basic education, nutrition, and family planning for village women in Oman.[1] Beyond a hazy idea that the country was likely to be fascinating, Oman was for me, like many others, largely unknown and shrouded in mystery.

Our host was the then-Ministry of Social Affairs and Labor. The ministry invited representatives of nongovernmental organizations and specialists from the American University in Beirut and the United Nations Children's Fund (UNICEF) to review the results of fieldwork that the Ford Foundation and UNICEF had sponsored in the historic towns of Nizwa and Sohar. Ultimately, these efforts resulted in the publication and distribution of a culturally appropriate manual for child care and nutrition,[2] recommendations for an instructional television series, and the design of accessible educational materials for women in rural areas.

In our travels throughout the country, we met national policymakers and we had discussions with, and received input and comment from, local leaders and villagers. The women of our delegation were also warmly welcomed into the inner sanctum of the private family quarter of Omani homes to share coffee, dates, conversation, and, sometimes, even henna tattoos with the ladies of the house.

As we traversed the country's rugged terrain on what at times appeared to be potentially impassable roads, a world unfolded before each and every one of us, a world unlike any we had previously experienced. Everywhere were scenes seemingly plucked from the pages of *One Thousand and One Nights*. Here was an ancient land, vast parts of it ensnared in relative isolation from the outside world, not for years but for decades, suddenly poised for a dramatic debut into the modern age. The Omanis' sense of purpose, combined with almost giddy optimism, was exciting to behold then as it is even now.

That brief interlude in Oman in the 1970s had a profound effect on me. What stood out in my mind, in particular, was the clear resolve and extraordinary courage, vision, and commitment of its young leader, Sultan Qaboos, whose determination to change the course of Oman's modern narrative has not wavered. Throughout the ensuing years, I continued to follow with great interest, albeit from a considerable distance, reports of the myriad changes that were transforming Oman into a dynamic and modern nation-state.

Imagine my delight, therefore, during a cold February day in 2006, at receiving an invitation from the Washington-based National Council on US-Arab Relations (National Council) to return to the sultanate after an absence of thirty-two years. On this journey, I would be accompanied by my husband, David, a select group of American educators, and some US Central Command (CENTCOM)[3] military personnel for a ten-day "Anthropological Immersion Experience in Oman."

Our Omani adventure would be led by two exceedingly capable gentlemen: the first, the National Council's founding president and CEO, John Duke Anthony—long an internationally respected specialist on Arabia and the Gulf, whose grasp of the history, culture, and dynamics of the countries that line that littoral, or coastline, of eastern Arabia, from Kuwait to Oman, plus Yemen and beyond, is unrivaled. In May 1981, Anthony, who first visited Oman in 1971, only a year after the accession of Sultan Qaboos to the throne, witnessed the birth of the Gulf Cooperation Council (GCC), an important subregional organization of six countries, including Bahrain,

Kuwait, Oman, Qatar, Saudi Arabia, and the United Arab Emirates. Since the organization's inception, he is the only Westerner to have been invited to attend each of the GCC Ministerial and Heads of State summits.

The second capable gentleman to accompany us was Peter J. Ochs II, or "Peachey," author of the *Maverick Guide to Oman*, the first English-language guidebook on the sultanate published in the United States. Peachey's intimate knowledge of Oman's unusual, rugged terrain would be invaluable, particularly as we frequently strayed far off the beaten path.

That study visit was designed as a broad cultural undertaking, intended to provide the participants with firsthand exposure to Oman's land, sea, and people. What an unprecedented departure this assignment would be for our military companions, whose previous experiences in the general region had been confined largely to the war-torn fields of battle in Iraq and Afghanistan.

The itinerary read like one that might have been plucked from the pages of *National Geographic*. During the course of our two-week adventure, we would explore the sultanate's picturesque coastal regions and pristine beaches. Our journey would take us across barren mountain ranges, venturing beyond paved roads in all-wheel-drive vehicles across great *wadis* (dried river beds) and massive sand dunes.

Stopping in remote villages and lush oases, we would meet with potters, weavers, and tribal folk. Who could resist the prospect of sleeping under the desert sky in a Bedouin camp or sailing with Arab mariners aboard a legendary dhow, or traditional sailing vessel, as they navigated with surprising dexterity around the majestic fjords of the Musandam peninsula near the all-important Strait of Hormuz?

It was a stunning and unforgettable experience. But after an absence of just over three decades, what struck me most were the changes I witnessed, which had transformed Oman from an isolated and stagnant backwater to a thoroughly modern emerging regional power and international player—without forfeiting its rich history or enduring culture. This astounding transformation inspired me to publish a seven-part multimedia series of articles from the perspective of one who had observed this remarkable "renaissance" from two distinct vantage points—on the one hand, from only four years after it began, and on the other, some three decades later, from the then-unfolding present.[4]

The enthusiasm generated by this publication led to a further investigation of Oman's distinctive paradigm of fast-paced, but measured, development. Subsequent visits to the sultanate have enabled me to appreciate, on a variety of levels, the profound historical underpinnings of the Omani renaissance while, at the same time, marveling at its many manifestations. I am indebted to the Office of the Adviser to His Majesty the Sultan for Cultural Affairs and to the Ministry of Information for their confidence in this project and for arranging travel, accommodations, and access to a broad spectrum of Omani society, including high-level officials. Meetings and interviews with Omanis of various backgrounds have led me to understand more fully many of the important cultural nuances that are often absent from some of the more familiar journalistic accounts of this country's transformation. My determination to share this story with others has been strengthened further by the Omanis themselves, whose sheer delight and sincere appreciation upon learning of a foreigner's interest in their beloved land is palpable.

Throughout this journey, I have been struck by the leadership, priorities, and resolve that have enabled the sultanate to make a relatively seamless transition to a dynamic present without a corresponding loss of traditional values. For more than four decades, Oman's citizens have been inspired by a single individual whose commitment to public welfare is acknowledged far and wide, whose independent foreign policy is in many ways unequalled in the region, and whose all-encompassing spirit of national identity is made manifest in a climate of optimism and unity.

As a lifelong student of the Middle East, I feel privileged to have been introduced to Oman relatively early in my career and to have had the extraordinary opportunity to witness firsthand the country's remarkable transformation. This is a story of national development in which *all* citizens, women as well as men, play a vital role. It is a story that is, in many ways, distinctly Omani—a logical extension of the sultanate's proud culture and history.

It is my hope that this book will enable me to share the inspiring story of an important—and, in many ways, a globally vital—country, together with its history, its people, and its emergence into the modern age.

Linda Pappas Funsch
Frederick, Maryland

ACKNOWLEDGMENTS

I owe a tremendous debt of gratitude to John Duke Anthony, founding president and CEO of the National Council on US-Arab Relations. It was at his invitation that I returned to Oman in 2006 after an absence of more than thirty years. This singular experience set into motion a chain of events, including several visits, that only heightened my interest in that enchanting country. His input has been invaluable as I have sought to unravel the essence of the Omani mystique.

Hunaina Sultan al-Mughairy, the ambassador of Oman to the United States, was the first to suggest that I write a book about her beloved country. Her continued interest in and support for this project has inspired me to write a scholarly account that I hope will prove worthy of her trust.

The Office of the Adviser to His Majesty the Sultan for Cultural Affairs has on several occasions facilitated my travel to Oman, in addition to providing logistical support within the country. I wish to express my gratitude, in particular, to Abdul Aziz bin Mohammed al-Rowas for giving so generously of his time through many hours of interviews. His unique perspective and valuable insights have led me to a deeper appreciation of the nuances of the Omani "renaissance." Substantive conversations with Said bin Nasser bin Ali al-Salmi, director general of the Office of the Adviser, have further enhanced my understanding of the country.

I am indebted to Oman's Ministry of Information and, in particular, to Abdulmunim bin Mansoor bin Said al-Hasani, and to his predecessor, Hamad bin Mohammed al-Rashdi, for providing opportunities for field research on several occasions.

In the early years of this project, I had the good fortune to meet Said Abdullah al-Harthy, a former public affairs specialist at the US Embassy in Muscat from the village of Mudharib. My understanding of Oman has been enhanced substantially by the knowledge gleaned from our many conversations.

Frances D. Cook, a former US ambassador to Oman (1995–1999), has been a valued friend and stalwart supporter of this project, providing me not only with her own learned opinions on the subject but also with a continuous flow of information from a wide variety of sources.

Several friends and colleagues reviewed and commented on earlier drafts of this manuscript. In this context I should like to acknowledge, in addition to John Duke Anthony, Graham Leonard, Heidi Shoup, Noel J. Guckian, and Jeremy Jones. Although their input was invaluable, responsibility for errors or omissions remains mine alone.

I would like to express my gratitude to Palgrave Macmillan for believing in, supporting, and publishing this volume. Special thanks go to Farideh Koohi-Kamali and to her highly professional team, in particular, Veronica Goldstein.

I am grateful to Margaret Procario for helping to put the manuscript in its final form. During endless days and evenings, she reorganized the text, tightened the verbiage, scrutinized the grammar, and doggedly attempted to persuade me that the *Chicago Manual of Style* trumped my own. Her skill, perseverance, and friendship have been invaluable.

I wish to pay tribute to my family for their patience and fortitude during this extended, if often inconvenient, journey into uncharted waters. To Alexandra and Catherine and, especially, to Andrew—who came to my rescue at the eleventh hour with a masterful map of Oman that serves to enhance the narrative—I thank you. Robert N. Wood III has been invaluable as my trusted counselor and literary reviewer. I am deeply appreciative to you all.

I am indebted to my parents, George and Margaret Pappas, quintessential educators both, for it was they who instilled in me from an early age a sense of adventure—a "wanderlust"—predicated upon respect for all traditions. From our family's earliest trips to the Middle East and beyond, they emphasized the importance of keeping an open mind, appreciating diverse histories and cultures, and seeking the common bond that unites people the world over.

David J. Funsch, my husband and partner, has been a source of strength and inspiration for nearly forty years. Steadfast in his support of my quest to understand and interpret the complexities of the Middle East, he has accompanied me on many international journeys and encouraged me in various professional pursuits, no matter how unpopular. It is my honor to dedicate the book to him.

Finally, I am indebted to the people of Oman for providing me with the inspiration to write about their beautiful country. Throughout my travels in the sultanate, I have been struck repeatedly by the kindness and hospitality of the Omanis. Theirs is a culture of welcome and promise. Theirs is a story that must be told. I hope that they will find in my account an accurate reflection of their beloved land.

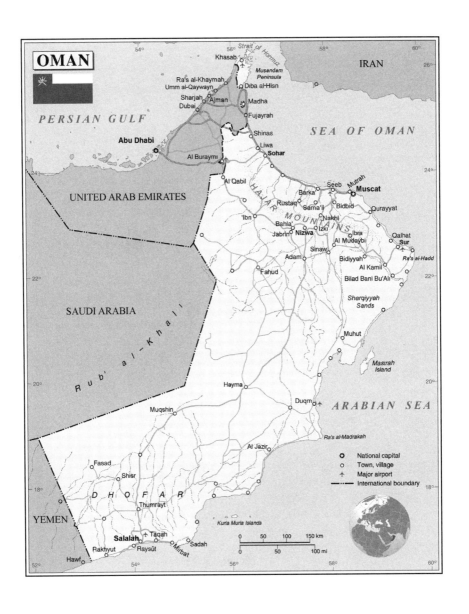

INTRODUCTION

A "GOOD NEWS" STORY FROM THE MIDDLE EAST

Oman is a country with a deep-rooted history, a distinguished character, which has its own philosophy in social life, and therefore we should not allow senseless imitation to impede our progress or passively affect our immortal heritage.

Qaboos bin Said

This book examines the variety of factors that have transformed the Sultanate of Oman from a medieval potentate, a veritable terra incognita to the outside world, to a modern nation-state in less than two generations. It analyzes the dynamics that have enabled this ancient country to make a distinctive yet almost seamless transition from an isolated, stagnant backwater to a strategic regional power—without a corresponding loss of national identity. Although increasingly "modern," Omanis adhere to a development model of their own invention, one that reflects their unique history and places a premium on independence and cultural authenticity rather than blindly embracing all that is Western.

Oman shares much in common with its neighbors in terms of geography and, to a lesser extent, in terms of natural resources, among which oil and natural gas deposits predominate. It shares with many others in the region a similar language, religion, and history. Yet, as this story unfolds, it will become abundantly clear that the sultanate is profoundly different from its neighbors in many ways, standing apart more often than not as "the exception to the rule."

The most notable distinction is that Oman has a long history *as a country*. Over the centuries, its people have cultivated a pattern of settled agriculture, time-honored fisheries, and maritime activity extending to the farthest reaches of the globe. Located within an area of the Middle East region that is largely dependent on hydrocarbon production, Oman is developing a robust, diversified economy while slowly, but steadily, divesting itself from an exclusive dependence on oil revenues.

Here is a country in which the notion of royalty is applied to some, but by no means all, members of the sultan's extended family—a surprisingly small number in comparison with those in neighboring states. In the case of Oman, the distinction between "royal" and "ruling" family is instructive, transcending mere semantics; for, central to understanding the political reality of Oman is the fact that it is the sultan alone who *rules*, albeit through an evolving and expanding system of institutions that has led to ever-greater levels of popular participation. While governing in other Gulf countries is largely a family affair, Sultan Qaboos's cabinet currently includes only two members of the royal family.

Mechanisms for power sharing, informed by culture and tradition, are woven into the political fabric of the modern Omani state. Foremost among these is the notion of *shura* (consultation). As the society has embraced modernization, Oman's tribal heritage continues to be revered. In today's sultanate, tribal leaders, rather than being relegated to the sidelines, are invited to participate in the evolving political discourse. Professional advisers, skilled technocrats, and representatives of merchant families complete the roster at the center of the functioning bureaucracy.

This combination of tradition and modernization is reflected as well in Oman's religious complexion. Within the prevailing Islamic milieu is the Ibadhi tradition, largely unique to Oman,[1] which contributes an additional dimension to the country's rich mosaic of diversity. For more than thirteen centuries, Ibadhism has served as a guiding principle for many people of this land, suggesting an appropriate dynamic between the ruler and his people while also providing a model of social interaction based on moderation and inclusivity. In a region currently fragmented by extremism and intolerance, the "irresistible glow of religious pluralism" that pervades Omani society is a refreshing and welcome departure.[2]

On the basis of primary and secondary research, independent observation, interviews, and data collected during my travels to the region, this book argues that the Sultanate of Oman, while remaining grounded in its traditional roots, has pursued a policy of political and social modernization, combined with cultural and religious inclusion that uniquely positions it as a moderating influence on the twenty-first-century world political stage. The case will be made that a distinct national self-awareness, based on the deep appreciation of a unique historical tradition, has contributed to the evolution of a relatively optimistic and cohesive society that, while culturally diverse and inclusive of other traditions, remains resolute in the affirmation of its Arab and Muslim identity as it journeys steadily, thoughtfully, and confidently into the modern age.

The architect of Oman's transformation is Sultan Qaboos bin Said, a widely admired, charismatic ruler who has galvanized a formerly battered nation, uniting its citizenry in a common cause. Under his leadership of more than four decades, Sultan Qaboos has managed to construct from this rubble an edifice that not only is decidedly modern but also retains at its foundation the Omani people's cherished customs and traditions.

The analysis of the sultanate's distinctive journey begins in chapter 1, "The Lure of Oman," with an examination of the country's unique geographic location in the Middle East, straddling the crossroads of ancient and modern trade routes, both by land and by sea. The familiar adage "geography is destiny" seems particularly apt in the case of Oman—historically, currently, and as the case will be made, in the future. This chapter explores the important, if frequently underreported, role of Oman in the global economy of old, including its illustrious seafaring history marked by prolonged interaction with remote lands and distant people, which contributed in myriad ways to the formation not only of a tapestry of ethnic and linguistic traditions in Oman but also of a characteristic cosmopolitanism or openness toward other societies and cultures.

The chapter continues with an examination of Oman's diverse culture and society, including the harmony that exists among various religious communities within the context of the indigenous Ibadhi tradition of Islam, a little-known, even misunderstood sect that is neither Sunni nor Shi'a. The origins and nature of Ibadhism are analyzed, as are the distinct historical influences that have shaped the Ibadhi weltanschauung.

Finally, social organization, including the primacy of family and the dynamics of life in both village and desert, are explored, particularly in the context of a rapidly evolving, modernizing state. Of particular note here are the ingenious systems the Omani people have devised to collect and distribute the country's most precious resource—water.

The maxim that "history informs the present" is nowhere truer than in the case of Oman. Chapter 2, "Setting the Stage: Oman Pre-1970," provides the historical framework for Oman's modern transformation. Replete with tales of colonization and empire building, daring confrontations and diplomatic triumphs, the history of Oman is traced from its earliest moments through the rise of power of the venerable Al Bu Said tribe, one of the oldest, continuously ruling dynasties in the world. The milestones in the country's history—as well as the inspiring accounts of its most legendary figures—will be essential to understanding the formation of the modern Omani identity, as well as the sultanate's distinctive approach to regional and international affairs.

By the mid-twentieth century, this once-thriving society had descended into poverty and isolation. Although the popular narrative places responsibility for this period of Oman's stagnation squarely on the shoulders of Qaboos bin Said's predecessor and father, Sultan Said bin Taymur, this chapter will reexamine the conditions that led to this critical interlude in Oman's history in light of interviews with Omanis at the highest levels and on the basis of current accepted scholarship. An effort will be made to understand the person of Said bin Taymur and reconsider his decisions, evaluating them from the perspective of the context in which they were made.

The personal journey of Sultan Qaboos bin Said, who became ruler of Oman in 1970, is the subject of chapter 3, "Qaboos bin Said: Renaissance Man." This is a story rich in drama, intrigue, and most important, stunning achievement. The chapter will begin by looking at his early life and background, including the circumstances that led him to wrest control of the sultanate from his father at the young age of twenty-nine. The enormous task confronting the new, still untested head of state at the start of his national career in 1970 is examined in depth. His response to the innumerable challenges that might easily have caused others to flee reveals insights into his quiet personality, his deeply considered mission, and his effective leadership style.

This chapter underscores the creative ways in which this virtually unknown sultan inspired a sense of national identity and unified the country behind an ambitious program of modernization. Winning the trust and confidence of his subjects, he unveiled his priorities, pledging to develop a modern national infrastructure, to build schools and hospitals, and to empower *all* citizens of Oman, women as well as men. His handling of two insurrections—one involving foreign interference and the other of a more homegrown variety—provides insights into Sultan Qaboos's governing style, including his penchant for building alliances and his willingness to reconcile and adapt. His leadership style is revealed as well in his speeches, which not only provide a record of his decisions but also provide important clues about his thought processes. The chapter ends by looking at Qaboos bin Said's vision for his country, one that would remain true to Oman's past while embracing its future, eschewing Westernization for thoughtful, measured modernization.

Chapter 4, "Creating a Civil Society," begins by discussing education and healthcare, the "twin pillars" of Oman's national development strategy. Particularly noteworthy are the little-known efforts of US citizens to address the educational and health needs of Omanis in the early decades of the twentieth century. More impressive still is the astonishing record of the country's success, at both governmental and private levels, in expanding these two vital sectors to reach virtually every segment of Omani society.

Of particular interest in the creation of a civil society in Oman is the role of women. The chapter dispels common misconceptions about the historical role of women in Muslim societies and looks at the increasing strides women are making in modern Oman.

The chapter continues by discussing the all-important nature of Omani political culture. This is examined from the perspective of both the inherent constraints on power, embodied in the tradition of *shura* (consultation), and the evolution of political participation—first, through the creation of representative institutions, culminating in the *Majlis Oman* (Council of Oman), and second, through the introduction of the Basic Statute of the State, also known as the Basic Law, serving as Oman's first constitution. Finally, the inevitable question of royal succession is explored. In this context, the relevant provisions of the 1996 Basic Law, as well as its 2011 amendments, are presented, including the mechanisms that have been set in place to ensure a smooth transition of power.

Modern institutions that reward creativity and entrepreneurship within a recognizable cultural milieu, that are compatible with tradition, and that provide a framework for a sustainable and diversified economy are the subjects of analysis in chapter 5, "Constructing a Modern Economy." As Oman contemplates the inevitable depletion of its oil reserves—a problem of far lesser concern to its Gulf neighbors—the central themes of economic diversification and greater utilization of Omani labor are highlighted, including the all-important expansion of the private sector. The government's stalwart support of entrepreneurship and investment, including generous incentives and legal guarantees, will be shown to contribute to a business-friendly climate.

The development of a modern infrastructure, essential to a competitive twenty-first-century economy, is examined in detail. Given the relatively primitive state of public services and access in Oman before 1970, sweeping government initiatives have virtually transformed the national landscape. Massive investments have been made in traditional areas such as agriculture, fisheries, water delivery systems, and ports as well as in the development of highways, airports, electrical systems, and telecommunication.

In a country with such outstanding natural beauty and friendly people, the most promising prospects for economic diversity lie in the tourism sector, with particular emphasis on developing venues relating to history and culture, ecotourism, and high-end luxury destinations. Mindful of the past, the government actively promotes the preservation and marketing of heritage crafts and consumer goods. In the arts, the sultan's commitment to the role of music and dance in building bridges across cultures is exemplified in the majestic Royal Opera House Muscat, a stunning achievement in both size and beauty. Taken together, these initiatives in so many diverse areas bode well for the continued economic growth and success of Oman in the twenty-first century.

"Foreign Relations: A Policy of Mutual Respect" is the focus of chapter 6. The sultanate has maintained a venerable tradition of friendship and longstanding cooperation both with Western friends, including Great Britain and the United States, with which it shares strong bilateral ties dating back more than two centuries, and with Eastern friends, such as Iran, whose history is inextricably linked to Oman's own. Because Oman's longstanding record of bilateral relations with the United Kingdom has been referenced in previous chapters, this chapter will highlight the lesser-known history of Oman's friendship with the United States, one that endures to this day.

The bulk of the chapter is devoted to Oman's foreign policy under Qaboos bin Said. Oman is distinguished from many of its regional neighbors in its steadfast embrace of a measured and independent foreign policy, designed to preserve its sovereignty and avoid interference in the internal affairs of other countries while simultaneously pursuing peaceful coexistence with all nations. This strategy effectively permits the country's leadership to pursue a path of "quiet diplomacy," engaging with various parties, when requested, in an attempt to serve as interlocutor and mediator in the cause of defusing regional and international tensions. In this context, Oman's venerable friendship with the Islamic Republic of Iran, unique among its Middle Eastern neighbors, is discussed in greater detail.

The final chapter, "Challenges and Opportunities in a New Century," examines not only how the Middle East's longest-reigning monarch has responded to the challenges inherent in a youthful and potentially restive population but also, and perhaps even more important, how he has succeeded in intuiting the mood of the nation, providing ever-greater pathways for opportunity and inclusion through meaningful decisions and effective communication.

While much of the Middle East appears to be hemorrhaging from chronic instability, Oman's leader of more than four decades remains a beloved figure. The regard in which Qaboos bin Said is held by his people was underscored, in particular, during the Arab Awakening of 2011, when in the midst of bloody protests and demands for regime change throughout the region, disturbances in Oman focused largely on domestic issues. In an attempt to defuse tensions, Sultan Qaboos responded to the concerns of the demonstrators, moving purposefully to enact economic, political, and legislative reforms.

The participation of young citizens in twenty-first-century Oman, including their expectations and anxieties, is examined in depth here. The chapter will explain how Qaboos bin Said, the "motivator in chief," has responded to youth in his speeches as well as outline the specific measures he has taken to alleviate their concerns and make them contributing members of Omani society.

Young people are not the only Omanis affected by the changes in lifestyle that have accompanied a rapidly escalating standard of living. The chapter will continue by showing the unintended consequences of these changes, such as traffic accidents and chronic, but preventable, illnesses. It will also highlight programs and public awareness campaigns, including frequent statements by Sultan Qaboos that are designed to reverse these trends. However, in Oman as elsewhere, changes in human behavior will take time and perseverance.

Among the most intractable twentieth-century challenges is the attempt of a few to hijack a venerable faith tradition for their own agenda. Quiet and humble by nature, and usually measured in his demeanor, Sultan Qaboos, a scholar of the faith, is nonetheless unambiguous with regard to those who would seek to pervert Islam. The chapter highlights his historic, unequivocal condemnation of religious extremism in any form. His personal jihad[3] takes aim at those who would distort the faith for subversive political ends. For Qaboos bin Said, there is no place in Islam for violence or intolerance.

The chapter concludes with an exploration of Oman's potential as a force for moderation in the region and beyond. While its commitment to peace, through quiet mediation and patient dialogue among political adversaries, seems firmly embedded in Oman's national psyche, the country is also emerging as a recognized venue for international cultural exchange and ecumenical discourse. Given Oman's history at the crossroads of mighty seas and great landmasses, combined with its tradition of diversity and inclusion, this modern manifestation of Oman's unique cultural perspective and potential is especially noteworthy.

This book is intended to demonstrate the degree to which Oman's paradigm for modernization is unique, particularly among its neighbors, reflecting the country's distinctive traditions and unique history. From the perspective of one who has followed the Omani renaissance since its infancy, I hope to demonstrate that the country's voyage of rebirth, while beset by inherent challenges, is on a solid course. Given the Omanis' singular heritage, it is reasonable to expect that they will continue to be guided by the culturally authentic modernization that has characterized their entry to the twenty-first century, motivated by an enduring sense of national identity, embracing the future with confidence and purpose.

CHAPTER 1

THE LURE OF OMAN

The Sultanate of Oman, the oldest independent state in the Arab world, is a unique and enchanting land. Its history, including its modern history, is unlike that of any other country in the Middle East. Although it was occupied in 1507 by the Portuguese, it regained its political authority and went on not only to reassert its territorial integrity at home but also to exercise a broad sphere of influence across the globe.

The political and administrative capital of Oman is Muscat, lying adjacent to the commercial port city of Mutrah, within the governorate of Muscat. Other major centers include Salalah, Nizwa, Sohar, Sur, 'Ibri, al-Buraymi, Ibra', Haima, Rustaq, and Khasab. Consistent with other "hyper-urbanizing" trends throughout the Middle East, almost three-quarters of Oman's people live in urban areas. But this similarity with the rest of the Middle East is one of only a few.

In terms of its geography, demography, and culture, Oman is a country of surprising diversity that defies the prevailing stereotypes about the Arab and Islamic world. Although the Middle East is often perceived as a monolithic region mired in social injustice, sectarian conflict, and endless bloodshed, Oman stands out as an "oasis of tranquility" amid a desert of discord. How did the small country of Oman escape the fate to which so many of its neighbors succumbed? What factors set in motion the series of events that would produce the traditional yet modern, Arabic yet cosmopolitan, nation-state we know as Oman today? For answers to these questions, we must first look to the past, to the sultanate's cultural landscape.

A LAND UNIQUELY POSITIONED

Situated at the strategic crossroads of Europe, Asia, and Africa, Oman is a noncontiguous country, hugging the southeastern coast of the Arabian Peninsula, sharing that ancient and storied landmass with seven other countries. Occupying an area of 82,000 square miles (309,500 square km),

roughly equivalent in size to the US state of Kansas or the nation of Great
Britain, the sultanate is bordered to the south by the Republic of Yemen
and to its north by the United Arab Emirates (UAE). The Kingdom of
Saudi Arabia lies to its north and west. Oman's northern governorate, or
administrative division, Musandam, a peninsula that juts into the Strait
of Hormuz, is separated geographically from the rest of the country, surrounded by the UAE. The small enclave of Madha, or Wadi Madha, is the
second noncontiguous territory within Oman, surrounded on all sides by
the UAE. This remote settlement of approximately two thousand residents
in the governorate of Musandam chose to become part of the nation of
Oman in 1942.[1]

In addition, Oman's domain extends to several small islands off the coast,
including the Salamah Island near the Strait of Hormuz as well as al-Masirah
Island and the Kuria Muria Islands in the Arabian Sea, of which only one,
Hallaniyah, is inhabited. The Islamic Republic of Iran lies almost within view,
on the eastern side of the narrow strait.

Oman is a land of dramatic landscapes and breathtaking natural beauty. A
striking feature of the country's topography is the rugged Hajar mountain
range, shaped like a human backbone. It extends along a great curve, from
Musandam in the north to Ra's al-Hadd in the south, where the sun first rises
in the Arab world each day. Within the governorate of Dakhiliyah, the Jabal
al-Akhdar (Green Mountain) region dominates this imposing chain, its large
plateau providing a fertile environment for a variety of fruits, herbs, and wild-
flowers. Towering above this imposing landscape is Jabal Shams (Mountain
of the Sun), one of the highest points in the Arabian Peninsula, rising defi-
antly some 9,800 feet (3,000 m) above sea level and frequently snowcapped
during the winter months.

The central interior plain of Oman is characterized by vast desert expanses.
Lying on the Tropic of Cancer, it is typically hot and dry. During the peak
summer months, coastal regions may experience extreme temperatures, high
humidity, and even cyclones. However, throughout the remainder of the
year, from mid-October to the end of March, temperatures throughout the
sultanate are typically moderate.

One highly anticipated feature of Oman's climate is the summer monsoon
(*khareef*), blowing in a southwesterly pattern from the Indian Ocean, bath-
ing the brown, rocky hills of the southern governorate of Dhofar in cool and
refreshing mists. The effect is to magically transform the provincial capital
city, Salalah, and its surrounding mountains into lush, verdant panoramas
with overflowing *wadis* (river beds) and inviting waterfalls.

Geologists the world over flock to Oman to study its gems, minerals, and,
in particular, its almost incomparable variety of rocks representing different
periods in the evolution of its geological formation. According to Peter J.
Ochs II, a geologist *extraordinaire* and the deputy leader of the author's
2006 study visit to the sultanate, "the geology of Oman represents a cross
section of almost all the rocks found on our planet,"[2] including white marble

and rare dark ophiolites, volcanic rocks from beneath the sea, rich in the minerals olivine, serpentine, and chromite.

Geography as Destiny

To a considerable extent, Oman's location has shaped its history and culture. Oman lies at the intersection of ancient landmasses and sea lanes. It is a meeting point between East and West. Strategically seated at the crossroads of Africa, India, and the rest of Asia, it stands not only as gatekeeper to the Strait of Hormuz and the Persian Gulf but also as a sentinel at the intersection of vital sea routes embracing the vast region of the Indian Ocean and routes to the Red Sea. During certain periods in its history, the vast, forbidding desert expanse at its back has served as an effective buffer, and indeed, in the opinion of some, even as a "blessing," against invading forces.

Oman's strategic location, combined with a sustained history of interaction with peoples of distant lands, robust trade relations, and extensive imperial exploits, contributed significantly to its rich cultural mosaic, including the relative ease with which its citizens interact with people from distant lands and various cultures.

While it is indisputably "Arab" in character, Oman—a member of the League of Arab States since 1971—is in many respects, particularly culturally and economically, far more oriented toward the East, that is, toward the Indian Ocean, the Asian subcontinent of India and Pakistan and beyond, than it is toward the Arabian Peninsula at its back door. It is illustrative to note that if only in terms of sheer proximity, the Omani capital, Muscat, is closer to Karachi, Pakistan, than it is to Salalah, the capital of the southern Omani governorate of Dhofar.[3]

"Jugular of the World's Economy"

At the far northern tip of Oman lies the Musandam peninsula, where barren limestone mountains and towering cliffs rise dramatically from the sea, strangely evocative of the fjords of Norway—a curious visual juxtaposition in this distant Arabian territory. Separated from the rest of the sultanate's territory by the UAE, the importance of this northernmost region of Oman, both to Oman and to an oil-hungry world, is immeasurable; for here, lying between this rugged landmass and Iran, separating the Persian Gulf from the Sea of Oman, is the vital Strait of Hormuz.[4]

Called the world's most important chokepoint,[5] the Strait of Hormuz is only twenty-one miles wide at its narrowest point, with shipping lanes measuring only two miles wide in either direction. Nevertheless, massive supertankers transport some seventeen million barrels of crude oil per day through the strait, accounting for 30 percent of the oil traded by sea. In addition to oil, liquefied natural gas is transported through the Strait of Hormuz, representing more than 30 percent of the global trade in that commodity each year.[6] It is little wonder then that modern pundits have termed this waterway "the jugular of the world's economy."

SEAFARING AND TRADE

Popular images of the Middle East do not generally include the sea; and while Arabs are perceived, particularly in the West, as a desert people, this image is far from complete. With more than 1,000 miles (3,165 km) of coastline, Oman has a long and illustrious history of seafaring. The sea, along with its attendant pursuits, trade and fishing, is central to the Omani national narrative and is reflected in many local customs, including dress, cuisine, and music.[7]

Even before the dawn of Islam, Oman's sailors were acknowledged masters of the ocean. Tales of fantastic voyages and splendid sailing vessels figure prominently in its people's accumulated heritage and oral traditions. It should be no surprise that one of the most fabled seafarers of all, Sinbad himself, of the immortal *One Thousand and One Nights* (also known as *Arabian Nights*), is said to have hailed from the port city of Sohar, once—and again now—a thriving, cosmopolitan city.

Omani sailors ventured great distances, armed with an intimate knowledge of astronomy and equipped with a compass and an astrolabe, an Arabian invention that, by measuring the movement and elevation of the stars, made it possible to calculate latitude and time of day. When they returned home, they brought with them delectable wares to sample as well as vivid tales of remote and exotic lands. Perhaps inadvertently, they introduced Islam to the broader world as they went, leaving in their wake some of the earliest recorded communities of Muslims in the Far East.[8]

Omani trade with China is documented as early as the eighth century. According to Arabic and Chinese documents, the trader 'Abu Obeidah 'Abdallah bin al-Qassem, "a master of the scientific principles of maritime navigation,"[9] traveled to Canton, China, in 750 CE. This milestone, followed by centuries of interaction with peoples of diverse customs and cultures, including not only China but also India and East Africa, markedly affected the Omanis' sense of their place in the world as a "seaborne national identity, forged over the millennia of interacting with—*not withdrawing from*—the outside world" (italics mine).[10]

The evolution of global trade and commerce continued largely unabated for centuries, contributing to a great extent to the development of a "cosmopolitanism" that is the very essence of the Omani national psyche. E. Harper Johnson shares a vivid account of the legendary *shaykh* 'Abdullah al-'Omani, a wealthy businessman from Sohar, who arrived in China in 1050 CE. After winning the respect of officials there "for his courage, ability, kindness, and astuteness," al-Omani, hailed by the emperor Jen-Tsung as the "good ethics general," was received at the Imperial Palace, where in a private audience with the Chinese ruler, gifts were exchanged amid great fanfare.[11]

In 1498, during the Western Age of Exploration, it is alleged that the Omani navigator, mathematician, and cartographer Ahmad bin Majid, seen by many as "a veritable repository of the seas,"[12] was employed by the legendary Portuguese explorer Vasco da Gama to serve as his maritime guide around the Cape of Good Hope in South Africa to Calicut on the western coast of India.[13] According to Kaplan, "Majid had sailed the Indian Ocean for half a century. . . . He knew the best entry point to the mouths of the Tigris and the Indus, the way to negotiate the shoals off Mozambique, and the best landfalls in India and on both coasts of the Red Sea."[14]

Undisputed masters of the seas, Omanis eventually left their mark on near and distant lands, including Iraq (Basra), the Asian subcontinent, and the coast of present-day Iran and Pakistan, including the interior regions of Baluchistan. In Africa they established a presence on the islands of Zanzibar and Pemba, and even farther into the interior of that continent, in Rwanda, Burundi, Tanzania, Kenya, and Somalia. These exploits help to explain the somewhat surprising use of Swahili, an African language, in the sultanate today, a legacy of the protracted interaction between the Omanis in Africa and the Africans who were brought to Arabia.[15]

The Dhow

The ancient ports of Salalah, in the southern governorate of Dhofar, Sur, south of Muscat, and Sohar, northwest of the capital city of Muscat, are inexorably linked to Oman's maritime history. Sur was renowned in ancient times, and until now, as the center of the country's traditional shipbuilding industry. It is here that Oman's trademark dhows—shallow-draught, broad-beamed ships with great lateen sails—were constructed to ply the waters of the Arabian Sea and beyond, crisscrossing the Indian Ocean as they traded with the peoples of South Asia and the Far East.[16]

Records suggest that in the fourth century BCE, during the legendary conquests of Alexander the Great, the maritime powers of the ancient world relied on the expertise of Phoenician shipbuilders and sailors to construct seaworthy vessels in the Red Sea and the Persian Gulf, explaining, perhaps, the coincidence (or not?) that two coastal cities, one in Lebanon, the land of the Phoenicians, and the other in Oman, are called Sur.[17]

To this day, Omani shipbuilders can be observed patiently working with wood and nails under the searing sun of Sur as they painstakingly complete construction of distinctively designed, handcrafted dhows (see figure 1.1). Although demand for these vessels has diminished somewhat in recent decades, the completed products stand as works of great beauty and utilitarian function, recalling Oman's proud and venerable seafaring tradition.

By the tenth century CE, Sohar, west of Muscat on Oman's northern Batinah coast, once the seat of a Christian bishopric as well as the location of a Jewish synagogue and cemetery, had developed into a flourishing and cosmopolitan trading hub. Shielded from stormy seas within the calm waters of the Sea of Oman, Sohar's merchants established lucrative trading relations with their counterparts in distant lands.

Figure 1.1　Modern homage to an ancient tradition: A dhow shipyard in present-day Sur
Photo by author (2014).

Today, after more than a millennium, a poignant reminder of Oman's seafaring legacy is featured prominently in the midst of a roundabout near al-Bustan Palace Hotel, half an hour's drive southwest of the capital of Muscat. In 1980 the British historian and explorer Tim Severin supervised the construction of the *Sohar*, a replica of a lateen-rigged, cotton-sailed Omani dhow that 'Abdullah bin Gasm guided to China in the ninth century CE. Meticulously handcrafted by an international crew in Oman, the *Sohar* was constructed from the bark of more than 75,000 palm trees, using four tons of coconut rope and not a single nail. Severin and his Omani crew set out in this eighty-seven-foot vessel for Guangzhou in November of that year, completing their often-harrowing journey of over six thousand nautical miles to China in eight months.[18]

In a related effort, the governments of Oman and Singapore announced plans in 2008 to collaborate on a project commemorating Oman's illustrious maritime history. Inspired by a discovery off the coast of Belitung Island, Indonesia, some ten years earlier, plans were made to design and reconstruct a ninth-century Omani dhow.

Tom Vosmer, an Australian maritime archaeologist and the world's leading authority on the history of Arabic shipbuilding, was invited to head the construction team. Guided by the salvaged Belitung shipwreck, Vosmer and his team were meticulous in their research, adhering scrupulously to historic Omani shipbuilding techniques. On February 16, 2010, after seventeen months of painstaking work, the newly constructed vessel, christened the

Jewel of Muscat by Captain Saleh Said al-Jabri, was launched amid great fanfare. Following ancient trade routes, the *Jewel* embarked on its historic journey from Muscat to Singapore—across the Sea of Oman and the Arabian Sea to the west coast of India and beyond, through the Strait of Malacca—finally arriving to a rousing welcome in Singapore 138 days later.[19]

Dignitaries from the two countries met in Singapore on October 15, 2011, to celebrate the success of this historic venture, a testament to Oman's history of maritime achievement and cultural interaction with peoples of distant lands and cultures. Today the *Jewel* is displayed prominently at the Maritime Experiential Museum, a gift to the people of Singapore from Sultan Qaboos bin Said to "mark the revival of the ancient trading routes that linked Asia to the Middle East."[20]

Frankincense and Myrrh: The Oil of Antiquity

For much of its history, Oman was known for supplying the ancient world with frankincense (Arabic, *luban*), a valuable gum resin extracted from a gnarly looking tree (Latin name, *Boswellia sacra*[21]). Frankincense is found in the southern Dhofari region of the sultanate; it appears in neighboring Yemen and Somalia as well, but it is much less abundant and of poorer quality. There is nothing about this nondescript tree to suggest it contains a coveted substance "for which the ancient world had a nearly insatiable appetite,"[22] prized more highly than gold and treasured by priests and kings, pharaohs and emperors.

When burned, frankincense produces an aroma that some find almost intoxicating, with an effect reminiscent of elaborate rites in Eastern Orthodox and Roman Catholic churches. Long before the Christian era, frankincense and its cousin myrrh, the aromatic resin of a small, thorny tree from the genus *Commiphora*, were burned at religious ceremonies and in the houses of the wealthy. It was and, in many cases, still is used to treat common illnesses, to slow bleeding, to heal wounds, to ward off insects, to freshen clothes, and to bless people:

> Lumps of the resin were added to drinking water to invigorate the body, especially the kidneys; it was thought to kill disease by activating the immune system and warding off evil spirits. Frankincense sweetened every funeral pyre in the ancient world and was used to embalm pharaohs. This resin was found inside the tomb of Tutankhamen in Luxor and . . . was stored in special rooms under priestly guard in the Hebrew temple in Jerusalem.[23]

Frankincense is sometimes chewed, but not swallowed, for its pleasant taste and presumed medicinal effects. Current research suggests that this rare and valuable resin contains properties that boost the human immune system by reducing inflammation, while additional studies have suggested that it has antibacterial and antifungal effects.[24] At present, the government of Oman has initiated a program of systematic cultivation of frankincense trees in Dhofar for the purpose of research on the medicinal properties of this valuable resin.

The importance of this milky-colored resin to the global economy of old can hardly be exaggerated. As Robert Kaplan put it, "Frankincense was to antiquity as oil is to the modern age."[25] With a near monopoly on this precious commodity, Oman was catapulted onto the world stage in antiquity, establishing its preeminence in the global marketplace. International trade in frankincense led to great wealth and a level of sophistication previously unknown in Arabia.[26]

Between the fourth century BCE and the fourth century CE, merchants set off from the southern Omani governorate of Dhofar laden with tons of this precious resin, either from the bustling port of al-Baleed, near present-day Salalah, or from the nearly impregnable pre-Islamic settlement of Sumhuram, located in the area of Khor Rori. (See figure 1.2 for an impressive reminder of the glory that was the ancient city of al-Baleed.) Sailing eastward and northward, across the Indian Ocean toward Persia and India, or in a southwesterly direction, toward the Red Sea, their precious cargo found its way to eager clients in Egypt and Rome. In exchange, Omanis returned from Africa with ivory, wood, and ostrich feathers, from Rome perhaps with gold, and from South Asia with diamonds, sapphires, lapis lazuli, and spices.

The center of the trade in frankincense and myrrh was the commercially vibrant province of Dhofar, which, along with neighboring Yemen, is also

Figure 1.2 The archaeological site of al-Baleed, an ancient port and pre-Islamic settlement near the city of Salalah

Photo by author (2014).

believed to have been the center of an area known in antiquity as *Arabia Felix*, or Happy Arabia. The name seems particularly apt considering the relative prosperity of the merchant tribes of this region by the standards of the day. Recent archaeological excavations in Sumhuram reveal an impressive array of pre-Islamic fortifications, temples, large frankincense storage rooms, and multistory homes, testifying to the affluence of a community where residents enjoyed lavish, even sumptuous, lifestyles. Significant objects of iron and bronze, as well as a workshop for metals, provide further evidence that the city was an important center of trade. It is fair to suggest that robust trade and commerce with people of far-flung lands instilled in the residents of Dhofar an appreciation of cultures and traditions far beyond their shores, a characteristic that endures to this day.

Reaching its zenith during the height of the Roman Empire, the frankincense trade lasted for some 1,500 years, propelling this remote region of Oman into international prominence. "Until about 100 BC the fulcrum of trade between East and West was here, in this seeming wasteland of southern Arabia."[27]

At the dawn of the Christian era, the New Testament recounts the story of the Three Wise Men, alternately known as Magi or Kings, who set off to Bethlehem carrying gifts for the baby Jesus.

> In the time of King Herod, after Jesus was born in Bethlehem of Judea, wise men from the East came to Jerusalem. . . . On entering the house, they saw the child with Mary his mother. . . . Then, opening their treasure chests, they offered him gifts of gold, frankincense, and myrrh. (Matthew 2:1, 11, New Revised Standard Version [NRSV])

It is quite likely that these travelers, known as Balthasar, Melchior, and Caspar (or Gaspar), may have hailed from Dhofar, journeying from the East westward across Arabia, along well-worn trade routes, to Palestine, bringing to the infant child gifts of the greatest value from their region.

Over the centuries, countless travelers have marveled at the economic importance and levels of sophistication in ancient Dhofar. On his return journey from the East, where he lived at the court of the Moghul kings, the legendary Venetian explorer Marco Polo wrote extensively in his *Travels* of his 1290 visit to al-Baleed. He characterized it as a wealthy and vibrant center of international trade:

> Dhafar [*sic*] is a great and noble and fine city. . . . It stands upon the sea and has a very good haven, so that there is a great traffic of shipping between this and India; and the merchants take hence great numbers of Arab horses to that market, making great profits thereby.[28]

He continued, describing its most famous export: "Much white incense is produced here, and I will tell you how it grows. The trees are like small fir trees; these are notched with a knife in several places, and from these notches the incense is exuded."[29]

During the following century, the renowned Moroccan traveler Shaykh Abu 'Abdullah Muhammad bin 'Abdullah, better known as Ibn Battuta, visited this area twice, in 1329 and again in 1349, exploring far more thoroughly than his Venetian predecessor the land we now know as Oman and describing in rich detail the manners and customs of its people.[30] Today, the Dhofari area, known as "Frankincense Land," encompasses a wide swath of archaeological sites in and around Salalah representing a nexus of international cultural importance, leading to its inclusion in 2000 on the United Nations Educational, Scientific, and Cultural Organization's (UNESCO) World Heritage List.[31]

Many unexcavated sites remain in Oman to excite the imaginations of archaeologists and historians alike. In the early 1990s, the legendary Lost City of Ubar (also Wubar) was identified by ancient maps, satellite photographs, and archaeological excavations near Shisr, a remote region of western Oman, north of Salalah and south of the Rub' al-Khali desert. The *New York Times* announced this discovery in glowing terms: "Guided by ancient maps and sharp-eyed surveys from space, archaeologists and explorers have discovered a lost city deep in the sands of Arabia, and they are virtually sure it is Ubar, the fabled entrepôt of the rich frankincense trade thousands of years ago."[32]

This five-thousand-year-old center of export for the prosperous frankincense trade was said to have been "swallowed by the sands" between 300 and 500 BCE. Popularized by both Ranulph Fiennes in his 1992 book *Atlantis of the Sands: The Search for the Lost City of Ubar* and Nicholas Clapp in his 1999 book *The Road to Ubar: Finding the Atlantis of the Sands*, the site and its significance remain shrouded in controversy.

Today, each drop of this precious resin is still harvested by hand, as it was centuries ago, by a select caste of skilled herders. Frankincense remains an integral element of Omani popular culture, economy, and tradition. In Dhofar it is an omnipresent feature of the governorate's cultural landscape. With its seductive fragrance wafting through the interiors of public buildings and private homes, welcoming both family and visitors, it provides a poignant reminder of Oman's glorious past.

CULTURE AND SOCIETY

During the course of its long history, Oman has been known by many names. The ancient Greeks referred to the frankincense coast of Dhofar as "Omana."[33] Archaeological evidence points to the existence of human settlements in this land spanning more than five thousand years.

Before the dawn of Islam in the seventh century CE, Sumerian tablets referred to Oman as the land of "Magan," meaning "big ship." At the crossroads of ancient trade routes, where civilizations from the Indus valley to Mesopotamia intersected, Oman would have been a prize for traders and conquerors alike. From this land, copper was exported to Mesopotamia. In combination with tin, copper produces bronze, one of the most critical materials to ancient civilization, guaranteeing the importance of Oman in antiquity.

In contrast to its neighbors in the Arabian Peninsula, Oman enjoyed a relative abundance of water in ancient times, permitting agriculture and leading to permanent settlements as well as a division of labor. During the pre-Islamic period, the Persian Sassanids, whose occupation was concentrated in the city of Sohar, referred to this land as Mazoun,[34] from the word *muzn*, suggesting clouds and abundant flowing water. Sohar is known to have been the site of permanent, continuous settlements for millennia. It remains a major center to this day. While water is far less abundant today than in the past, this city, representing Oman's famed North Batinah governorate, continues to be at the center of the country's agricultural sector.

Ultimately, the origin of the word "Oman" is not entirely clear. It may be linked to an ancient Arab settlement in Yemen called "Uman," a famous person of ancient times, or the Arabic word denoting "settled."

Early Migrations

From a historical perspective, mass human migrations to Oman are generally acknowledged to have originated in or around the ancient site of Ma'rib, a fortified city in southwestern Arabia in the modern Republic of Yemen. Ma'rib is famous as the location of the pre-Islamic state of Saba' (115–950 BCE), the center of the Sabaean civilization referenced in the Bible.

The civilization of Saba' (or Sheba, as it is known in the West) was exceptionally prosperous, trading with ancient Sumer, in what is present-day Iraq, and serving as a transit point for Eastern luxury goods destined for the West. In addition to copper, heading the list of highly coveted products were two rare and expensive aromatic resins—frankincense and myrrh. According to the Old Testament's Book of Kings, the Queen of Sheba, Belqis by name, visited King Solomon in Jerusalem around 900 BCE, accompanied by "a very great retinue, with camels bearing spices, and very much gold, and precious stones" (1 Kings 10:2, NRSV).

Ma'rib was renowned for its great dam (Suadd Ma'rib), an engineering marvel of antiquity, constructed of meticulously hand-hewn stone blocks that, according to modern estimates, spanned almost two thousand feet. As Stewart explains,

> According to inscriptions, the dam was built in the seventh century BC, . . . but it was maintained, for centuries after, by successive generations of skilled Sabaeans and, later, by the kings of Himyar, a civilization that succeeded the Sabaeans as a potent force in South Arabia.[35]

Between the fifth and sixth centuries CE, the Ma'rib dam broke and was repaired, if only temporarily. According to early Muslim historians, the dam collapsed in 570 CE. The cause of the collapse, whether an earthquake,

exceptionally heavy rains, or the absence of knowledge sufficient to effect
much-needed repairs, continues to be the subject of scholarly debate to this day.

More significant than the cause of the dam's demise and the subsequent
collapse of an ancient civilization in southern Arabia, however, was the far-
reaching effect that this momentous event would have on human migration
and the formation of modern societies in the wider region.

Following the collapse of the dam, the peoples of the Ma'rib region and,
in particular, members of the predominant tribe of al-Azd, began to migrate
along three major routes: to the north, toward present-day Iraq; to the east,
toward central Arabia and Bahrain; and to the southeast, toward Oman.[36] By
the second century CE, Malik bin Faham al-Azdi led his tribe into the territory of present-day Oman, already populated with Arabic-speaking peoples.
The Persians, who controlled large portions of the country at that time, vig-
orously opposed Bin Faham and his people. Ultimately, the Azd prevailed.
The victory of Malik bin Faham's forces, strengthening the Arab presence in
Oman and leading to the end of Persian rule in the country is an event that
is recalled with great pride in Oman to this day.

A Polyglot People

The population of Oman today is more than four million. In contrast to its
neighbors—in particular, to the UAE, where the proportion of expatriates
hovers around 85–90 percent—the number of foreigners in the sultanate is
especially low, accounting for 44 percent or less of the population.[37] Nevertheless, Omani society is exceptionally diverse, representing a rich mixture
of ethnicities. Most citizens identify as Arab in origin; others are descended
from Omanis who migrated in waves from East Africa, Baluchistan, and the
Indian subcontinent throughout many centuries of trade and commercial
interaction.

Another distinguishing feature of Oman lies in the fact that its citizens are
employed in virtually all sectors of society, including business, service, and
industry.[38] In addition, the role of merchants and "guest workers," particularly from the Asian subcontinent, is central to the modern history of trade
and commerce in the sultanate. Given their geographic proximity to Oman,
South Asians, primarily Indians, have been actively engaged in the country's
commercial life for generations, selling imported goods in shops along the
coast and venturing even farther into the country's interior, financing exports
to sell in foreign markets. Others, from Pakistan and especially Baluchistan,
have immigrated in great waves, each bringing with them the languages and
customs of their native lands, further contributing to the cultural tapestry
that characterizes Oman.

In 1955 the American physician Donald Bosch and his educator wife,
Eloise, arrived in Oman to begin a lifelong commitment of service to its
citizens.[39] Their journals record their surprise at the large numbers of peoples from distant lands, or the "imported Omanis,"[40] they encountered in
the capital region of Muscat and Mutrah, many of whom not only assisted

in improving education and healthcare but also contributed to the broader modernizing efforts of the sultanate. Even today, the languages of South Asia are commonplace in Oman, as is the inclusion of dedicated pages in daily newspapers reporting on current events, popular culture, and even "home team" scores from India and Pakistan—underscoring the prevailing spirit of inclusivity that characterizes Oman's societal dynamic.

Oman is a polyglot nation. While Arabic prevails as the official language as well as the predominant language of communication, English, Hindi, Urdu, and even Swahili are in evidence throughout the broad spectrum of the Omani cultural landscape. Linguistic diversity is further enhanced by the existence of ancient languages of southeastern Arabia that are believed to predate Islam, among which are Shahri (Jabali), a spoken language of the tribal people within the governorate of Dhofar, and Mahri, used in both Dhofar and neighboring Yemen.

AN INCLUSIVE FAITH TRADITION

As in much of the modern Middle East, the Islamic ethos prevails in Oman. During the lifetime of the Prophet Muhammad (570–632 CE), the inhabitants of Arabia, including Oman, observed a variety of religious traditions. Magianism (*Majusiyyah*), associated with Zoroastrianism, which was practiced by the Persians, was the predominant religion, followed by idolatry and Judaism.[41]

Islam was introduced into Oman in the seventh century CE. According to oral tradition, during the life of the Prophet Muhammad, Mazin bin Ghadhuba, from Sama'il, journeyed to Medina, in present-day Saudi Arabia, and dedicated himself to the new faith, becoming the first Omani to embrace Islam. While several delegations from Oman are reputed to have traveled to Medina to meet with the Prophet and his companions, the definitive moment in the mass conversion of Omanis to the Islamic faith was delivered in the person of 'Amr ibn al-'As. As the personal envoy of the Prophet Muhammad, he was charged with delivering a letter to the two kings of Oman, brothers 'Abd and Jayfar, sons of al-Julanda bin al-Mustakbir.[42]

The message of the Prophet Muhammad was quickly embraced by leaders and people alike. According to tradition, after reading his letter, 'Abd and Jayfar "called for a general council meeting of the Omani sheiks and they resolved to accept Islam peacefully. . . . They then sent envoys to different parts of the country . . . and, according to Omani sources, all of these regions accepted the teachings of Islam."[43]

After more than fourteen centuries, the people of Oman continue to identify with Islam, albeit most profess a variation of that faith that is little known and even less understood by people outside of its borders, including many in the world's greater Muslim community (*ummah*). Ibadhism is a distinct sect within a worldwide Islamic milieu in which the other two more widely recognized traditions, Sunni and Shi'a, predominate. While Ibadhism is observed primarily in Oman, together with Sunni and Shi'a Islam, Ibadhism is also practiced, to a far lesser extent, in East Africa, especially in Zanzibar, on the island of Jerba in Tunisia, in the Mzab valley of Algeria, and in the Nafusa Mountains of Libya.

Within the Islamic mosaic, this third major tradition, or school of thought, was inspired by the teachings of Jabir bin Zayd al-Azdi (630–710 CE), who was born near Nizwa, Oman's historic center of religious devotion. As a respected scholar of Islam and the author of the encyclopedic *Diwan Jabir*, he was known throughout the first-century Islamic world. From his base in Basra (present-day Iraq), he attracted an enthusiastic following, among whom was a particularly idealistic student, 'Abdullah bin Ibadh al-Tamimi, after whom Ibadhism takes its name.

Neither Sunni nor Shi'a,[44] Ibadhism has its origins in an early Islamic movement whose adherents differed over the question of leadership. While early followers of Islam, identified as Sunnis (from *Sunnah*, followers of tradition), selected as their leaders men from the Quraysh, the tribe of the Prophet Muhammad, others, of the Shi'i tradition (from *Shi'at 'Ali*, or partisans of 'Ali), held that legitimate leadership should be hereditary, derived from the *family* of the Prophet Muhammad, beginning with 'Ali bin 'Abu Talib, the first cousin and son-in-law of the Prophet.

Countering with yet another perspective on leadership that some might contend is peculiarly democratic, a third group, the Ibadhis, held that the leader of the faithful should be an imam (one who sets an example) *elected* on the basis of his knowledge and piety. Without regard to lineage or race, the leader is determined by a consensus of tribal *shaykhs* (tribal leaders),[45] who exercise both religious and temporal rule, *as well as by* public acclamation. Further, from the Ibadhi perspective, the community of elders reserves the right to depose their elected leader if he is determined to be unjust.

According to Valerie Hoffman, the last "true imam" to unite Oman was Ahmad bin Said Al Bu Said (r. 1744–1775), founder of the Al Bu Said dynasty that rules to this day. His descendants eschewed the title "imam," with its connotations of religious leadership, in favor of *sayyid* (lord) a title instead suggesting the noble origins of any member of the royal family.[46] In time, the descendants of Ahmad bin Said adopted the title "sultan," implying lawful authority and power, "thus, relinquishing all pretense of spiritual authority."[47]

Unlike the Sunni majority in Islam, Ibadhis accept the notion of *ijtihad* (independent reasoning), in which sacred text is continually open to interpretation, with an eye toward historical dynamics, suggesting, as Jeremy Jones points out, "a potential for political change, for they contain within themselves an orientation toward flexibility and an embrace of the new and the other."[48] Also significant to the Ibadhi narrative is the emphasis on conciliation and peaceful resolution of disputes.[49]

Holding fast to the conviction that all believers are equal in the sight of God (*Allah*), Omanis are egalitarian in both theory and practice. For many, this is valued as democracy in action at the most basic level, meaning that people of all ranks not only pray together as equals but also greet, eat, and deal with one another with the same courtesy and acceptance. Thus, official visitors may be observed dining with their drivers and escorts, just as individuals from the middle class work side by side with members of the royal family in various government ministries, each sharing equally in the comprehensive benefits available to all citizens of the sultanate.

Ibadhism in the Islamic Mosaic

Over time, Ibadhi beliefs evolved to embrace moderation and inclusivity, particularly vis-à-vis other Muslims. Rather than meeting unbelievers and sinners—either in their own sect or in others—with enmity or hostility, Ibadhis broke off relations with "the ungrateful" (al-kafirun) by withholding friendship from them.[50]

Omanis have largely integrated all variations of the Islamic faith tradition into a singular national ethos, or, as one Omani insisted, "We are all Omani citizens and Muslims." Within the sultanate's religious milieu, Ibadhis and other fellow Muslims pray side by side, focusing more on what unifies them than on what potentially divides them. Representatives of each religious denomination share positions of power and authority throughout the land, including at the highest levels, as cabinet ministers, as advisers, and as members of the Majlis Oman (Council of Oman), the country's bicameral parliament.

Ibadhism in the Larger Culture

As travelers have discovered throughout the ages, Omani moderation and inclusivity have extended beyond the boundaries of Islam, embracing people with different religious and cultural traditions. For generations, seafaring Omanis ventured far from home, interacting with diverse cultures. In the course of their travels, Omani sailors and merchants introduced Islam to the peoples of East Africa, Indonesia, and the Far East and at the same time introduced the cultures of those lands to Oman.[51]

The experience of prolonged interaction with diverse societies has had a profound impact on the Omani people, instilling in them a respect for religions and cultures different from their own. The prevalence of this welcoming atmosphere, a distinctive feature of Omani culture, was borne out by the observations of a visitor to the sultanate more than a century ago. In a National Geographic article from 1911, an American visitor noted that the Arabs of Oman are

> remarkably free from fanaticism, simple in their habits, and wonderful in their hospitality. Most of them belong to the Abadhi [sic] sect, which has many beliefs in common with Christianity, and the experience of our missionaries has been that the people are not only accessible, but willing to learn, and many of them eager not only for medical help, but for teaching.[52]

Decades after the publication of that *National Geographic* article, Ray F. Skinner, reflecting on his two-year assignment at the Protestant Church in Oman (1987–1989), wrote in his introduction to *Christians in Oman*,

> Until recently, free discourse and travel has been difficult in Arabia, and remains so in many regions within the peninsula. However in the Sultanate of Oman, there has traditionally been a welcome for the courteous visitor. The expatriate community is allowed to build churches, and its clergy have no restrictions put on them, within the bounds of non-proselytisation.[53]

Indeed, in today's Oman, religious pluralism[54] clearly extends to other faith traditions as well as to other sects of Islam. Hindu temples and Christian churches, erected on land donated by the sultan, coexist with mosques. Although proselytizing is illegal, freedom of religion is assured, consistent with the teaching of the Qu'ran:

> Verily! Those who believe and those who are Jews and Christians and Sabians, whoever believe in God and the Day of Judgement and does righteous good deeds shall have their reward with their Almighty God, on them there shall be no fear, nor they grieve. (Surat al-Bakhrah 2:62)

Oman's venerable history of religious pluralism and mutual understanding (*tafahum*), within both an Islamic and a non-Islamic context, has made it an ideal venue both for inter-Islamic discourse and for dialogue among the other Abrahamic faiths.[55] In recent years, foreign visitors have engaged in "travel seminars" in Oman in which participants attend lectures and meetings with religious leaders and scholars, engage in interfaith dialogue with students in the Institute of Shari'a Sciences, and meet members of the American Protestant Mission in Oman, exploring further the ecumenical context of Oman with visits to Hindu temples. They also attend interfaith summer programs to promote communication and further understanding.[56]

Several observers have remarked on the "calming" aspect of Ibadhism, commenting on the country's innate serenity, "curiously aided by its Ibadhi form of Islam."[57] This sense of calm is readily evident as one engages in interpersonal dialogue throughout Oman. Visitors to the sultanate, both past and present, invariably remark on the prevailing etiquette of courtesy and hospitality that seems to permeate Omani society. Whether in public or private, a certain pattern of mannerly social interaction appears to underscore a deeply internalized pattern of social behavior that Fredric Barth terms the "ideology of politeness."[58]

This observable characteristic of Omani society has been recorded by visitors to the country for a very long time. In 1663 John Ovington, chaplain to King James II of England, described the citizens of Muscat in glowing terms:

> These Arabians are very courteous in their deportment, and extremely civil to strangers; they offer neither violence nor affront in any way; and tho' they are very tenacious in their own principles, and admirers of their own religion,

yet do they never impose it upon any, nor are their morals leven'd with such furious zeal, as to divest them of humanity and a tender respect. . . . In fine, these are a People naturally temperate and just, and imbued with those excellent qualities which Grecian philosophers and Roman moralists endeavoured to inspire into their subjects, tho' they missed their aim.[59]

More than three hundred years later, Alston and Laing concurred with Ovington, writing, "Those who have had the privilege of knowing the present-day inhabitants of Muscat will say that these judgments remain valid."[60]

In the nineteenth century, James Raymond Wellsted, a lieutenant in Her Majesty's British Indian navy, was granted permission by the sultan to visit Oman. In the book *Travels to Arabia*, Bayard Taylor recounts Wellsted's 1835 journey, remarking, in particular, on the hospitality of the people he encountered. Welcomed by the tribe of the Beni Abu-Ali, deep in the country's interior, the Englishman was received with "every demonstration of friendship. Sheep were killed, a feast prepared, a guard of honor stationed around the tent, and in the evening, all the men of the encampment . . . assembled for the purpose of exhibiting their war dance."[61]

On another occasion, Wellsted wrote of a casual encounter with the wives of a Beni Geneba Bedouin chief, a highly unusual experience for a Western male in early nineteenth-century Arabia. At their small encampment, "they conversed with him, unveiled, gave him coffee, milk, and dates, and treated him with all the hospitality which their scanty means allowed."[62]

As in days of old, visitors to Oman today routinely characterize its people as "comfortable in their own skin" or, alternately, "at peace with themselves," an observation that, sadly, cannot be applied to vast numbers of beleaguered citizens of the Middle East today.

SOCIAL ORGANIZATION

Today, as in the past, family continues to be the indisputable, primary unit of social organization in most societies of the Middle East. The state apparatus, including the opportunities and services provided by modern, centralized governments, is of relatively recent vintage in this region and elsewhere. Throughout much of history, individuals have had to rely almost exclusively on family for assistance, particularly during periods of economic hardship and political turmoil. One's very identity was understood largely through the prism of kinship patterns, providing a basis upon which to understand social relations, including its members' expectations and responsibilities. Recognizing the primacy of family, including the clan or tribe, which serves as an extension of families related through a common bloodline, is critical to appreciating the dynamics of the social fabric, as well as the political organization, of cultures in the Middle East.

Traditionally, Omani society has been organized into tribes. This system predates Islam. Historically, tribes have functioned as small, autonomous communities, each with its own identity, historical narrative, and territory. In harsh environments, such as those that have existed in Oman and elsewhere, the social cohesion and shared responsibility typical of tribal organization were indispensable for individual and group survival. The tribe, in addition to offering a social safety net for the community, observed an established code of conduct, demanded accountability from its leaders, and provided respectability for its members. In this context, it should be noted that "volunteerism," as it is understood in modern Western life, is largely alien to the traditional societies of the Middle East, because all manner of support and assistance has traditionally been available through the institutions of family and tribe.

Village Organization

During one of my early trips to the governorate of Sharqiyah with a small delegation of visitors, we were introduced to tribal organization and culture by the leader of a community that, in many ways, is representative of the traditional village dynamic not only in Oman but throughout much of the wider Middle East.

Escorting us first to a vantage point overlooking this ancient community, our host explained both the physical plan of the village and the time-honored responsibilities of its inhabitants. Before the advent of large urban communities and strong, centralized governments, he explained, villages were largely self-sufficient entities, insuring protection from hostile forces from the outside while providing security for the residents within their walls.

In this community, seven major families predominated; there was a corresponding number of watchtowers, gates, and "big houses." Our host explained that each family chose from its group an individual to serve as its leader for a period of four years, during which time he occupied the "big house." Periodically, the leaders of each family met in joint session (*majlis*)[63] for consultation (*shura*)[64] on local issues of importance. Local issues requiring broader, national assistance were handled, he explained, by a *wali*, an appointed representative of the sultan, serving as liaison between the villagers and the central government—today as in centuries past.[65]

In the past, villages were organized into committees through which deliberations were held and decisions made. Not surprising, the most important of these was the water committee, overseeing the cleaning, maintenance, and fair distribution of this precious resource in the community. A second committee, the education, or "Islamic," committee was responsible for the maintenance of schools and mosques and for paying the salaries of their employees. The "social" committee served as a sort of "safety net," providing for the welfare of the inhabitants, including widows and orphans who might be struggling with illness or economic hardship. Finally, historically there was an "economic" committee, whose raison d'être in Oman has been largely eclipsed since 1970 by the effective outreach of the national government.

The fourteenth-century traveler Ibn Khaldun, often hailed as the father of sociology, carried the notion of tribal identity to a new level when he wrote of *'asabiyah* (group feeling), a kind of esprit de corps or group solidarity based on personal relations. It is characterized, he said, by "boundless and unconditional loyalty to fellow clansmen" in which it is assumed that "the clan or tribe . . . is a unit by itself, self-sufficient and absolute."[66]

However, while *'asabiyah* represented the fundamental bond of human society and the basic motivational force of history for Ibn Khaldun, the *hadith* (traditions) attributed to the Prophet Muhammad condemns an exaggerated notion of tribal solidarity as contrary to the essence of Islam. From the outset, the message delivered by the Prophet was designed to replace traditional alliances and to bring about a new social order in which devotion to the *ummah* (or "nation" of believers) would transcend narrow tribal loyalties.

Although a commitment to tribal solidarity remains an enduring feature of Omani society today, since 1970 the dominant themes of *national unity* and *political cohesion* have gradually eclipsed narrow regional loyalties in the political culture and social dynamics of Omanis.

The Desert and Its People

While Oman boasts more than a thousand miles of coastline, including seasonally lush, tropical regions in the south and dense areas of cultivation in the north, a vast expanse of barren desert lies behind the deep *wadis* (water courses) and rugged mountains of the interior. In fact, two-thirds of Oman's area is arid.

Sharing the sultanate's border with Saudi Arabia and the UAE is the fabled and forbidding Empty Quarter (Rub' al-Khali), immortalized in Wilfred Thesiger's dramatic narrative *Arabian Sands*. The Empty Quarter of Arabia, the world's largest sand desert, is regarded as one of the most inhospitable places on earth. It was of little interest to the rest of the world for much of human history—that is, until the early twentieth century, when unimaginable reserves of petroleum were discovered far beneath the desert sands.[67]

Searing heat and hundreds of miles of waterless terrain would seem a hostile environment for human existence. And so it is, except for the tribal *bedu* (Bedouin), the fabled nomads of the desert, who have managed to exist in this harsh environment for millennia. The Bedouin of Arabia are proud and fiercely independent. The challenges of their difficult surroundings have bred strong survival skills, a resilient spirit, and tight social cohesion.

Bedu culture is unique in many ways. Distinguishing themselves from their settled cousins in nearby towns and cities, they are proud to consider themselves the "original" Arabs. Their unquestioned hospitality toward strangers is the stuff of legend. Their reliance on the camel, the "ship of the desert," as well as the date palm, is central to their way of life.

Desert Journey

There is something almost hypnotic about the desert; the all-enveloping silence, the stillness, even the certain vulnerability that one feels within such a vast expanse is somehow deeply moving.

During one of our daytime adventures through a section of the Omani desert region known as the Sharqiyah Sands, the infinite peace of this setting was temporarily but dramatically interrupted as our party of foreign guests was invited to explore massive dunes at breakneck speeds in four-wheel-drive vehicles navigated by fearless teenagers from a local tribe. For the white-knuckled passengers belted inside, this modern "sport," known as "dune bashing," is as thrilling and unforgettable an adventure as any to be experienced at an amusement park.

After regaining our composure and settling into our comfortable, if Spartan, lodgings, we prepared for the evening ahead, the highlight of which was a feast called *shuwa*, a meal traditionally prepared in Oman on festive occasions. Preparation is elaborate and undertaken with great ceremony. Meat, including lamb, or goat in our case, is rubbed with a variety of spices, for which Omani cuisine is renowned, and then wrapped in dried leaves of palm or banana. Thus enveloped, the meat is then slowly roasted for twenty-four to forty-eight hours in a special oven in a covered underground pit.[68] Accompanied by rice, the succulent, flavorful meat that emerges is an unforgettable delicacy for those lucky enough to be invited to partake in this feast.

Following such a sumptuous meal, we reclined on ample cushions to enjoy an evening's entertainment provided by local musicians whose beats were more evocative of the percussive rhythms of Africa than of the familiar string cadences of the Levant, or the countries of the eastern Mediterranean. As guests gradually returned to their *barasti* (palm frond) huts, many opted to sleep under the stars to delight in a sky ablaze with dazzling constellations, rarely visible in the industrialized world (see figure 1.3 for an image of this characteristic desert dwelling). Sleep would not come easily in the presence of this veritable light show. The desert, a captivating place of mystery and beauty, makes for a perfect retreat.

Awakened before dawn by the bleating of camels, we arose to embrace a new day. There was an almost reverent hush in the air as we silently set about assessing our surroundings, In the morning's faint light, we could just barely discern the outline of massive dunes, mountains of sand, all around us. Barefoot and disheveled, we raced to retrieve our cameras and, as if on cue, began climbing the dunes of soft, cool sand in anticipation of a magnificent sunrise. As the first brilliant orange glow appeared and then intensified on the eastern horizon, we were mesmerized by the indescribable, almost sacred beauty of the place.

Figure 1.3 *Barasti* hut, constructed of native palm fronds, provides shelter from the wind and sand in the desert regions of Oman
Photo by author (2014).

Although they represent a relatively small percentage of the overall population, these storied nomads constitute an important piece of the Omani cultural mosaic. While some *bedu* live along coastal areas, fishing in winter and harvesting dates in the summer, most are confined to more arid regions, where, accompanied by their herds of camels, goats, and sheep, they wander in search of water.

And yet, modernity is gradually altering the traditional lifestyles of the Bedouin not only in Oman but in the rest of Arabia as well. As the demand for education and modern conveniences grows, pastoral nomads of the desert regions are gradually migrating closer to villages and towns. As their children are transported to schools, parents communicate easily by cell phones while herding their livestock in pickup trucks. As in the rest of the world, Omani society is dynamic and changing.

Water and Human Ingenuity

The relatively recent discovery and production of oil in Oman has blessed the government with the means by which to create a modern national infrastructure. Yet, as one drives through the small towns and villages of the country's interior, it becomes apparent very quickly that *water*, scarce and precious, has long been, and will remain, this country's most valued commodity. In a region of arid and semiarid zones, devoid of rivers and lacking adequate rainfall, the challenge of sustainable agriculture has been of utmost concern to the inhabitants of Oman for millennia. Long before the modern Christian era, the people of this ancient land combined laws of physics, human ingenuity, and simple, if backbreaking, technology to devise an ingenious system of water distribution and irrigation, known as the *falaj* (plural, *aflaj*) or, less frequently, the *qanat* system.

Older accounts have suggested that the origin of this system was Persian, dating from the first millennium BCE; however, recent archaeological excavations in Salut in the Omani province of Bahla confirm that *falaj* systems were in use in southern Arabia at the end of the second millennium BCE, predating those in present-day Iran.[69] According to legend, the prophet Solomon (*Sulayman*), son of David (*Da'ud*), flew over Oman on a magic carpet and commanded an army of genies (*djinns*) to fashion a network of channels, both above and below the earth, through which life-giving waters would flow.

For the past three thousand years, until today, these subterranean channels and tunnels have been dug by hand and painstakingly maintained, tapping into mountain aquifers as they carry fresh water downhill by the force of gravity. Designed with numerous branches, or tributaries, *aflaj* distribute water to the mosques, homes, and farms of grateful villagers. See figure 1.4 for a 1974 photo of a *falaj* winding its way through the landscape of the Dakhiliyah governorate.

Figure 1.4   A *falaj* or water distribution system in the governorate of Dakhiliyah, combining human ingenuity with social organization

Photo by author (1974).

The *falaj* system continues to serve as a lifeline for the people of Oman's interior regions, permitting settlement and cultivation in an otherwise barren land. Of more than four thousand *falaj* canals that were built, some three thousand are still in operation today. Together they deliver 410 million cubic meters across Oman, supplying 38 percent of the country's fresh water.[70]

Falaj networks involve both engineering skills and social cooperation. Most *aflaj* are privately owned; as such, they can be sold, leased, or mortgaged. A typical system is owned by farmers of a single village, who contribute money for its maintenance and upkeep. According to this time-honored system, the owner of each agricultural plot (or *jasbah*) is allotted a number of shares based on a specific time period (called either *athar* or *badda*). During the day, the fair distribution of water is determined by a sundial (*amud*), with gradations indicating how long each plot receives a stream of water. At night the timing of water distribution is measured by the stars. The distribution manager (*bidar*) uses a wooden device or stones wrapped in mud and cloth (*suwar*) to open or close the distribution channels of the *falaj* to allow or to obstruct the flow of water to individual plots according to the number of shares to which each owner is entitled.[71]

Referring to this consensus-based tradition of water distribution as a "highly structured collectivist system" that has persisted in Oman for centuries and, indeed, well into the modern era, Jones and Ridout note that villagers today respect and adhere to these practices "as strictly as they would were they governed by more formal legal means."[72] Further, they maintain that the social dynamics that underpin the success of the *falaj* system, including self-regulating social reciprocity, have been internalized within Omani culture, extending even further into the realm of foreign policy—which, as we shall see in chapter 6, is marked by a consensual, dialogue-based approach.

REFLECTIONS

The sultanate's location along the littoral of the Indian Ocean, at the crossroads of major land routes and vital sea lanes, as well as its illustrious maritime history, has infused within the Omani national psyche a certain *sense of place* characterized by openness toward peoples of varying traditions. This legacy of interaction with other cultures is manifest today not only in an impressive cultural mosaic, reflecting a variety of races, languages, and ethnicities, but also in the spirit of hospitality and cosmopolitanism that permeates the country, making it an ideal venue today for international business, tourism, and dialogue.

Having carried Omani seamen to distant lands for centuries, the dhow, at the same time both delicate and resilient, remains an object of national pride. A resurgent demand from across the world for that superbly crafted yet graceful vessel has revived this industry, as new orders are being filled by skilled craftsmen today as in centuries past, in the historic shipyards of Sur.

And while frankincense, that milky resin from a gnarly tree, is no longer an internationally traded commodity worth its weight in gold, its alluring fragrance, a poignant reminder of a glorious past, endures as an omnipresent fixture in the homes, shops, and offices of modern Oman. As the current government has begun to subsidize cultivation of *Boswellia sacra* in the governorate of Dhofar, exciting new research is under way on the potential medicinal benefits of this legendary substance.

With four UNESCO World Heritage Sites to its credit, Oman's record as a region of settled people, with a distinctive civilization reaching back into antiquity, is of interest to archaeologists and historians alike. From ancient Greece to Mesopotamia to Saba', Oman was an important destination for trade and commerce as well as an acknowledged center of culture and sophistication. Much remains to be learned from additional excavations throughout the land. This sense of history informs the Omanis' "sense of self" even today, reinforcing their national identity and fueling their optimism as they venture headlong into the twenty-first century.

It has likely been a surprise to many that Oman is the center of a third sect within the Islamic ethos. Ibadhism, inadequately understood if known at all, is a tradition dating to the first century of Islam. It is important not only from a historical perspective but even more for understanding what makes Oman unique. Ibadhism is democratic, it is dynamic, and it is moderate. A bold statement, to be sure, but one that will be borne out in the pages to follow.

Although *the tribe* has predominated as the central focus of cultural life throughout the course of Oman's history, Qaboos bin Said, sultan since 1970, has galvanized his people into a *national entity*. He has accomplished this in an evolutionary fashion, initially by inviting traditional leadership figures into new political institutions and then, gradually, by expanding mechanisms for wider popular participation. Throughout this process, certain traditional features have remained in force, especially the notion of *shura* (consultation), a particularly democratic practice that has been a hallmark of Omani political life in the past as well as in the present.

Oman is a country of contrasting visual images, on the one hand calling to mind the desert, including its fabled dwellers, and on the other, lush oases, harboring the most precious natural resource of all, water. Between these two extremes lie formidable mountain ranges, whose summits reach for the sky. Throughout the ages, the people of Oman have exhibited extraordinary resilience and determination in overcoming harsh and challenging circumstances, characteristics that might explain a spirit of independence and resolve that underscores their modern history and national policies even today.

The *bedu*, nomadic people of the desert, have prevailed since time immemorial through difficult natural conditions. Independent and resourceful, they crisscross the land in search of green pastures, while their settled brothers and sisters, agriculturalists, faced with chronic uncertainty and harsh terrain, construct villages and towns with perseverance and ingenuity. In the process, the village folk of Oman devised an ingenious system whereby water, precious and scarce, could be diverted from great distances to their fields, bringing life to an ever-expanding variety of crops while allowing for a stable and increasingly diversified lifestyle and, eventually, giving rise to the traditional arts and crafts that are treasured to this day.

Here, then, is the cultural landscape of Oman, its land and society. Chapter 2 will explore the early history of modern Oman, including foreign incursions, the rise of heroic figures, valiant conquests, twists of fate, empire building, and an interlude of seeming stagnation.

CHAPTER 2

SETTING THE STAGE: OMAN PRE-1970

An appreciation of the history of Oman—one of the oldest independent nations on earth—is indispensable to understanding both Oman's people and its modern policies. It is history, long remembered and routinely celebrated through oral tradition, the arts, and cultural tourism that is at the very heart of Oman's collective identity, informing its domestic behavior and guiding its foreign relations. It is history, including victories, defeats, and lessons learned that renders Oman's particular journey into modernity unique unto itself.

EARLY INCURSIONS

Oman is a country with a long tradition of independence. Nevertheless, Oman's history has been punctuated by a series of invasions by the Persians as well as by an occupation by the Portuguese. From these foreign incursions, the Omanis would develop a national consciousness, intent on preserving their sovereignty and independence, one that would also embolden them to achieve supremacy on the seas, expanding their own borders and engaging in international commerce that would contribute to the cosmopolitan character of Oman as we know it today.

The "Neighbor" to the North

For centuries, Oman's fortunes have been intertwined more closely with Persia (present-day Iran) than with any other Middle Eastern power. In ancient times, and even into the modern era, Oman has borne the brunt of repeated incursions and periodic occupations by its mighty neighbor to the north.

Persian hegemony in Oman was first challenged by Malik bin Faham, celebrated leader of the tribe of al-Azd, which emigrated from the Ma'rib region of Yemen following the collapse of the great dam in the first or second century CE.[1] The Persians, who controlled vast portions of the country at the time, resisted the intrusion of the Azd tribe, confronting them at every turn. According to the Omani historian Isam al-Rawas,

> The repeated refusal of the Persians to allow Malik and his tribe to settle pre-
> sented the Azd with no alternative but to fight. The resultant battle in the
> desert of Salut near Nizwa between the troops of Malik and the Persian gover-
> nor of Sohar led to the defeat of the Persian army. The subsequent campaign
> brought total victory to the Azd, who succeeded in expelling the Persian colo-
> nists from Oman altogether. They left Sohar with their families and sailed to
> Fars [present-day Iran]. Thereupon Malik is said to have become king, estab-
> lishing [an] Arab kingdom in Oman.[2]

In time, Oman was populated by additional waves of migrants, from the powerful Azd tribe as well as from other groups. A loose federation of vari- ous peoples eventually formed, united only by their opposition to Persian incursions.

By the sixth century CE, Persian control of Oman reemerged but was confined largely to the region around Sohar, the center of maritime activity along the coast. Under the banner of the Sassanian Empire, the Persians, in competition with the Byzantine Empire for control of the Middle East, were determined to prevail on both sides of the Persian Gulf, including in "Mazoun," the name then most commonly associated with Oman. In addi- tion to Sohar, the major outposts of Sassanid power were Daba, at the north- ern end of the Batinah plain, and Rustaq, at the base of the Jabal al-Akhdar.[3]

European Imperialism

The Persians would return to Oman intermittently, well into the eighteenth century, but not before the country was first exploited by the Europeans. Oman's first brush with European colonization came from Portugal in the early sixteenth century. Following Vasco da Gama's successful discovery in 1497–1498 of a sea route around the Cape of Good Hope, which connected Europe with the Far East, Portugal became the preeminent maritime power of the day. To a significant degree, the object of its desire was the lands on the littoral, or coast, of the Indian Ocean, "which began its modern history as a Portuguese imperial lake."[4]

The motivation of the Europeans was purely commercial; their aim was to challenge Arab dominance of the important sea lanes connecting the distant lands of the East—in particular, the strategic region around the Strait of Hormuz. Victory over these routes would ensure the Portuguese a virtual monopoly over the growing and immensely lucrative spice trade. In time, the contenders were victorious, "gain[ing] control of the eastern trading routes much to the demise of Arab maritime traders operating in other than the local Indian Ocean region."[5]

Given its strategic location at the hub of vital and heavily trafficked trade routes, Oman, in particular, was soon to feel the blow of Portugal's insatiable ambitions. In 1507 the Portuguese lay siege to Muscat and other ports along the Persian Gulf. That great naval power could not have chosen a better location. Oman was ideally suited as a port of call for ships traversing the all-important maritime routes to the Indian subcontinent and beyond. It served as an ideal staging point for the Europeans' maritime ambitions: "For Lisbon, Muscat was a base . . . and Omanis provided a pool of labor. They left alone those who accepted their rule but suppressed those who complained."[6]

Alfonso de Albuquerque (1453–1515), an ambitious and notoriously brutal commander serving under Vasco da Gama, had a singular ambition: to establish Portuguese hegemony over all the sea lanes and strategic coastal lands in the Indian Ocean region. Arriving in Oman in 1507, the Portuguese commander assessed Muscat, the "principal *entrepôt* of the Kingdom of Hormuz," quite favorably, as "a very large and populous city. . . . There are orchards, gardens, and palm groves, with pools for watering them with wooden engines. The harbor is small, shaped like a horseshoe and sheltered from every wind. It is a very elegant town with very fine houses."[7]

Yet, these initial glowing, almost poetic accounts of Muscat's charm and natural beauty, resembling Lisbon with its gardens, orchards, and palm groves, did little to deter the Portuguese general from initiating an unrelenting campaign of treachery, brutality, and oppression against both citizens and infrastructure, unprecedented in the recorded history of Oman. The commander and his foot soldiers left a trail of destruction in their wake, burning towns, destroying fishing harbors, and disfiguring inhabitants. Accounts of this wanton cruelty remain permanently emblazoned in the memories of Omanis and others in the region who experienced the force of Albuquerque's might.[8]

Portuguese dominance in the Indian Ocean region had a profound impact on the dynamics of global trade as well as on the economy of Oman. The effect was not only to deprive the Omanis of control of the highly lucrative international maritime routes to the East, effectively restricting their commerce to the domestic sphere, but also to marginalize Omani Arabs in East Africa, effectively isolating them from their accustomed interaction with brethren in Arabia. Only in the nineteenth century, during the reign of Said bin Sultan, would these relations be restored.[9]

The Portuguese ruled over Oman's capital city, Muscat, and its coastal cities for almost 150 years, propelling the country to international attention as "one of the most important Portuguese strongholds in the Indian Ocean."[10] During this period, Portugal's dominance of the seas, including the most lucrative trade routes in the Persian Gulf, the Red Sea, and the Indian Ocean, went unchallenged, striking a cruel blow to Oman's former maritime glory.

At the same time, rival powers colluded to undermine Portuguese hegemony. From the early seventeenth century, an ascendant Britain with growing interests in the region, operating under the mantle of the "East India Company," and its ally, Persia, joined forces to challenge Portugal's maritime dominance in the Gulf.[11] In 1622 these new political bedfellows succeeded in expelling the Portuguese from Hormuz, the most important commercial center in the Persian Gulf. As Britain and Persia conspired to loosen

Lisbon's grip on Oman—sometimes in tandem and sometimes not—a local campaign, led by Nasr bin Murshid al-Yaʻrubi (r. 1624–1649), the founder of an ascendant dynasty, would finally succeed in ridding the country of the Portuguese forever.

The Struggle for Independence

At the turn of the seventeenth century CE, Oman was in disarray. Its strategic coastal regions were occupied and controlled by the Portuguese. Racked by intractable internal divisions, rival Omani rulers vied for power in the towns of Rustaq, Nakhl, Samad, Ibra', and Sama'il. The country's fortunes took a positive turn in 1624 when a delegation of *ʻulama'* (learned scholars), in keeping with the Ibadhi tradition of determining a leader through the consent of the governed, elected Nasr bin Murshid al-Yaʻrubi[12] of Rustaq to the exalted position of imam (leader).[13]

The accession of Nasr bin Murshid (r. 1624–1649), founder of the illustrious dynasty that bears his name (Yaʻrubid or Yaʻrubah), marks the beginning of Oman's struggle for independence from Portuguese control. Gifted with a charismatic personality, the imam (a title that would be assigned to all future Yaʻrubid rulers), was a persuasive leader, inspiring courage as he united Omanis in their overriding common goal: the expulsion of the colonial rulers. Assembling a powerful naval fleet, he launched several successful campaigns, ultimately succeeding in wresting a string of strategic coastal areas from Lisbon's grip. Upon the death of Imam Nasr[14] in 1649, his successor, Sultan[15] bin Sayf al-Yaʻrubi (r. 1649–1679), again proclaimed as imam by public acclamation, successfully accomplished Imam Nasr's objective by liberating Oman from the last vestiges of Portuguese control in 1649–1650.

The legacy of the Portuguese colonial period is everywhere evident in Muscat today, albeit in fairly benign manifestations. Multiple watchtowers, reminiscent of the past, are perched on hilltops surrounding the capital, while below, flanking Muscat's natural deepwater harbor, are two forts, al-Mirani, originally "Forte do Capitão" (1588), used primarily as a garrison, and al-Jalali, originally named "Forte de São João" (1587), later a notorious prison—both, imposing, fearsome sentinels designed to secure Portugal's hold on the Gulf against inroads by the Ottoman Turks (see figure 2.1 for a view of al-Jalali fort today).

In retrospect, the Portuguese legacy was significant in the evolution of Oman's collective identity, representing "the first impression that a European [power] left on Muscat and its people"[16] and searing into the Omani psyche a profound commitment to protect its national sovereignty. The sad chapter of Portuguese rule reawakened "a determination in the Omani people to shake off the shackles of subjugation,"[17] with the result that the country would never again be ruled directly by a foreign power.[18] To a significant extent, this brush with foreign occupation would solidify Oman's determination to preserve its sovereignty and independence, unassailable cornerstones of the sultanate's national policy today.

Figure 2.1   Al-Jalali Fort at Muscat Harbor, built by the Portuguese (as Forte de São João) in 1587 and used as a prison until 1970

Photo by author (2012).

EXPANDING DOMINIONS

Ironically, it was the Portuguese themselves, vanquished and forever driven from Omani soil, who contributed inadvertently to Oman's eventual reemergence as a respected and feared maritime power. During their 150-year-long occupation of Oman, the Europeans introduced improved techniques in building, operating, and maintaining ships. The Omanis were quick to learn these skills and, in time, would use this knowledge impressively to their own advantage.

At the same time that Oman was attempting to free itself from Portuguese control, Britain began to focus its attention on this small but strategically important country. British interest in Oman was understandable, given not only the latter's location on the Arabian Sea but also its proximity to the increasingly important subcontinent of South Asia, including India, which would become the centerpiece of Britain's growing empire. In 1645, in the first recorded link between the United Kingdom and Oman, the British East India Company, buttressed by the most formidable maritime fleet of the age, requested trading privileges from Imam Nasr bin Murshid al-Ya'rubi. Nasr acquiesced by granting the British a trading station in the northern port of Sohar.

Following the expulsion of the Portuguese, Nasr's successor, Imam Sultan bin Sayf al-Ya'rubi, in a stunning display of role reversal, developed a diversified and formidable naval fleet, including warships capable of carrying as many as eighty canons. Throughout the years following the restoration of sovereignty, Oman enjoyed a resurgence of power and prestige, as its navy gained fame as "one of the most powerful in the Arabian Sea."[19]

As the Omani naval forces pursued the vanquished Portuguese relentlessly on the high seas, their exploits, extending to lands far beyond the shores of Arabia, would ultimately leave an indelible imprint on the culture, the economy, and, perhaps most important, the mindset of the population of Oman.

In time, England's link with Oman strengthened, growing more and more exclusive. Nevertheless, Britain wasn't the only one to benefit from the relationship. The Omanis not only gained access to vital navigational charts developed by British seamen but also, by the early eighteenth century, began to modernize their own fleet, placing orders for well-constructed ships from the dockyards of British India.

Migrations to East Africa

One conspicuous feature of the Omani narrative, distinguishing it even further from that of its neighbors, is its almost unbroken history of interaction with the African continent. It is believed that Omani migration to East Africa began in the seventh century CE. Written accounts, including those of the celebrated fourteenth-century traveler Ibn Battuta, corroborate the presence of Omanis along the coastal cities and even into the deepest interior reaches of East Africa going back for centuries.

In 1652, when the Arabs of Mombasa (Kenya) requested Omani assistance in ousting the Portuguese from their shores, Imam Sultan bin Sayf dispatched an impressive fleet to East Africa, battering European outposts along the coast, including the islands of Zanzibar (part of present-day Tanzania) and Pemba (Mozambique) before ultimately defeating the Europeans in Mombasa in 1660. Solidifying his claim to these three territories, the imam appointed Omani *walis* (imperial governors) to oversee them.[20]

Not satisfied with subduing the Portuguese on the African continent, Oman's ambitions then turned to the Asian subcontinent, occupying the strategic enclave of Gwadar, located on the western corner of the historic Makran coast, today part of the Baluchistan province of Pakistan.[21] With a massive and powerful fleet, Imam Sultan commanded the vital sea lanes of the Indian Ocean, pursuing the Portuguese as far as Goa, their beloved colony off the coast of India. As the vanquished turned into conquerors, "Imam Sultan . . . and his immediate successors pursued a policy of prolonged attacks on Portuguese shipping in the Indian Ocean and systematically raided and plundered their settlements and trading posts on the Indian and East African coasts."[22]

During the second half of the seventeenth century, Oman further consolidated its strength and expanded its profile as a global power. This was a "high water point in the heroic struggles of Oman's history" in which the Omanis not only attacked "the Portuguese on their own shores but also in the Indian Ocean: in the water and on the land."[23]

As Oman's domains in East Africa were revived and further expanded, the country's prosperity and newfound wealth, garnered in part from participation in the international slave trade, soared to new heights. Back home in Arabia, much-needed resources and amenities were introduced. Imam Sultan launched a massive program of infrastructure improvements, introducing critical repairs to the country's neglected and crumbling *falaj* irrigation system. Construction was launched on a string of impressive forts that stand to this day in the "land of 500 forts" as a poignant reminder of a period of economic stability and political unity.

Oman's *imperium* had begun. While this era would usher in a period of unprecedented national wealth, Oman's bold exploits would attract, not surprisingly, unwanted attention from the international maritime powers of the day—Portugal, England, Persia, and India—as they all scrambled among themselves to create alliances to thwart Omani ambitions.[24]

After the death of Imam Sultan bin Sayf al-Ya'rubi in 1679, the leadership of Oman fell to his two sons: the first, Bal'arab bin Sultan, followed by his brother, Sayf bin Sultan. The second of the two, Imam Sayf bin Sultan (r. 1692–1711), considered by some to have been "the greatest of the Ya'ruba princes,"[25] embarked on an ambitious program of building and infrastructure repair throughout the country. He is credited with the restoration of *falaj* irrigation systems and the expansion of well excavation, which ushered in an era of intense agricultural productivity, particularly along the Batinah corridor, a region that would become, and remains to this day, the agricultural hub of Oman.

During the reign of Imam Sayf bin Sultan, Oman's international stature grew dramatically. Its naval strength, manpower, and defenses were so formidable as to cause the Europeans, reportedly, to be terrified that the Omanis would ultimately control the whole of the Gulf region.[26] After seizing several cities along the coast of East Africa in 1698, Imam Sayf proclaimed Zanzibar the second capital of Oman. Over time, substantial revenues were directed to these new territories in East Africa for the development of agriculture and commerce—unfortunately, it would appear, at the expense of maintaining a healthy infrastructure and a sustainable economy back home in Oman.

Acquisitions in South Asia

After consolidating his control over East Africa, Imam Sayf turned his attention further afield to South Asia and, in particular, to the vital port of Gwadar in Baluchistan. Securing and occupying this strategic seaport at the mouth of the Persian Gulf near the Strait of Hormuz, he assigned a *wali* to oversee this important acquisition and to report directly to the ruler of Oman, an arrangement that would endure for more than two hundred years.

By the early eighteenth century, Oman had achieved a pinnacle in its long and illustrious history. This was a period of unprecedented national independence. The country's economy was strong and vibrant. And with a formidable naval fleet, Oman's maritime dominance was irrefutable.

Respect for the Omani navy was not confined to its regional neighbors. According to modern historians, Oman's "naval force was superior to all others in the region and was successful in many campaigns. The English and Dutch fleets did their best to avoid any contact with the Omani navy. Whether they were European traders or those from the Arabian Gulf and the Indian Ocean, all respected the Omani forces."[27]

The death of Imam Sayf bin Sultan in 1711 was widely mourned as "a disaster for national unity, the state of the Ya'rubid dynasty, and the general public."[28] Regrettably, his passing was followed by a period of civil war and internecine struggles for supremacy of the imamate.

Following his death, dissension over the selection of a new imam swelled within the ranks of rival Omani tribes. Sultan bin Sayf II (r. 1711–1718) was chosen to succeed his father. He constructed a fort at Hazm, a strategic location between the coast and the interior, and made that his capital, effectively thwarting Persia's ambitions to expand its reach into Oman's interior. Most notable, perhaps, was Imam Sultan's role in liberating Bahrain from the Persians. At the time of his death, Oman's sphere of influence was formidable, reaching out beyond the Persian Gulf, to the shores of India, to the coast of East Africa, and even to some Arab countries on the Red Sea that fell under Ottoman influence.[29]

Following the death of Sultan bin Sayf II in 1718, his son, Sayf bin Sultan II, was installed as ruler. Although only a boy of twelve years, he had the support of the populace. In time, his lackluster conduct and failure of leadership inflamed the impatient Ya'rubid clans, who conspired to depose him. When he was unceremoniously removed from office in 1732, he called on Persian forces, led by Nadir Shah, to intervene on his behalf—against his own people. Seizing the opportunity, Persian forces, commanded by Latif Khan, launched a naval offensive on the Omani coast, not to aid the deposed ruler, but rather to advance Nadir's own colonial ambitions in the Gulf. His strategy was unambiguous: "to invade Oman and Bahrain and put them under the complete control of Persia and then to dominate the entire Gulf region."[30] Robert Geran Landen describes this as part of a broad, calculated strategy:

> The wily Nadir, a conqueror who had built up a huge Persian empire stretching from Iraq to the Punjab, was searching for an opportunity to expand in the Persian Gulf. He eagerly dispatched his newly constructed fleet and an army to Oman. Intervention by the Persians resulted, predictably enough, in the occupation of Oman's coast, the fall of the Ya'aribah [*sic*] dynasty, and the temporary supremacy of Iran in the Persian Gulf during the 1730s and 1740s.[31]

This marked yet another chapter in Persia's storied history of occupation in Oman, stemming from at least the fourth century BCE. Yet, just as, a century earlier, the Omanis had successfully rallied to oust the Portuguese invaders, they would unite again, and ultimately prevail, under the banner of a strong, charismatic tribal leader who would restore sovereignty to his people and his country.

ASCENDANCE OF THE AL BU SAID DYNASTY

The sovereignty of Oman hung in the balance as the Ya'rubids, in deep disarray, appeared defenseless against the advancing Persian forces. As the Persians, commanded by Nadir Shah, seized one city after another along the Omani coast, their momentum was broken in Sohar, an important city on the Batinah coast. The instrument of their undoing was none other than Sohar's *wali*, a merchant and shipowner from the remote town of Adam, on the edge of the Rub' al-Khali desert, who had made a name for himself in this prosperous coastal city.

Ahmad bin Said Al Bu Said (r. 1744–1775), a "first-class politician" who was highly respected by the local *shaykhs* and clan leaders for both his strength and his resolve, successfully defended Sohar throughout a punishing nine-month siege. He negotiated a ceasefire agreement with the Persians, who then recognized him as the governor of Oman. Having successfully expelled the invading foreign forces, including their Ya'rubid confederates, Ahmad bin Said was unanimously elected by the Omanis as imam. The year was 1744, a milestone in the modern history of the Omani nation, particularly because it marked the first time a strong-willed ruler was able to unite the country, consolidating his power over a land historically riddled with disputing tribes.

Building on his Ya'rubid conquests, Ahmad bin Said was hailed as imam not only of Oman proper but also of Zanzibar and Kilwa in East Africa, territories that stretched far beyond the shores of Arabia. The installation of Imam Ahmad effectively marked the end of the Ya'rubid state and the birth of the Al Bu Said dynasty, which has presided over Oman for more than 250 years, into the twenty-first century.

Imam Ahmad used his power at home to further enhance Oman's profile abroad. Building on his career as a merchant and shipowner, he involved himself in extensive economic enterprises abroad, creating within the country "an atmosphere conducive to commercial activity within the overall system of basic agriculture" as well as creating alliances with other powers of the day, including the Ottomans.[32]

In 1756 an event known the "Basra campaign" would establish the foundation for an alliance between Oman and Iraq that would endure for generations. In that year, at the request of the Ottoman *wali* of Baghdad, Imam Ahmad agreed to thwart a Persian attempt to overtake Basra in the southern region of present-day Iraq. Commanded by his son, Hilal, an Omani expedition of ten thousand men, ten large ships, and several smaller vessels set sail for the Shatt al-Arab (Stream of the Arabs), a river at the confluence of the Tigris and Euphrates. Forcing their way across the iron chains that had been constructed by the besieging Persians to prevent relief from reaching the city, they overcame the occupiers in a fierce naval battle. In gratitude for their victory, the Ottoman sultan ordered the *wali* of Basra to pay an annual land tax (*kharaj*) to the Omani leader, a practice that continued well into the nineteenth century.[33]

In another, related, mission, Oman's forces engaged and destroyed a pirate fleet in the Persian Gulf en route to the Shatt al-Arab, thereby ensuring safe passage and security for merchant shipping through this strategic waterway. Once again, Oman's undisputed supremacy on the seas was validated.

Upon his death, Ahmad bin Said Al Bu Said left behind an impressive legacy that continues to this day. During his long reign, not only did he unite the various tribes within Oman but he also expanded the country's power and influence throughout the Gulf region, including much of the territory of the present-day United Arab Emirates.[34] By establishing Oman's preeminence in the Gulf through the formation of a powerful regular navy, Imam Ahmad held foreign ambitions in that region in check, elevating Oman to the level of an independent and formidable Indian Ocean power. His leadership and success, including the stability he brought to Oman, won him the respect of European powers. Their merchants were eager to establish commercial ties with Omani cities, "particularly Muscat which, according to a report issued by the British East India Company in 1790, had become one of the leading cities in Asia."[35]

By the end of the eighteenth century, in a move that would surely presage the forward momentum and direction of Imam Ahmad's realm, his successors, Said bin Ahmad (r. 1775–1779), Hamad bin Said (r. 1779–1792), and Sultan bin Ahmad (r. 1792–1804), would move the seat of government from Rustaq, a traditional religious center in the interior, to Muscat, a vibrant port city and growing hub for international trade. Flanking the capital city with forts and towers and equipping its defenses with formidable canons, the nation of Oman, known by the end of the eighteenth century as "Muscat and Oman,"[36] enjoyed both great strength and increasing prosperity.

In 1792 Sultan bin Ahmad,[37] a son of the iconic founder of the Al Bu Said dynasty, assumed the political leadership of all Omani territory, including not only the country of "Muscat and Oman" within Arabia, but also Zanzibar in Africa. In 1798 he signed a treaty with Great Britain that explicitly prohibited French and Dutch ships from gaining access to Omani ports. In addition, this agreement established a factory of the British East India Company in Bandar Abbas, then an Omani territory, on the Persian coast.

Within two years, Imam Sultan bin Ahmad entered into a second treaty with Britain, introducing a "Resident British Political Agent," an "English gentleman of respectability," to reside permanently in Oman. The treaty, signed by Captain John Malcolm on behalf of the British Crown, concludes with the wish that "the friendship of these two states may remain unshook to the end of time, til the sun and moon have finished their revolving career."[38] Far from implying any dependence on Britain, these two treaties recognized Oman as a leading Indian Ocean maritime power and, as such, represented an alliance between equals.

During his tenure on the throne, Imam Sultan successfully defended Oman and Bahrain against Wahhabi[39] forces advancing into his realm from deep within the interior of Arabia. On another front, his triumphant excursions into South Asia's Makran coast, including the port of Bandar Abbas, marked the beginning of a historic relationship with Baluchistan (part of present-day Pakistan) in South Asia, precipitating a wave of immigrants, whose descendants today form an integral part of Oman's demographic mosaic.

The death of Imam Sultan, who was killed by pirates during a journey between Basra and Oman, tragic though it was, would be followed by the emergence of a figure that would come to personify the "golden age" of Omani power and prestige in the nineteenth century.

AL BU SAIDI POWER: FROM APOGEE TO DECLINE

Said bin Sultan Al Bu Said (r. 1807[40]–1856), grandson of Imam Ahmad bin Said Al Bu Said, founder of the Al Bu Said dynasty, came to power as a teenager. This exceptional young prince, with a quick grasp and "affable manners,"[41] ruled over a vast territory, including Oman and much of the rich East African littoral (arguably "one of the most lucrative trading axes in Asia"[42]) until his death in 1856. With legendary diplomatic skill and considerable political acumen, Sultan Said presided over the apogee of the Omani empire.

Waves of Omanis first migrated to Zanzibar as early as the seventh century CE.[43] It is reported that when the impressionable Said bin Sultan, as a young boy of twelve years, first saw this enchanting land, he was "bewitched" by its natural beauty.[44] As he grew and matured, he became conversant not only in Arabic but also in Swahili, Hindi, and Persian—useful, to be sure, for the head of an ever-expanding dominion. He elevated Oman's international stature substantially as he acquired new territories, such as Gwadar, a strategic port on the coast of Baluchistan, as well as Zanzibar, making Oman the only non-European country in the nineteenth century to hold possessions in Africa. For a map highlighting Oman's international influence at its height in the mid-nineteenth century, see figure 2.2.

Zanzibar provided an ideal venue from which Said could effectively oversee his substantial, and expanding, African domain. The initial spell that the island had cast upon the young royal never waned, and he spent ever-longer periods of time in residence there. In time, Zanzibar became a twin capital, along with Muscat, of all territories under Oman's control,[45] elevating Said bin Sultan to the title "First Sultan of Oman, Zanzibar and Gwadar."[46]

During Said bin Sultan's illustrious tenure, the cultivation of cloves, for which Zanzibar is still justifiably famous, was launched. Following their forbearers' venerable tradition of seafaring, Omani sailors introduced this fragrant spice, indigenous to Indonesia, to East Africa, where the hot, humid climate of Zanzibar proved ideal for its cultivation. When combined with other crops, the export of cloves yielded revenues that represented a third of Oman's budget; that, in addition to the sale of ivory and other material goods, as well as the highly profitable global slave trade, brought considerable prosperity to Oman.

Figure 2.2   Dark-shaded areas indicate Omani domains in the mid-nineteenth century
Courtesy of the Office of the Adviser to His Majesty the Sultan for Cultural Affairs.

Although the slave trade and the practice of slavery have marked regret-table periods in the history of nations across the globe, a distinction can be made between the robust, commercially driven nature of the international slave trade in the West and that which was practiced primarily by the Arabs in East Africa, whose slaves rarely ventured farther than the Arabian Penin-sula and the East Coast of Africa.[47] In Oman, slaves served a variety of roles and "would typically have been understood as members of the household, without legal rights of full citizens, but often entrusted with positions of effective social and political power within those households."[48]

Britain declared the buying and selling of slaves illegal in 1807 and began a campaign to end the slave trade in the Indian Ocean. In 1822, after Said bin Sultan signed the Moresby Treaty, a British initiative abolishing international trafficking in slaves, the Zanzibari economy over which he ruled experienced a shift in emphasis, as did the nature of slavery there. By midcentury, the treaty had effectively transformed the Zanzibari economy from one that was based on the sale of slaves to one that was based on the products of their labor. "Whereas once the slave himself was the commodity, according to the new system, it was the labour power of the slave that would become the commodity."[49] Since Zanzibar's wealth in the nineteenth century was largely dependent upon clove plantation agriculture, manual labor was of paramount importance. And African slaves provided the labor. The irony of this consequence of British efforts to end the slave trade was not lost on Jones and Ridout, who note that

> the response in Zanzibar to British efforts to limit the slave trade may have actually encouraged or at least hastened the development of a slave economy that rather more closely resembled the kind of slavery prevalent in the Americas—which had most animated the abolitionist movement—than it did the form of slavery that had been part of Omani life for centuries.[50]

Nevertheless, they claim that the transformation in the nature of slavery in Zanzibar was never complete. And, as Kaplan adds, "It should be said that on the whole Omani slavers were not nearly as cruel as their European counterparts. Rather than enforce a living death upon the poor Africans they captured, they often integrated them into their families, clothed them, and provided them with wives."[51]

Meanwhile, throughout the nineteenth century, as the fortunes of Zanzibaris[52] soared, the situation for most Omanis in Arabia was deteriorating. The economy was beginning to falter, as remittances from abroad were too often put toward the construction of ostentatious palaces and the accumulation of personal wealth rather than toward improvements to local infrastructure. Most important, as the maintenance of water resources and management systems (*aflaj*) suffered from neglect, so did the country's agricultural sector. Profits from Zanzibar would soon begin to decline as well, as Said began to cooperate with British efforts to curtail the slave trade. Said's sons Turki and Barghash eventually signed treaties with Britain abolishing Oman's slave trade in 1873.[53]

In 1856, while sailing from Muscat to his beloved Zanzibar, Said bin Sultan, "the Sultan of Zanzibar," whose vast dominions included Muscat, died suddenly at the age of sixty-five. Putting the impact of this legendary figure in its historical perspective, Landen claims that "he was the last ruler of any importance in the Persian Gulf whose career was successful in the context of the region's traditional civilization and its ancient system of political dynamics,"[54] adding, presciently, that within a few years of his passing, the impact of Western imperialism would destroy the overall structure of the old order in the Gulf.

For the moment at least, Oman's supremacy vis-à-vis its neighbors appeared to be secure: "In 1856 the Gulf still reflected, for the most part, the civilization of its post-sixteenth century 'silver age.' Oman was still the leading political power among the Gulf states and Masqat [sic] still retained its place as the region's leading commercial and shipping center."[55] Sadly, that was not to last.

Following the death of Said bin Sultan, dissension quickly arose, as claims to his title as well as to the disposition of lands he controlled were contested by the late monarch's numerous sons—in particular, Majid and Thuwayni. In an attempt to avoid a prolonged war of succession that would have a profoundly destabilizing effect throughout the entire western Indian Ocean basin, including the key shipping routes to India, the British government intervened.

The official British residency in Oman, which had been constructed on land adjacent to the royal palace in Muscat's harbor and open for business since April of 1800, ensured that Anglo-Omani relations remained firmly, and inextricably, entrenched for generations to come. Throughout the course of the nineteenth century, as Anglo-French rivalry in the Indian Ocean escalated, the Anglo-Omani alliance deepened and was renewed, periodically, by increasingly proprietary treaties of friendship and commerce. Although there were times when Britain's geostrategic interest in Oman worked to the latter's advantage, there were also times when it had quite the opposite effect. British interference in the succession process after Said bin Sultan's death is one such example.

When the acrimonious struggle between Majid and Thuwayni threatened British commercial interests, the British government dispatched Charles John Canning, governor-general of India, to restore unity by securing from the princes a promise to abide by the results of arbitration. Lord Canning's solution was the 1861 Canning Award (also called the Canning Arbitration), an arrangement that would not only undermine the authority of Oman's ruling family but also portend British entanglement in Oman's domestic affairs, effectively compromising Oman's economic independence for more than a century.

This "foreign-imposed settlement, over what was essentially an internal matter,"[56] advanced "a typically British solution of partition" in which the once-sprawling Omani empire would be divided into two parts: a prosperous African domain governed from Zanzibar and "a poorly endowed Asiatic principality governed from Masqat [sic]."[57] Under the terms of this agreement, brothers Majid and Thuwayni would divide the spoils of their father's legacy, with Majid appointed to rule in Zanzibar and Thuwayni assigned to reign in Muscat.

Addressing the obvious inequality of the brothers' inheritance, the agreement obliged Majid, heir to the far-wealthier domain in Africa, to pay to his brother in Muscat an annual tribute, guaranteed by the British, as compensation for relinquishing his claim to Oman's rich African territory. Under the terms of this arrangement, the British "decided to place Zanzibar under British protection and, to seal the deal, issued a joint declaration with the French that recognized the award as well as their joint obligations to respect the independence of both Muscat and Zanzibar."[58] In reality, Zanzibar's independence effectively created two "sultanates."

THE "HERMIT KINGDOM"

In time, Oman's influence ebbed, as the country, racked by internal divisions and threats of foreign incursions, became increasingly more insular. During much of the late nineteenth century and into the twentieth century, Oman, once a great international power, languished as one of the most forgotten quarters in Arabia—except, that is, by the British, who while singularly focused on the Indian subcontinent to the East (the proverbial "Jewel in the Imperial Crown"), managed Oman as if it were a protectorate, albeit an unofficial one.[59] British officers commanded Oman's military, while British civil servants were assigned to the highest posts in the Omani government.

As the twentieth century burst onto the scene with unprecedented optimism, accompanied by revolutionary transformations in communication, transportation, and technology, Oman gradually withdrew from the global stage. By midcentury, it was described as one of the most backward and underdeveloped places on earth, either as the "Tibet of Arabia" or as the "sick man of the Gulf." As late as 1966, Wendell Phillips, the American archaeologist and oil consultant, dubbed the country "unknown."

Oman under Said bin Taymur

Said bin Taymur (r. 1932–1970), who assumed leadership while the country was still known as "Muscat and Oman," was staunchly conservative and resolutely resistant to change, particularly *Western* change. According to the accepted narrative, Sultan Said imposed draconian measures on his people, effectively isolating them from the modern age.

Representing a dynasty that, over the course of two centuries, had catapulted Oman to international status, both in Arabia and abroad, the new sultan would leave behind a legacy of a very different sort. Unlike his predecessors, Sultan Said would be remembered as the ruler who virtually sealed off his country from the outside world. After almost four decades with Said at the helm, the country was little more than a medieval potentate, a quintessential Arab "hermit kingdom," impoverished, xenophobic, and afflicted by a stubborn Marxist-inspired insurrection in the south and chronic civil unrest in the north.

In 1970, Oman had six miles of paved roads, no municipal water system, no newspapers, radios, or televisions, and only a single electrical power plant. Within the country, education was limited to three primary schools—open only to boys—with an enrollment of fewer than a thousand. Because there were no public healthcare facilities, the Dutch Reformed Church operated a small general hospital in Mutrah, adjacent to Muscat, and an even smaller maternity hospital in the capital city. The average life expectancy in Oman was forty-seven years.

According to one eyewitness of the period before 1970,[60] significant business, to the extent that it existed in Muscat, was conducted primarily by Omani and Indian traders and merchants. Exports consisted almost exclusively of dates, dried limes, leather, and frankincense. From 1948 to 1968, the British Bank of the Middle East was the sole financial institution in the sultanate. Communication was limited to cable telegraph and wireless technology. The postal system, a small British facility, serviced a few people of eastern Arabia and the Gulf. Foreign residents were affiliated with either the British military or "the Company," namely, Petroleum Development (Oman) Limited, originally part of the Iraq Petroleum Company and, by 1960, largely controlled by Shell Oil Company/Royal Dutch Shell, the major force in petroleum extraction and export in Oman.

By the standards of the post–World War II industrial era, Oman was an anachronism. Private cars were illegal. Permission was required to wear eyeglasses, which were viewed as a Western "corruption." Smoking in public was strictly forbidden; if caught, violators would be sent, unceremoniously, to the notorious Jalali prison on the edge of the Muscat harbor.[61]

Promptly at eight o'clock in the evening, a canon boomed and the heavy wooden gates of the capital city, Muscat, were sealed shut, secured by a foot-long metal key. There were no streetlights, lest Omanis be tempted to carouse after dark. Within the confines of the walled area of the Old City, pedestrians were required to carry a small kerosene lantern during nighttime hours, presumably for purposes of identification. Recollecting the mood of Muscat in 1968, a Western visitor recalls,

> It was dark and we were ready to sit down to dinner when our host pulled back the curtain and beckoned me out onto the balcony of the British Bank of the Middle East which is situated just outside the city walls . . . and the main gate of the city. As we stepped outside into the darkness a roar of gunfire sounded and we saw in the distance over the harbor a red flash outlining the battlements of Fort Mirani, black against the night sky.
>
> Our host pointed to the gate. Slowly it was beginning to close—we could even hear the rusty hinges and the bolts being drawn. I was transported back to the Middle Ages, even more so later when we crept round the narrow streets with our oil lamps. . . .
>
> And this was only the tip of the iceberg, the part that was visible. Beneath the surface Muscat and the whole of Oman seethed and chafed under the restrictions imposed by their autocratic Sultan. . . . The whole country was an incredible anachronism.[62]

How, one might wonder, had a country such as this, with a long and distinguished history of regional dominance, global exploration, and international commerce, succumbed to this state of stagnation and apparent inertia?

A Twentieth-Century Enigma

In many ways, Sultan Said bin Taymur was an enigma, for "while he left the country in a medieval state, he was not a man of medieval habits."[63] Born in 1910, he had traveled extensively, as had previous generations of Omanis. From 1922 to 1927, he left Oman for British-controlled India, where he was educated at Mayo College in Ajmer, the "Eton" of India, the famed "school of Maharajahs" that his father had also attended. In Baghdad he studied Arabic literature and history.

Impeccably dressed and courteous, Sultan Said "possessed a sternness and strength that belied his appearance."[64] By all accounts, he was a quiet man, "satisfied with a modest and private lifestyle . . . enjoying a frugal life governed by affordability."[65] Fluent in several languages, including Arabic and English, in addition to some Hindi and Urdu, he traveled extensively. Despite British opposition,[66] he set out on a world tour in 1937, stopping in Tokyo before making a trip across the United States. In Washington he was received at the White House as an official guest of President Franklin Delano Roosevelt and feted at a state dinner. Before returning to Muscat in 1938, he completed his international goodwill tour with visits to Rome, Paris, and, finally, London, where he was received as an honored guest of King George VI.

These ventures, so far from home, were said to have "invigorated" the sultan. An American missionary in Mutrah remarked that Said returned to Oman "filled with ambition to make something better of his country. Already the government offices show much improvement, and there is a fine school building going up."[67] For many, however, the promise of such improvements went unfulfilled.

SAID BIN TAYMUR IN PERSPECTIVE

In an attempt to understand this dark period in Oman's history before the dawn of the modern era that is now widely celebrated as *al-nahda* (the renaissance), it would be useful to consider both the complex dynamics of Oman in the mid-twentieth century and the realpolitik within the region during the tumultuous decades of his reign.

Said assumed responsibility for the welfare of Oman following the abdication of his father, Taymur bin Faysal Al Bu Said (r. 1913–1931). Sultan Taymur had bequeathed to his son a country weakened by deepening fiscal chaos, fitful attempts at national reconciliation, and diminished authority vis-à-vis formidable international powers.

Domestic Challenges

From the outset, Said inherited an empty treasury and crippling debt. In the 1920s, fierce competition from new date plantations in the United States and Iraq dealt a severe blow to the global demand for Oman's chief export product. Combined with the disastrous effects of a post–World War I recession, followed by the Great Depression and intense fluctuations in the value of the sultanate's local currency, the Maria Theresa dollar (or thaler), Oman's economy struggled to honor its obligations to its creditors. Assistance from Great Britain did little, ultimately, to resolve the country's systemic weaknesses. (The realization of much-needed revenues from recently discovered petroleum deposits in the interior region of Fahud was a long way off, not to be felt for decades.)

For many years, the very integrity of Al Bu Saidi authority over its subjects had been challenged by persistent and intractable rebellions within the country. From the late nineteenth to the mid-twentieth century, the authority of the sultan in Muscat was challenged by tribal leaders vying for political supremacy, particularly in the north. In the first part of the twentieth century, Sultan Taymur suffered a series of debilitating defeats at the hands of resurgent tribes, pledging allegiance not to the sultan but rather to ambitious imams.

The Seeb Agreement of 1920 was designed to achieve a modus operandi between the sultan and his provincial adversaries. Arbitrated by the British and signed, on behalf of the sultan, by Britain's "political agent in Oman," Major R. E. L. Wingate, this agreement offered a kind of olive branch, recognizing both tribal autonomy and the authority of the imam in the interior, effectively granting him autonomy as the "imam of the Muslims." At the same time, the treaty's signatories acknowledged the nominal sovereignty of the sultan in Muscat over *all* his people, guaranteeing nonaggression by the tribes and *shaykhs* against the inhabitants of coastal towns. This peculiar arrangement reinforced the somewhat-confusing designation of the country as "Muscat and Oman," an appellation that remained in force until 1970.

According to Landen, the Seeb Agreement was, in many ways, a flawed and imprecise document, for it resembled "something more than an armistice but something less than a definitive, clear settlement on all the issues that clouded relations between the two branches of Omani Ibadhism."[68] Ultimately, it proved fragile because ambitious imams in Oman's interior continued their campaigns to undermine the authority of the sultan of Muscat well into midcentury.

The Role of Britain

British influence in the internal affairs of the sultanate reached its peak during the reign of Sultan Taymur (1913–1931). It has been asserted that the grandfather of the current ruler was inclined to consign the details of government affairs to the wisdom of foreign, particularly British, advisers, representatives of the country with the most at stake in the Persian Gulf and Indian Ocean region in the early twentieth century. Apparently comfortable with this arrangement, Sultan Taymur "took frequent trips to India and even visited Britain and Europe in 1928."[69]

Upon ascending to the throne, his son and successor, Said bin Taymur, was considerably more circumspect in his dealings with the British, attempting from the start to assert his independence whenever he could. It is said that he was both "resentful and skeptical of the work of the British advisers imposed on his father."[70] By all accounts, he was decidedly uncomfortable with the somewhat officious Bertram Thomas, financial adviser to Sultan Taymur, who described himself toward the end of his first five years in Muscat as "virtually regent."[71]

Although Sultan Said continued to rely on several British and other foreign advisers during his thirty-eight-year reign, "he realized that a prime reason for the erosion of the country's independence was its chronic insolvency and consequent dependence on British support," with the effect that "a hallmark of his reign was his emphasis on restoring the freedom of action and *de facto* as well as *de jure* independence of his sultanate."[72] In many ways, Sultan Said's characteristic reluctance to accede automatically to the meddling of British representatives in Oman's national affairs foreshadowed the determination of his son and successor, Sultan Qaboos, to protect and maintain Oman's independence.

Regional Trends

As Sultan Said's reign continued through the global depression and the Second World War, the entire region around him was in a state of flux. The countries of the Middle East, embroiled in wars of independence, successive coups d'état and political assassinations, were at the epicenter of the Cold War theater, where antagonists from each side were playing for ever-higher stakes. The United States had embraced its "twin pillar" policy, relying on its friendship with both Saudi Arabia and Iran to contain the spread of communism.

The 1952 Free Officers Revolution in Egypt had overthrown King Farouk, a close friend of Sultan Said's, ending a dynasty that had endured since 1805. Gamal Abdel Nasser, ascending to the presidency of the new republic, advocated sweeping pan-Arabism, nonalignment, and "positive neutralism"; at the same time, he aggressively courted the Soviets for military and development assistance, calling into question not only the trajectory of regional alliances but also the security of monarchies.

Within the tiny countries of the Persian Gulf region, unimaginable wealth, in the form of petrodollars, began to pour into the coffers of ruling families. Eager to reap the benefits of this sudden good fortune, many indulged in well-publicized excesses, threatening to undermine the values inherent in their traditionally conservative societies. It is reported that Sultan Said was deeply alarmed by these extreme displays of affluence, likely reinforcing his determination to maintain the status quo within his still-impoverished country.

The Jabal al-Akhdar War

Within Oman itself, the mid-twentieth century was a time of great upheaval. In 1957 Talib bin 'Ali, the brother of Ghalib bin 'Ali al-Hina'i, a former imam who had ruled over the interior of the country, returned from Saudi Arabia prepared to stage an insurrection against the sultan's forces. Armed with three hundred well-equipped fighters, the Oman Revolutionary Movement moved against the central government, gaining momentum as its forces spread to towns and villages in the north. Sultan Said had no choice but to call on the British for support. With armored-car detachments and Royal Air Force (RAF) aircraft, British forces, along with the Trucial Oman Scouts—a paramilitary force established in the mid-1950s and commanded by the British—intervened to support the Omani Armed Forces, gradually pushing the rebels into the hills of the Jabal al-Akhdar (Green Mountain).[73]

The insurgents stood their ground for two years, mining roads and ambushing Omani and British forces. With Arab supporters on both sides of the divide, the "Question of Oman" rose to international attention as partisans succeeded in bringing the issue to the agenda of the General Assembly of the United Nations. Prolonged and intensified efforts led to the final, dramatic defeat of the rebels in 1959. As the forces loyal to the sultan prevailed, the rebels fled. The 1920 Treaty of Seeb was revoked, and the office of the Imam of the Muslims was abolished. For the first time since 1871, the sultanate was united.

In a further effort to put the policies of Sultan Said in perspective, W. D. Peyton, in an engaging and balanced description of pre-renaissance Oman, suggests that, following the country's reunification after the Jabal rebellions of the 1950s, "the Sultan felt it wise to impose a touch of conservatism in order that the men of the Interior would not regard their fellow countrymen of the coastal areas as unduly frivolous or impious."[74] Viewed in the context of the current Middle East, where forces between religious extremism and secular Westernization, anarchy and democracy, collide in deadly battles for supremacy, the difficult circumstances and myriad challenges confronting Sultan Said might well suggest a more sympathetic assessment of his choices.

Interestingly, after the rebel defeat in the Jabal al-Akhdar, Sultan Said bin Taymur never returned to Muscat, remaining in Salalah, in the southernmost governorate of Dhofar, to the end of his reign. "Govern he certainly did, but it was in absentia and done through emissaries, by cable, by telephone. He had plans for Oman, but they were his own plans, to be carried out in his own time."[75]

The Dhofar Rebellion

No sooner had the insurrection in the interior been quashed than another revolt started to percolate in Dhofar, the preferred pied-à-terre of Sultan Said. Physically isolated from the rest of the country, this stark and mountainous area, once the fabled center of the illustrious frankincense trade, had experienced a recurring series of tribal rebellions.

In 1964 a separatist movement calling itself the Dhofar Liberation-Front launched what would become a major threat to Omani sovereignty.

A protracted insurrection against the government of the sultan, it was abetted by Soviet-inspired leftist forces, including the Marxist-dominated Popular Front for the Liberation of Oman and the Arab Gulf. The rebels, armed and financed by the People's Democratic Republic of Yemen (also known as South Yemen), had as their objective the overthrow of all traditional Arab regimes in the Gulf region.

Put into a wider, international perspective, the stakes could not have been higher: "The war in Dhofar was the first proxy war in the Arabian Peninsula between the West and the Soviet Union, as South Yemen, the only Marxist regime in the Arab World, was a client of the Kremlin,"[76] as well as of Communist China and East Germany. The war was seen as a clarion call for action, not only from the friends of Oman in Britain and the United States but also from neighboring monarchies on both sides of the Persian Gulf.

The secessionist war in Dhofar would represent one of the most prolonged and debilitating challenges to the sultan's authority. Even after the introduction in 1966 of the British-trained and subsidized "Sultan's Armed Forces," this stubborn rebellion continued to drain Oman's resources well beyond the end of Sultan Said's reign.

Newfound Oil Wealth

It was not until 1964, a mere six years before the end of Said's reign, that oil was finally discovered in commercially viable quantities in Oman, long after the petrodollar windfall began to transform the lives of citizens in neighboring countries. By 1967, commercial exports had begun, followed by great expectations for change. It is widely reported that many people attempted to persuade Sultan Said to aggressively invest this new wealth in national development projects.

Having served as the ruler of a poverty-stricken and debt-ridden country for more than thirty-five years, Sultan Said was, by this time, "not only extremely cautious about spending money not actually in his treasury but also sincerely concerned about how modernization and education would affect the people of Oman."[77] Leery of the potentially disruptive effects of sudden wealth on conservative societies in his own region, he resisted the urge to open the flood gates to modernization, which, at that time, was a buzzword for Westernization. He was, in the words of one eyewitness, "not sure that opening up Oman would be good for the Omani people, . . . questioning the shock of its impact on their traditional life, [and] sincerely worried about the impact from the outside."[78] He looked to his neighbors in the Gulf, whose societies were reeling from the effects of sudden oil wealth and a "rush to prosperity," believing that unprecedented wealth had been responsible not only for an erosion of traditional values and bad behavior but also for a succession of family feuds and palace coups.

In an unabashedly paternalistic tone, Sultan Said is reported to have asserted that "the people shall not have what they want but what I think is good for them."[79] And although he did introduce a few small changes, for example, opening *saidiyyah* (government) schools in Mutrah and Dhofar and financing a twenty-two-bed hospital in Salalah, change came far too slowly for the Omanis—as well as for many in his inner circle who were growing increasingly impatient with the status quo.

Throughout the decade of the 1960s, Said bin Taymur gradually withdrew to the relative isolation of Salalah, far from the nation's capital, within the protected confines of al-Husn Palace. To quote Allen and Rigsbee, he explained his self-imposed solitude in terms of "a desire to relieve himself of the embarrassment of being unable to satisfy the constant demands for money with which his subjects would beleaguer him."[80]

Frustrated by the stifling stagnation at home, many Omanis fled the country, opting for greater opportunities and more lucrative employment, particularly in the rapidly developing economies of the Persian Gulf, while others, unable to flee, carried on, enduring the most challenging of circumstances. And while the momentum for historic change was gaining strength, the sultan of Oman was removed, to a large extent, from the very people he served.

REFLECTIONS

As we will see more clearly in the chapters to follow, the seeds of the Omani renaissance, a brilliant achievement by any measure, were planted long before 1970, the year in which Sultan Qaboos began his efforts to modernize his country. It is this continuity, this very convergence of tradition and modernization that makes Oman's story so compelling.

Throughout many centuries of foreign incursions and sporadic occupations, the Omanis have managed to prevail. Throughout periods of wealth as well as periods of desperate economic decline, they have endured. Historically, the Persians have been Oman's most formidable, and determined, adversaries, invading the country at various intervals. Expelled by the rulers of the Ya'rubid dynasty, they returned only to be routed, for all time, by Imam Ahmad bin Said Al Bu Said, the founder of the dynasty that rules Oman to this day.

The interlude of Portuguese occupation, from 1507 to 1650, is particularly instructive. In a stunning example of "role reversal," the Omanis, experienced navigators and able seamen, pursued the Europeans relentlessly into the Indian Ocean and beyond, to distant coasts in Asia and Africa, ultimately seizing for themselves many valuable domains from their former colonizers. These experiences, and others, have instilled into this nation's citizenry a palpable sense of national pride as well as a preoccupation with the importance of *independence* and *sovereignty*—themes that are at the heart of Oman's current national policies.

Oman's long association with Africa may seem surprising in the historical narrative of this Arabian sultanate. By most accounts, Omanis have been a continuous presence in Africa since the seventh century CE, not only along the regions of that continent's eastern littoral but also deep into the interior reaches of the continent.

Before the modern era of relative affluence fueled by the export of oil, Omanis, particularly those living in Zanzibar, the "twin capital of Oman," amassed great fortunes through trade and commerce with countries and cultures throughout the world. Theirs was a cosmopolitan society whose people would, in time, prove invaluable to the success and the character of the modern sultanate. In a similar vein, Oman's reach into South Asia and, in particular, the Makran coast helps to explain the diversity that is everywhere apparent in the sultanate today.

No history would be complete without a retrospective analysis of Oman in the mid-twentieth century, a period that is often sensationalized but insufficiently understood. Following World War II, as countries throughout the industrialized world were rebuilding and modernizing, many corners of the Arabian Peninsula appeared frozen in time and untouched by development, none more so than Oman.

The common narrative associated with the "hermit kingdom," the term used to describe, somewhat dismissively, the sultanate during the period preceding 1970, generally puts the blame squarely on the shoulders of its leader, Said bin Taymur. Although decidedly controversial, the decisions of the sultan can be judged less harshly when viewed from a more multidimensional historical—and cultural—perspective that considers the formidable range of domestic and regional challenges with which he was confronted.

To a considerable extent, the legacy of Sultan Said will continue in chapter 3, as we introduce Qaboos bin Said, the person who inherited the "hermit kingdom" from his father and set into motion what we now know as the modern Omani renaissance.

APPENDIX: AL BU SAID DYNASTY*

Rulers of Oman

Ahmad bin Said Al Bu Said (r. 1744–1775)
Said bin Ahmad (r. 1775–1779)
Hamad bin Said (r. 1779–1792)
Sultan bin Ahmad (r. 1792–1804)
Badr bin Saif (r. 1804–1807)
Said bin Sultan (r. 1807–1856)
Thuwayni bin Said (r. 1856–1866)
Salim bin Thuwayni (r. 1866–1868)
'Azzan bin Qais (r. 1868–1871)
Turki bin Said (r. 1871–1888)
Faysal bin Turki (r. 1888–1913)
Taymur bin Faysal (r. 1913–1932)
Said bin Taymur (r. 1932–1970)
Qaboos bin Said (r. 1970–)

*Source: Vincent McBrierty and Mohammad al-Zubair, *Oman: Ancient Civilization, Modern Nation* (Dublin: Trinity College/Muscat: Bait Al Zubair Foundation, 2004), 27.

CHAPTER 3

QABOOS BIN SAID: RENAISSANCE MAN

The long history of Omani independence had prepared the country for its entry into the modern age. Now all that was necessary was the right leader to effect the country's transition. That leader was Qaboos bin Said, a man who has come to personify a transformation so dramatic it can only be called a renaissance (*nahda*). Qaboos bin Said is by any measure an exceptional man. He has shepherded a country, formerly stagnant and suspended in time, into the twenty-first century. Oman is today a "good news" story, a story of success: stable, harmonious, and optimistic. This herculean task has been accomplished with courage and conviction, intelligence and vision.

This chapter will explore the forces that have shaped the present sultan of Oman, from his childhood in Salalah to his experiences abroad, from his tenure in the royal compound to his accession to the throne. It has been an extraordinary journey, all the more so because of its success, a success borne of careful thought and abiding respect for the history and traditions of his people. While there is much about this account that suggests great drama and intrigue, it is in actuality a deeply human story of a journey, the journey of an inspiring leader and his equally remarkable people.

EARLY YEARS

The leader destined to transform Oman from a backward and stagnant medieval potentate to a progressive twenty-first-century state was born Qaboos bin Said al-Said,[1] on November 18, 1940, in Salalah, the provincial capital of the governorate of Dhofar. A rare name in the Arab world, "Qaboos" is said to be of pre-Islamic origin; early written records reveal that the ruler of the Lakhmids, the first Arab dynasty, had given the name to his son.[2] Representing the fourteenth ruler of the Al Bu Said dynasty, Qaboos bin Said was the only son of Said bin Taymur and Mazoon bint Ahmad al-Mashani. Raised in the picturesque coastal village of Taqah, Mazoon al-Mashani belonged to the Jabali people, a group that embraces an ancient culture and unique language.

Relatively little is known of Qaboos's childhood. We do know that he was educated at home by teachers from the *saidiyyah* school, Salalah's only educational establishment, who were brought to al-Husn Palace to tutor the young prince.[3]

Nevertheless, his education quickly made him aware of the world outside Oman. As a child, Qaboos traveled with his father to India, where he met his grandfather, the former Sultan Taymur, who had retreated to the subcontinent following his abdication in 1931. Then, in 1958, upon completion of his studies in Salalah, the eighteen-year-old Qaboos set sail for Great Britain to further his education.

In England, he was tutored privately for two years by Philip Roman, an academic who offered pre-university training to private pupils. The young Omani prince lived with Roman's family in the village of Felsham, ten miles east of Bury St. Edmunds, Suffolk. The Romans were solidly middle class and held to conservative values; they treated their foreign guest with kindness and discretion, introducing him to a world vastly different from any he had known in Oman. It was during this period that the future sultan developed an abiding love of European classical music, including organ music, a passion that continues to this day. During these years, Qaboos also spent time at the Suffolk County Council observing the dynamics of local government.

While studying in the United Kingdom, Qaboos was closely chaperoned by Major Leslie Chauncey, whose association with Oman was deep, and with its ruler, Sultan Said bin Taymur, profound. Having assumed the post of British Consul in Muscat in 1949, Chauncey retired from the Foreign Service in 1958, only to return to Oman as the sultan's personal adviser. It was an ideal partnership: "Cast in the old colonial mould, for better or for worse, Major Chauncey, ex-Indian Army, took his job very seriously. He and Sultan Sa'id were very much akin in character—autocratic, obstinate, but with great integrity and even greater determination that Oman should progress only in their way and in their time."[4]

Qaboos entered the Royal Military Academy at Sandhurst, in Berkshire, as an officer cadet in 1960, graduating two years later. Joining the First Battalion of the Cameronians (Scottish Rifles) infantry regiment, one of the oldest regiments in the British Army, he was given a staff appointment and served in Germany for one year.

Following his discharge as a second lieutenant in the Cameronians, the future sultan set out on a three-month world tour, arranged by his father. From the perspective of Sultan Said, who had himself traveled extensively as a youth, his son's "grand tour" was intended as more than a mere sightseeing interlude. In fact, Said hoped that after Qaboos's five years in Europe, the trip would "make his son aware that the Western model of development was not the only possible option."[5] History and Qaboos's future record of governance would demonstrate that this lesson was thoroughly learned.

Major Chauncey and his wife were charged with accompanying the young man "to restrain any youthful enthusiasm that the sultan himself so distrusted." Qaboos's interlude in Europe would seem to indicate a spirit of largesse on the part of his father, Sultan Said. However, as Chauncey added, portending the future that awaited Qaboos upon his return home, "This broad-minded action toward his son was to be the last."[6]

Having successfully completed his education abroad, served with distinction in the British Armed Forces, and experienced travel far beyond the shores of Arabia, Qaboos ultimately returned to Salalah in 1964. The next chapter in his remarkable journey is rife with conjecture. One foreign observer, an intimate of the Royal Court,[7] records that Qaboos's reception was most unexpected, for his father, Sultan Said, placed his son under virtual house arrest. There, in the palace, he would immerse himself in the history of Oman and religious studies, only to appear in public for official functions or weekly walks with the *wali* of Dhofar on Friday afternoons.

No one can presume to know with any certainty why Sultan Said decided to confine his son to the palace. We can, however, attempt to shed light on Said's action by examining the context in which his decision was made as well as its effects on the future sultan, Qaboos.

Against the backdrop of Cold War gamesmanship, in which Moscow's appetite for vulnerable "third-world" countries in the Middle East and other postcolonial societies seemed insatiable, the Omani leadership found itself entangled in a debilitating series of domestic political challenges. A stubborn rebellion in the north was increasingly overshadowed by an incipient and potentially far more devastating threat in the southern governorate of Dhofar. Here, a heavily subsidized and crippling insurrection, launched from the People's Democratic Republic of Yemen, a Marxist state on its borders, raged throughout the late 1960s, threatening Oman's sovereignty, draining the country's coffers, claiming its sons, and straining its resolve.

Lacking internal security, modern infrastructure, or effective means of communication, it would be an understatement to claim that Omanis were not terribly mobile during that decade. By all accounts, even the sultan, Said bin Taymur, had become something of a recluse. Attending to the pressing affairs of state, including Oman's newly discovered oil wealth, which he viewed as a "mixed blessing," Said eschewed travel outside of Salalah, even to the capital of Muscat, which he had not visited since 1958. With no roads connecting the two cities, even at a mere 540 miles (870 km) apart, the temptation to venture beyond the confines of familiar, and safe, surroundings was minimal. Thus, amid the uncertainty and instability of that turbulent decade, it is safe to say that the royal family in Oman felt that the wisest course of action was to "stay put."

Throughout the years following his return to Oman, Qaboos remained in Dhofar, where, ensconced in a small house within the palace compound, he studied Islam and Omani history, tutored by religious scholars. People personally acquainted with Sultan Qaboos maintain that during this period, the future ruler was seldom seen in public, except on prayer days or on ceremonial occasions, and at those times mostly in the company of either his father or the *wali* of Dhofar.[8] Instead, it is reported that he seized upon the opportunity of this respite, devoting his time to intellectual pursuits, immersing himself not only in the prescribed curriculum but also in serious contemplation of his country's destiny.

In later years, as Oman began its transition from a medieval-style potentate to a resilient regional power, Qaboos himself would reveal that his interlude in Salalah had been an investment in his country's future. In a 1995 interview, the sultan of Oman reflected on this period, expressing gratitude to his father for enriching his education:

> My father's insistence on my thoroughly studying my religion and the history and culture of my country were a profound help in forming my consciousness of my responsibilities toward my people and to humanity at large. Also, I had the benefit—one might say as a counterbalance in a sense—of a Western education and exposure to life as a soldier.[9]

Throughout the course of his strict regime in Salalah, the young Qaboos occasionally took time away from his studies to read international newspapers or to meet with friends for conversation or a game of bridge, a favorite pastime.

Meanwhile, frustration continued to mount, particularly among the British advisers who had long been ensconced in the inner corridors of the royal palace. The Communist-inspired insurgency in the south showed little sign of being crushed, inflicting great pain on families and depleting the country's treasury. There was great concern over the failure of the sultan's forces to prevail decisively over the rebels in Dhofar. It was simply a matter of time before Oman's political landscape would be dramatically altered. When sympathetic but impatient palace insiders queried the sultan about the timing of his son's assumption of the responsibilities of state, Said bin Taymur, still only in his fifties, is reported to have replied, "When he is ready he will take it."[10]

ASCENSION TO POWER

And take it he did. On July 23, 1970, after six years of imposed confinement, twenty-nine-year-old Qaboos bin Said replaced his father with the help of British military advisers. This affair might have gone down as a bloodless coup but for the fact that one palace insider who attempted to oppose the sultan's removal was killed;[11] in the melee that followed, Sultan Said pulled a pistol from his *dishdasha* (long white garment), only to wound himself accidentally in the foot.

The reign of Said bin Taymur, sultan of Muscat and Oman for thirty-eight years, had come to an end. Throughout one of the most challenging periods in Omani history, he had succeeded in putting the country back on a secure financial footing and reunifying restive tribal groups in the north. It was time, however, for a new head of state, one who would build upon the legacy of previous generations of Al Bu Saidi rulers and lead his people into the modern era. Before being flown to England, where he remained at the

Dorchester Hotel until his death in 1972, Sultan Said signed an instrument of abdication, signaling the end of an era of darkness and the beginning of a bright new chapter in the long and intriguing history of Oman.

Assisted by a trusted inner circle of British advisers and others, including resident businessmen from the Indian subcontinent, Qaboos, now sultan, was poised to lead his country into the twentieth century. He immediately made preparations to travel to Muscat, his first-ever visit to the capital city. On July 23, 1970, he issued a call to all who longed to restore Oman to its rightful place in the world. His words were unambiguous:

> I promise you to proceed forthwith in the process of creating a modern government. My first act will be the immediate abolition of all the unnecessary restrictions on your lives and activities.
>
> My people, I will proceed as quickly as possible to transform your life into a prosperous one with a bright future. Every one of you must play his part towards this goal. Our country in the past was famous and strong. If we work in unity and cooperation we will regenerate that glorious past and we will take a respectable place in the world.
>
> I call upon you to continue living as usual. I will be arriving in Muscat in the coming few days and then I will let you know of my future plans. . . .
>
> My people, my brothers, yesterday it was complete darkness and with the help of God, tomorrow will be a new dawn on Muscat, Oman and its people.
>
> God bless us all and may He grant our efforts success.[12]

And so began the reign of Sultan Qaboos, the longest-ruling leader in the Middle East today. (See figure 3.1 for a photograph of the young sultan addressing the nation in July 1970.)

Twenty-seven years later, reflecting on that fateful day, Qaboos bin Said addressed his fellow citizens from the "eternal city of Salalah," the very place from which he had launched his historic rise to power:

> This city was the first to embrace the rays of this true dawn that dispersed the darkness, and spread happiness, gave life and eliminated the traces of the years of stagnation which had held back the progress and stultified the resources of our country, so it was unable to keep pace with the passage of time and the advancement of other nations. Yes, from this land, the blessed process took its first steps in nation-building and modernisation.[13]

Domestic Challenges

Imagine, if you can, an ancient land, trapped in virtual isolation for much of the twentieth century, suddenly faced with a dramatic debut into the modern age. How would the people of Oman, the beneficiaries of a rich and unbroken history, reconcile modernization with the cherished institutions of their culture and tradition?

Given the virtual absence of any civil infrastructure upon which to build a modern, functioning government, the challenges were formidable.

Figure 3.1   Qaboos bin Said in July 1970 addressing the nation after assuming the throne
Used with permission of the Sultan's Armed Forces Museum, Bayt al-Falaj, Muscat.

Confronting the young sultan were "the obstacles of illiteracy, isolation, high mortality rates, insufficient social development, inadequate or non-existent healthcare, dwindling educational opportunities, unsurveyed natural resources, and a civil war."[14]

A further obstacle toward achieving a functioning modern state was the difficult task of promoting a spirit of Omani "nationalism." Nationalism and the "rule of law" (as understood in a contemporary context) are notions that supersede traditional and deeply entrenched tribal loyalties. Thus, they were in 1970 and continue to be today elusive and, indeed, contentious ideas for many peoples of the postimperial Middle East. For many Middle Easterners, the idea of pledging fealty to a larger polity beyond the tribe or clan is a cultural anomaly.

In 1970 most Omanis had never even heard the name "Qaboos." Virtually unknown, even to his countrymen,[15] the twenty-nine-year-old sultan broke dramatically with the reclusive style of his father. Following his impressive debut in Muscat, he embarked on a massive "meet and greet" campaign throughout the land. (See figure 3.2 for a photograph of Sultan Qaboos reviewing Omani troops.) Exuding great charisma and offering hope to his long-suffering countrymen, he shared his vision of the new Oman through

Figure 3.2   Qaboos bin Said reviewing the troops in 1970
Used with permission of the Sultan's Armed Forces Museum, Bayt al-Falaj, Muscat.

impassioned, yet measured and heartfelt, speeches, quickly establishing a personal rapport with his people, uniting both men *and* women in a common cause.

In the words of the eyewitness Eloise Bosch, an American teacher who had lived in Oman since 1955 with her physician husband Donald Bosch, "People began to talk about a New Oman which would be full of exciting opportunities and hopes for a brighter future. It seemed as if a tight band around the chest had been removed and the people could breathe freely again."[16]

A New Dawn

Upon assuming power in 1970, one of the first and, symbolically, most important acts of Sultan Qaboos was to release all but a few prisoners from the notorious Jalali prison, constructed by the Portuguese in 1589 high atop the cliffs adjacent to Muscat's harbor. According to Pauline Searle, "The prisoners themselves must have been completely overwhelmed . . . [because] for days they wandered around still toting bits of chain and leg irons attached to their ankles . . . with a glazed look on their faces."[17]

Bent on achieving unity throughout the land, the new ruler announced a change in the name of the country, from the historically divisive (and slightly confusing) "Muscat and Oman," to "the Sultanate of Oman." As the nation's former flag, on a field of solid red, was retired from service, a new flag was unfurled, in red, green, and white hues, featuring crossed swords over a *khanjar*,[18] Oman's traditional curved dagger (see figure 3.3 for a photograph of Qaboos bin Said receiving the new flag of Oman).

Figure 3.3 Signaling the dawn of a new era, Qaboos bin Said receives Oman's new national flag in 1970 from Sayyid Tariq Al Bu Said
Courtesy of the Office of the Adviser to His Majesty the Sultan for Cultural Affairs.

The transformation of Oman would require all Omanis to work together. As restrictions on movement were lifted for all citizens, Sultan Qaboos reached out personally to tribal leaders throughout the land to join him in this common cause, emphasizing repeatedly the importance of the "collective effort." To attract the help of educated Omanis, Sultan Qaboos invited Omani expatriates to return home to lend their talents to the formidable tasks that lay ahead. At that time, many were living in East Africa and in other parts of the Middle East, particularly in Iran, Egypt, and the Gulf countries, as well as in Syria and Iraq, where the Ba'athist regime provided free education of a relatively high quality. Returning expatriates were guaranteed the restoration of their citizenship, considered by Omanis to be immutable.[19]

Signaling an end to Oman's long period of isolation, in 1971 the sultan expressed his intention to restore connections with the family of nations in the Gulf region and beyond by joining both the League of Arab States and the United Nations. Over a period of some time, he sought and concluded agreements on long-simmering border disputes with Oman's neighbors, including Iran, Yemen, the United Arab Emirates, and Saudi Arabia.

National Unity

As Oman's international profile reemerged, its young leader, Qaboos bin Said, attracted the attention of many observers, in both Eastern and

Western circles, through his deft handling of both domestic and foreign affairs. After more than four decades in power, the longest-serving head of state in the Persian Gulf region continues to be admired as one of the brightest visionaries and most effective reformers in the Middle East. He is credited with unifying disparate elements of his country through keen political acumen and effective communication. Most important, perhaps, is his unwavering determination to safeguard Oman's independence and sovereignty.

Building on his understanding of Omani history and society, the young sultan understood from the outset that for the monarchy to survive as a political institution *and* for modernizing efforts to succeed, his conservative subjects would need to be persuaded to unite in a sweeping national effort that would reconcile tradition with modernization. To a significant extent, this would require the recognition and co-option of the tribal dynamic that had been central to Omani society from time immemorial. Accordingly, Qaboos embarked on a campaign to reach out to people throughout the country for their input and support.

Respect for Oman's tribal organization and cultural tradition was incorporated into the sultan's strategy for nation building. "It was his opinion that everything valuable from the past ought to be brought forward into the future."[20] Instead of marginalizing traditional leaders, relegating them to nominal positions of irrelevance (as has been attempted, repeatedly, through the present day, in countless other societies throughout the world, with predictably disastrous results), he invited them to join him in this new national endeavor.

Initially, he met with tribal leaders in Dhofar, endeavoring to win their trust and loyalty. In August 1970, in an unprecedented radio appeal, Qaboos invited the *shaykhs* and elders throughout the land to unite with their fellow countrymen in this unprecedented, if massive, national undertaking. Traveling throughout the country, he embarked on a "charm offensive," a classic counterinsurgency strategy, gradually unifying disparate elements, many of which surely must have viewed this unproven young man with a degree of skepticism.

The successful outcome of the sultan's campaign to engender a sense of national identity might well have been aided, in part, by the absence of any *single* dominant group or tribe within the country. Be that as it may, as he traversed the land, he delivered a consistent and compelling message, one that included a promise of fairness and inclusivity. His openness and clearly articulated goals "coupled with the state's power and its even-handed policy in creating equal opportunities for all citizens regardless of their background . . . mitigated any cleavages within Omani society and thus any potential societal conflict."[21]

Oman's transformation is all the more striking when one considers the repeated debacles of other twenty-first-century Middle Eastern societies that have failed to satisfy the aspirations and concerns of individual citizens and minority groups within a historically diverse cultural mosaic.

Moral Victory in Dhofar

From the moment of his accession to the throne, Sultan Qaboos, as a sea-soned military man and a professional soldier, considered his country's secu-rity to be of paramount importance. Foremost in his mind was ending the ongoing war in Dhofar. The protracted insurgency in Oman's southern gov-ernorate, bordering the Marxist People's Democratic Republic of Yemen, had put a serious strain on the country's meager financial resources since 1963. There seemed to be no end in sight.

It was the height of the Cold War, which made the conflict in Dhofar far more than an issue of national sovereignty for the deeply religious and tra-ditionally conservative Omanis; it was a war against Communism, evil, and godlessness. Shrewdly tapping into the Omani people's sense of religious commitment and tradition, Sultan Qaboos established *firqats*, or armed groups, in 1972, to "fight against the terrorism of the communist gangs in the mountains of Dhofar," declaring that Omanis had a "sacred duty" to wage war "against atheism."[22]

Having trained in Britain and served in Germany, Qaboos assumed a "hands on" approach toward resolving that long and debilitating conflict. The monarch later "readily admitted that his own military experiences, spe-cifically, Sandhurst, his service in the British Army on the Rhine, and the Dhofar war, were major influences in his life."[23] He was well-primed and uniquely equipped for the formidable task ahead.

Qaboos's military training in Europe served him well. The young sultan aggressively pursued his foes on the battlefield. His approach to the insur-rection was akin to a "carrot and stick" method, "attempting to undo the damage caused by [his father's] petty restrictions on the population while simultaneously engaging in a heavy military build-up to reverse the tide of battle."[24]

Employing not only the sword but also the olive branch, Qaboos announced his intention in August 1970 to extend a general amnesty to all Dhofari guerillas who had fought against his father in exchange for their surrender and oath of loyalty. This proved attractive to many of the "tribal" and "nationalist" rebels. Many surrendered voluntarily and were retrained by the sultan's British advisers as "an irregular unit" of the country's Armed Forces. He introduced a nonconscripted army to assist in ending the hos-tilities. The opportunity to join this young, visionary leader in an exciting, unprecedented national endeavor proved irresistible to many of these hard-ened warriors, several of whom became prominent leaders in the national government, serving to this day.

In Dhofar, Sultan Qaboos addressed social and economic problems, order-ing the construction of new roads, bridges, and wells in the communities of those who proved loyal. Schools and health facilities sprung up, as if over-night. As their lot improved, the people of this long-neglected region were persuaded that a new day finally was at hand. Not only had the young leader advanced his position on the military front but he had also made "a good deal of progress . . . toward replacing a situation of mistrust and neglect with a spirit of unification and mutual cooperation throughout the Sultanate."[25]

By 1975, the armed portion of the Dhofari rebellion was crushed. The stubborn and costly insurgency in the south was over. The moral battle was won. Celebrating the final, hard-fought victory of the Sultan's Armed Forces[26] over the protracted rebel insurrection, Sultan Qaboos reflected on "this subversive principle . . . [that] knows no religion," proclaiming that "our people do not accept that virtue be replaced by evil, and righteousness by falsehood."[27]

Reporting to his countrymen on the occasion of the fifth National Day,[28] in 1975, Qaboos vilified the adversary that had persistently threatened national unity during the first five years of his rule. Acting to galvanize popular support for his patriotic vision of Oman, the sultan declared that "the Communists spread hardship among their citizens. They open prisons and detention camps while we build schools and hospitals. They lay obstacles, sow thorns and choke the freedom of the people, while we remove obstacles and make the hardships of life easy."[29]

After purging the "Communist corruption" in 1975, Qaboos's joy could hardly be contained as he described the victory in Dhofar as a milestone, in a wider context, proclaiming, "Our Victory . . . is the first to be achieved by an Arab country over world communism in the battlefield."[30] At the same time, he struck a cautionary tone, warning both Omanis and their neighbors to remain ever vigilant to the threat of world Communism.

Building Alliances

At this critical juncture in his country's history, the sultan was aided by a number of influential figures and important allies, including many from the United Kingdom. This was hardly surprising, since British influence on the ruling families and power brokers of Oman and its neighbors had been a dominant feature throughout the Gulf for as long as anyone could recall. Providing guidance and professional expertise on a number of levels, several British officials were instrumental in the formation of the modern Omani state, frequently attaining high positions within the government as a result.

Chief among Qaboos's supporters was Reza Pahlavi, the shah of Iran, who aided Qaboos's efforts in myriad ways. Throughout the 1970s, Qaboos's genuine respect and personal admiration for the shah was widely recognized. In addition, the sultan never forgot the support and sacrifices of the Iranian people, who aided his country in a time of great need during the protracted war in Dhofar. Iranian support, including paratroopers and ground forces, played a defining role in the state's victory, particularly in the latter stages of the rebellion.[31] Among Oman's few friends in the region, the Iranians sustained alarming losses, by some estimates as high as a thousand men.[32]

When the shah was removed from power by the supporters of Ayatollah Ruhollah Khomeini in 1979, Oman's cordial relations with Iran remained firm. Even after the sultanate's neighbor renamed itself the Islamic Republic of Iran, Oman's friendly ties to that nation persisted, attesting to Sultan Qaboos's appreciation of a time-honored bond.[33]

It is characteristic of the Omanis, including their head of state, to place a high value on friendship; indeed, it is one of their most enduring attributes. Historic alliances, and in particular, those with Iran, continue to inform the trajectory of Omani foreign policy to this day, casting the sultanate into a role of invaluable interlocutor in the international and, particularly, diplomatic arenas, as we shall see in chapter 6.

QABOOS'S GOVERNING STYLE

From a historical perspective, the similarities between the legendary Ahmad bin Said, the eighteenth-century founder of the Al Bu Said dynasty, and his descendant, Qaboos bin Said, the leader of Oman's modern renaissance, are striking. As each assumed his respective reins of leadership, conditions within the country were not dissimilar: "Imam Ahmed [*sic*] came to power after many years of administrative decay. Devastation and misery surrounded him. The great history of the country had begun to fade from memory and to restore the dignity of Oman, the people's faith in the possibility of renewal also had to be restored."[34]

And so it was, also, for the young Qaboos, whose knowledge of Oman's history, including that of its illustrious rulers—including his own ancestors— was extensive. As the leader of an underdeveloped country fraught with deep and seemingly intractable divisions, he began his reign by extending an impartial hand to people from every corner of his realm. This was a time to heal, and Qaboos bin Said was equal to the task. He would prove to be a ruler with a flair for reconciliation and flexibility, a head of state not only willing but also seemingly compelled to explain the rationale for his actions while meeting his subjects face-to-face. A man of culture and erudition, he was determined to expand the opportunities of all of Oman's citizens.

National Reconciliation

From the start, Qaboos attempted to form a partnership with *all* citizens— men, women, and children—from every corner of the land. On July 23, 1970, immediately after his accession to the throne, the young monarch, in a conspicuous departure from the modus operandi of his father, left Salalah to travel the then-formidable distance to Muscat. There, in the capital city, in an unprecedented move, Sultan Qaboos addressed his fellow citizens with a blend of empathy and conviction. In words that resonated deeply with a captive and expectant audience, he announced his intention to extend Oman's bounty to *all regions*, distributing the nation's resources throughout the land for economic and social development programs. Giving Omanis reason to hope for a brighter future—perhaps for the first time—he stressed the importance of their personal long-term investment in this new national endeavor.

The prospect of reconciling the needs and aspirations of a population historically divided along ethnic, religious, cultural, and even linguistic lines was enormous. However, Qaboos soon won the trust of his countrymen, becoming emblematic of the hope and confidence that only a few years back would have been unimaginable. His words rang not only with a sense of pride in the idea of an Omani "nation"—as he evoked his country's illustrious past—but also with an unmistakable modern imperative as he emphasized the importance of individual commitment and "ownership" of its successful rebirth.

Unprecedented Adaptability

From the earliest years of his rule, Qaboos bin Said has demonstrated an affinity toward moderation and flexibility in contrast with the authoritarian legacy for which his father is remembered. These characteristics represent what Riphenburg has referred to as an "adaptive traditional monarchy," asserting that while Qaboos's style "is definitely rooted in that of the traditional monarch,"[35] it has evolved to respond to the needs and realities of the modern world.

This adaptive style is particularly striking in the context of his pronouncements about Islam and its relevance in today's world. Oman's ruler steadfastly maintains that within the Islamic tradition, it is not only *appropriate* to "renew and revise [Muslim] thinking in accordance with the needs of the modern world"[36] but also *absolutely essential* to do so. He asserts without qualification that Islam is consistent with modernity and fully capable of interacting confidently and independently with the rest of the world, insisting that "in order that Muslims not remain backward, while others advance, they are required by the Law of Islam to . . . renew and revise their thinking, so that they can apply the right solutions to modern problems that are facing the Islamic community." He warns further that "obstinacy in religious understanding leads to backwardness, prevalence of violence, and intolerance," which are "far removed from Islam which rejects exaggeration and bigotry."[37]

This inclination, or "willingness to make adjustments to changing conditions in a pragmatic manner,"[38] is deeply suggestive of an earlier era in the history of the greater Middle East, including largely Muslim Iberia, particularly during the era of the Abbasid caliphate, when openness, dialogue, and adaptation, merging ancient Greek philosophical traditions with an Islamic spirit of openness and inquiry, gave rise to unprecedented levels of scientific and artistic expression. In the early centuries of Islam, it was this adaptation, this synthesis, that enabled the medieval *ummah* (Islamic community) of the "Golden Age" to surmount internal challenges at home while, at the same time, ascending to extraordinary heights, leaving in its wake an incomparable intellectual legacy that spread to every corner of the earth.[39]

In the case of Qaboos bin Said, this characteristic inclination toward adaptation and openness suggests an unassailable confidence, derived not only from his knowledge of world history but also, very likely, from his understanding of Oman's unique journey, the success of which is based, in large measure, on its historic resilience and regular interaction with people of other cultures and ideas.

Communicator-in-Chief

It has been observed that Qaboos bin Said is the only head of state in the modern Arab world to have created a written record of his leadership through regular speeches to his countrymen. For more than four decades, the sultan of Oman has addressed his people on Oman's National Day (November 18, the sultan's birthday), on the occasion of the opening of the Council of Oman (the bicameral legislative branch of government), or at other events of national significance, such as the dedication of major national enterprises, like Sultan Qaboos University, Oman's premier center of higher education, or the opening of major regional events, such as Gulf Cooperation Council summit meetings.

The speeches of Oman's ruler warrant careful analysis. While they stand as a permanent record of his philosophy, decisions, and actions, they reveal much about the man himself. They are thoughtful and sincere, blending conviction and compassion, and characteristically laced with references to his country's illustrious history. One cannot help but wonder about the effect of his early adult years, especially his time of private study and reflection in Salalah, on the development of his vision for Oman; for surely this extended interlude would have provided him with the opportunity to carefully consider the myriad responsibilities with which he would someday be charged. Kechichian concurs with this assumption, emphasizing that the sultan's regular practice of accounting to his countrymen, unprecedented in the country's history, is "itself an indication that he had given the idea some thought before acceding to the throne and, equally important, [that he realized] its ultimate value both as a communication technique as well as a permanent record of his positions."[40]

This comprehensive collection of orations provides scholars and others with a valuable and readily accessible trove of information; for here is a rich historical record that reveals important insights into the philosophy and thought processes of the ruler himself. Careful review of these speeches, the very words of the master architect of Oman's journey into modernity, provides an invaluable perspective for anyone attempting to understand the country's domestic program of development as well as its characteristically independent foreign policy.

The sultan's pronouncements are always powerful, but without the expected measure of hyperbole that typically characterizes the speeches of many of his counterparts in the modern Middle East. The measured tenor of his remarks, often fatherly, sounds alternately stern and tender. Like a successful coach, his words are always inspirational, persuasive, and upbeat. As he addresses the youth of his country, he exhorts them in the path of "diligence, hard work, patience, perseverance, and sustained effort,"[41] reflecting a spirit not unlike that of the "puritan ethic" so revered in the West.

In his dual role as both teacher and philosopher, the sultan's pronouncements incorporate both history and religion. He draws extensively on the teachings of Islam, including the Qur'an and *hadith* (teachings of the Prophet), of which he has a deep and abiding understanding. He admonishes Omanis to be mindful of human excesses, including envy, pride, and the failure to save money. Rarely vague, the sultan's exhortations are generally action oriented, patiently explaining the rationale for national projects, whether contemplated or under way.

What is most compelling about these speeches, however, is that underlying them all is a pervasive spirit of unity (esprit de corps), the sense that "we are all in this together"—young and old, male and female, urban and rural. Qaboos is, ultimately, the unifying voice of Oman.

A Face-to-Face Leader

From the earliest days of his reign, Qaboos bin Said embarked upon the now-legendary practice of annual "Meet the People" tours, also known as "Open Parliament" sessions. This well-organized institution is particularly interesting, having evolved into the stuff of legend. It personifies his unique style, reinforcing his popularity by bringing the ruler ever closer to his people.

During a part of each year, the sultan journeys to a designated area of the country, often to very remote locales, accompanied by cabinet ministers and trusted advisers. Enthusiastically received by the local population, he sets up a base camp, often an elaborate tent compound, for extended, and substantive, visits with his subjects. Conducting one-on-one audiences with citizens from all walks of life—ordinary citizens (*bedu*, mountain dwellers, fishermen, and farmers) as well as dignitaries (village elders, *shaykhs*, and local administrators)—he invites their petitions, hears their grievances, and mediates their disputes.

Listening attentively to their concerns and petitions, he deliberates carefully before issuing, then and there, specific directives for action to the appropriate cabinet members in attendance. High-ranking officials may be instructed to make site visits; for example, while the minister of health is dispatched to clinics and hospitals, the minister of education is likely to be sent to visit schools. In some cases, if further consultation is required, the sultan refers the issues to the *Majlis al-Shura* (Consultative Council) for additional study and recommendations.

These "Meet the People" events provide an opportunity for Qaboos to meet with his fellow citizens face-to-face and to reinforce a connection between ruler and people that, in this case, is almost palpable. Throughout the course of these sessions, he has the opportunity to hear the needs of Omanis, appreciate their problems, understand each region's particular challenges in the context of development priorities, observe the progress that has been made on the implementation of government projects, and explain the government's current priorities and rationale for funding.

By means of this highly anticipated ritual, as well as others throughout the year, Sultan Qaboos has remained at the forefront of the Omani national consciousness for more than four decades. Each year, these outings are eagerly anticipated by all Omanis and are televised nationally. They provide a rare opportunity for citizens to interact with their monarch in an informal setting; as the regent listens patiently to his people's concerns and acts on their requests, he quietly explains, at the same time, his vision and plans for the nation's future.

Renaissance Man

The current ruler of Oman, Qaboos bin Said, now a soft-spoken septuagenarian, a gentleman of exceptional sophistication and urbanity, has been described as the "best-informed, most thoughtful, most well-read and articulate leader—in both Arabic and English—in the Middle East; he is the only one in the region you can truly call a renaissance man."[42] This judgment is echoed by virtually everyone who has known the sultan of Oman. As one former US diplomat assigned to Muscat asserted, "He is one of the most unique individuals in the region: incredibly smart, endowed with great wisdom while, at the same time, warm, personable, and exceptionally humble."[43]

Interested and knowledgeable in a variety of subjects, including world history and religions, language and literature, science, astronomy, and the environment, he is an experienced military man as well as an adept marksman. An accomplished equestrian as well, Sultan Qaboos sponsors an Annual Royal Horse Racing Festival event in Muscat, a showcase for purebred Arabian horses and thoroughbreds.[44]

Sultan Qaboos is that rare and exceptional leader who represents the quintessential global citizen, embodying a blend of the West, in which he spent his formative years, and the East, namely, his beloved Oman. He has managed, almost seamlessly, to reconcile the two harmoniously as the country has been transformed into a modern state that is, in many ways, uniquely "Omani." To a great extent, the success of this enterprise bears his signature alone.

Patron of the Arts

Although Oman's head of state has identified basic education, health services, and the development of human resources as top priorities since his accession to power, he has endeavored to cultivate among his compatriots an appreciation not only of Oman's unique cultural heritage but also of the artistic legacy of other countries and cultures, particularly in music and dance. This may be a reflection, in part, of his own youthful experiences in Europe and beyond; at the same time, it is undeniably in harmony with Oman's long tradition of interaction with the peoples and customs of distant lands.

The leader of the Arab world's oldest independent state is a committed patron of the arts in many forms. The inclusion of bagpipes into the standard musical repertoire of Oman might well strike a first-time observer as something of an anomaly. Yet, the adoption of bagpipe music into the national repertoire of this Arabian sultanate thousands of miles from the Scottish highlands represents just one in a long line of adaptations from other cultures that the people of Oman have embraced.

The origin of this phenomenon stems from Qaboos bin Said's youth, when during his training in an English military academy and subsequent service with the Scottish Cameronians, he developed a taste for Western military bands and, in particular, bagpipe music. After his accession to power, several military wind bands and bagpipe bands were established in Oman, where today their music has become an integral part of the national cultural scene. Some observers have remarked that bagpipes can be used effectively in Arabic music because their intervals match some Arabic scales better than do those of wind instruments.[45] The Oman Military Music Festival (Tattoo)[46] is today a major event in the sultanate, presided over by the head of state himself.[47] Omani pipers compete regularly in the international arena as well, winning both acclaim and recognition for their skills.

Despite his fondness for military music, Sultan Qaboos is passionate about music of all genres. He composes music and plays the 'oud, a stringed instrument indigenous to the Middle East that is the forerunner of the European lute. An avid aficionado of Western classical music, Qaboos is said to be particularly fond of Aaron Copland and Gustav Mahler. It is reported that he is an accomplished organist as well. Pipe organs feature prominently not only in every royal palace but also in many Christian churches throughout the land, representing gifts from the country's ruler.[48]

In 1985 Oman's ruler established the 120-member Royal Oman Symphony Orchestra, a classical ensemble consisting entirely of young Omani musicians drawn from the indigenous population. This initiative was the first of its kind in the Gulf and is distinguished from other, newer orchestras around the region by virtue of the fact that the members of this orchestra are all Omanis.

The creation of an all-Omani orchestra was partly a matter of choice and partly one of necessity, given "that the country is more populous, that it has a longer-standing urbanized tradition, and that it is less wealthy than the other states."[49] Yet it was precisely that mixture of characteristics that enabled this ensemble to become "an Omani orchestra that is embedded in the nation."[50] Beginning their tenure as members of this prestigious symphonic ensemble while very young, children are provided with the opportunity to mature personally and professionally, honing their talents and artistic skills well into adulthood.

Reaching around the globe to promote cultural and artistic dialogue on all levels, Oman has enjoyed a close collaboration with many international institutions, including the world-renowned John F. Kennedy Center for the Performing Arts, in Washington, DC. In 2009 young dancers from the sultanate joined with their American counterparts to perform a lively, extravagant production. The musical extravaganza, *OMAN . . . O Man!*, choreographed by Emmy-award-winner Debbie Allen, a joyful celebration of discovery of the differences and similarities between cultures, strikingly reminiscent of Oman's own historical narrative of global interaction, was a tour de force. (For a detailed discussion of Sultan Qaboos's crowning achievement in the arts, highlighting the 2011 opening of the Royal Opera House Muscat as well as other cultural endeavors, see chapter 5.)

VISION FOR THE FUTURE

From the day of his accession to power, on July 23, 1970, Sultan Qaboos stressed the importance of shared responsibility for the enormous tasks that lay ahead. As Oman stood poised to enter the modern age, he addressed the men and women of Oman, invoking their country's glorious history and illustrious achievements, proclaiming that the realization of a new Oman would mean that "every one of you must play his part towards this goal."[51]

Throughout his reign of nearly half a century, his themes have remained consistent. On the occasion of the first National Day, on July 23, 1971, Qaboos emphasized that development would be achieved "only when the people share the burden of responsibility and help with the task of building"[52] and that "hard work is the only way to meet our objectives."[53] That message (don't expect government to do all the heavy lifting), frequently repeated, is as relevant today as it was forty-plus years ago.

During the early years of the young sultan's reign and, particularly, as the war in Dhofar was winding down, additional revenue became available for the massive infrastructural changes that would transform Oman. A national building boom was under way, proceeding at an astonishing rate, not only in the capital city of Muscat and its environs but also throughout the farthest reaches of the land.

During what one oil executive called "the intoxicating years of the early 1970s," there was no time to waste. Omani manpower alone would not be sufficient to achieve the tasks at hand. Highly educated professionals, many from the West, and unskilled laborers, particularly from India, Pakistan, and Bangladesh, would be recruited to accomplish the enormous tasks that lay ahead. The atmosphere was electric; the pace of change, fast and furious.

Modernization, Not Westernization

As Sultan Qaboos surveyed his Gulf neighbors' frenzy to develop as quickly as possible, often equating modernization with Westernization, he knew well what he did *not* want to do. Unlike his friend and ally, the shah of Iran, the Omani ruler rejected the wholesale adoption of Western values with their material trappings. Throughout the course of his country's transition, he frequently articulated his commitment to preserve his people's cultural values, creating "harmony between the fruits of the present and the values of the glorious past."[54]

Here the distinction between the terms "modernization" and "Westernization," often applied interchangeably, is significant. Westernization, writ large, implies the uncritical adoption of things associated with the West, including ideas and cultural trappings. When applied on a large scale to a developing society, it renders its adherents powerless, particularly in terms of innovation and enterprise, because it is a practice merely of imitation. Modernization, on the other hand, is an empowering process. It encourages people to think independently, to make decisions critically, and in the context of national development, to select, if they choose, innovations that are consistent with their national program as well as compatible with their culture and tradition.

This distinction, to a great extent, underlies the vision that Qaboos bin Said has embraced for his nation. In 1993 he told the students of Sultan Qaboos University that "Oman is a country with a deep-rooted history, a distinguished character, which has its own philosophy in social life, and therefore we should not allow senseless imitation to impede our progress or passively affect our immortal heritage."[55] In order for this strategy to succeed, he has emphasized the need "to preserve a careful balance between . . . two paramount factors—the acceptance of modernity and the retention of old established values."[56] As E. Harper Johnson puts it,

> His Majesty understood the implicit relationship between self-identity and a sense of self-worth in a fast-changing global society. No aspect of this evolution would be made at the expense of knowledge of the past, or the valued heritage of the land. It was a system of integration, a strengthening of age-old foundations.[57]

Past Merges with Future

In recent years, the sultan has focused increasingly on the growing contingent of young people in Oman. As he listens to their concerns, he urges them to be guided by their past as they work to invest in their country's future. He seizes upon every opportunity to remind the country, particularly its young citizens, of their illustrious history; for this is the basis from which Oman's national model for modernization derives its inspiration, strength, and resolve. Since the first day of his accession to the throne, he has articulated the theme that "our country in the past was famous and strong. If we work in unity and co-operation, we will regenerate that glorious past and we will take a respectable place in the world."[58]

In an effort to rally Omanis together toward a united, national endeavor, the sultan emphasizes the importance of remaining mindful of the country's past while, at the same time, looking to a future of peace and stability. Standing at the epicenter of this paradigm for development is an emphasis on national identity and cultural authenticity. The goal is selective modernization rather than blind imitation, a program that encourages the adoption of appropriate information and technologies from other societies while, at the same time, remaining true to Oman's unique heritage, including its cherished norms and values.

Reclaiming Cultural Roots

Shortly after Sultan Qaboos's accession to power, Omanis, even those who had lived, studied, and worked abroad for extended periods, began to rediscover and embrace the symbols of their country's culture. For most, this began with the adoption of traditional dress. By the early 1970s, many Omanis, particularly government employees living in the capital region, had begun to favor some variation of contemporary Western dress, a perceived embodiment of "modernization." Within a very short time, however, this trend was reversed as young, urban Omanis transitioned into more traditional attire as an affirmation of their country's culture.

Today, traditional dress, across a wide spectrum of forms, colors, and styles, is the hallmark of modern Omani material culture. The norm for men is the dishdasha, a flowing, ankle-length robe, at whose neckline hangs a fragrant, usually incense-scented, tassel. Their heads are covered with either an embroidered skullcap (*kumma*) or a brightly colored, patterned turban (*ammama*).

In government offices, and on official and ceremonial occasions, men proudly sport the iconic *khanjar*, a distinctive curved dagger, meticulously crafted from silver and, occasionally, even gold filigree. This hallmark of Omani national identity is featured prominently on the national crest itself, which depicts a *khanjar* over two crossed swords.[59]

Women in urban and rural areas dress modestly but fashionably, covering their bodies with long robes or tunics (*thob*), frequently constructed of beautiful fabrics, dazzling colors, and elaborate patterns, worn over trousers (*sarwal*) with richly embellished cuffs. In urban areas, women wear simple or ornate headscarves, while women of the tribal areas, including the *bedu*, enhance their appearance even more dramatically by covering their faces with the eagle-like black or indigo-colored mask (*burka*) that offers protection from the sun while, at the same time, it has been suggested, adding a certain measure of allure to the wearer.

The Cultural Milieu

In an increasingly globalized and culturally homogenized world, the goal of respecting and preserving national identity while simultaneously pursuing a course of modernization can be a formidable challenge. In this context, the new Oman differs considerably from its neighbors in the Gulf region. To a great extent, this difference in approach can be directly attributed to the country's leadership, for whom history and tradition were sufficient precedents around which to construct a modern society. While the pace of development in Oman has been staggering, "the country's leaders seem committed to avoid the ugliness and garishness that characterize so much of modern development, especially in the capital cities of the developing world."[60]

In Oman, development is characterized in many ways by a distinctively "Omani" touch. New construction routinely blends modern building requirements with traditional architectural motifs. Whitewashed or traditional pastel facades with graceful Islamic arches and signature domes are omnipresent, whether featured on grand governmental complexes or on the most modest of private homes.

For most observers, the startling absence of so-called modern skyscrapers stands as a refreshing departure from the apparent competition among Oman's Gulf neighbors to "sprout record-setting concrete-and-glass monstrosities to fuel tourism, [while] Sultan Qaboos forbids anything taller than six [actually, twelve] floors, excluding minarets."[61] The result is a pleasing continuity and authentic blend of style, height, and materials.

Cultural symbols, including oversized incense burners, dhows, and traditional coffee pots, adorn "thematic" roundabouts and public places throughout the capital city and beyond. Colorful flowers and blooming shrubbery delight the senses along the miles and miles of meticulously maintained roadways in Muscat, leading not only to schools, hospitals, businesses, and government ministries but also to public parks, gardens, and sports stadiums.

The overall effect is calm and pleasing, particularly because it represents a conscious effort to integrate history and modernity into a culturally authentic, uniquely national tableau. Whether it is the importance placed on the choice of national dress or the emphasis placed on traditional construction and design, Omanis, as a veteran Oman-watcher has observed, "are comfortable in their own skin."

Comprehensive efforts are ongoing to restore and preserve castles, forts, and private palaces (discussed in depth in chapter 5), reminders of Oman's great and glorious national past. Unabashedly proud of their history and faithful to their culture, Omanis are forging a future in which tradition, in fact, serves as a springboard for modernization.

REFLECTIONS

The transition, in 1970, from Sultan Said bin Taymur to his son, Qaboos, marks a major turning point in the history of Oman. Well into the future, historians will surely include Qaboos bin Said among the pantheon of important statesmen in the Middle East and beyond. His impact has been profound, not only on his own people, whose lot he has improved immeasurably, but also on the people in the Middle East and in the wider world community, for this is a head of state who safeguards his country's sovereignty assiduously while, at the same time, inviting visitors of disparate backgrounds to its shores for the exchange of ideas—political, economic, and cultural.

When he assumed leadership by ousting his father, the young leader faced challenges that were daunting to say the least. The economy, though no longer riddled with debt (thanks to his father's abstemious practices), was being drained by a prolonged, and seemingly endless, war in the south. While individual citizens labored under inexplicable personal restrictions, limiting their freedom of movement as well as their use of modern conveniences, the national infrastructure, including transportation, utilities, and health and educational facilities, was abysmal. Many skilled Omanis had long since left the sultanate for more fulfilling opportunities abroad.

It was a formidable challenge, to be sure. However, it is clear that the new ruler had a plan, or at least a vision, well in place, most likely formulated during his early adult years in Salalah, during which time he focused on the study of Oman's history and traditions while, simultaneously, acquiring valuable insights from his father and those who knew the dynamics of Omani society.

Qaboos was decisive. He traveled to the capital city, for the first time in his life, to announce the dawn of a new day. Uniting the country under a new flag, he lifted restrictions, freed political prisoners, and invited expatriate Omanis to return "home" to assist him in the colossal endeavors that lay ahead. Eyewitness accounts at the time suggest that Oman's citizens were virtually giddy with excitement and expectation.

If Omanis were to enter the modern age, the Dhofari insurrection would need to be resolved. This was accomplished rather decisively by Qaboos, a veteran military man, who led the Sultan's Armed Forces to final victory with the assistance of stalwart friends, whose contribution to the ultimate victory would not soon be forgotten.

In the contentious international climate of the 1970s and 1980s, the young sultan preserved his country's sovereignty in the face of formidable adversaries. At the same time, he campaigned domestically to build a new national consensus, weaving traditional institutions into the fabric of new ones. He adapted, reconciling the old with the new; communicated, through speeches and personal visits; and, at every turn, took the opportunity to remind his countrymen of their glorious legacy, which would provide a compass for their success in a modern, global age.

Central to the message of Sultan Qaboos was, and remains, the relevance of tradition to modernization. The lessons of Oman's history, specifically, an illustrious legacy built on maritime exploits, international conquests, cultural synergy, and resiliency, would surely be sufficient to guide Omanis through the murky waters that lay ahead. This message, in so many manifestations, has clearly resonated with the citizens of Oman, including those who were persuaded to abandon comfortable lives abroad to return to a land they hardly knew. This is the story of a leader who not only possesses an exceptional knowledge of both the East and the West but also pursues a clear vision for his country as it ascends to new, and culturally authentic, heights. It is the story of a "renaissance man" who, by virtue of deft communication and an outstanding track record, exemplifies the optimism of the modern Omani state.

By every account, the septuagenarian ruler of Oman who, in the opinion of some who have studied him, most closely approximates the Platonic concept of "philosopher king"[62] is the very essence of cosmopolitanism, reflecting, perhaps, the unique history of the country over which he has presided for more than four decades. In the chapters ahead, we will explore how this exceptional leader has delivered even more, in quiet pursuit of international peace and diplomacy.

CHAPTER 4

CREATING A CIVIL SOCIETY

Upon assuming the leadership of Oman in 1970, Qaboos bin Said was confronted with a variety of challenges, not least of which was constructing a framework of institutions to provide for the health, education, and well-being of his countrymen. From the beginning of his reign, Sultan Qaboos invested considerable acumen and resources toward neutralizing disparate political factions throughout Oman. Having restored political stability in the country, he lifted the harsh restrictions on movement previously enforced throughout the land and promised a new era in the lives and fortunes of his people.

However, the advancement of the Omani people would prove to be a formidable challenge. Over the better part of the twentieth century, Oman had become a country beset by illiteracy, with fewer than a handful of schools—and what schools there were, open only to boys. Added to the affliction of illiteracy was an alarming rate of disease, which, combined with inadequate healthcare facilities, meant that the average Omani couldn't expect to live past the age of fifty. And so, from the beginning of his reign, Qaboos bin Said singled out education and healthcare as the twin pillars upon which his country would be reconstructed.

To understand the scope of the progress that has been made in these crucial areas, it will be necessary to look at conditions in Oman before and after Sultan Qaboos took power, giving special recognition to the foreign volunteers who labored tirelessly, and often at immense personal cost, to help the Omani people before national institutions were able to take their place. In doing so, we also need to draw attention to the advances made by women—which are remarkable by any standard. But we can't stop there. The sweeping reforms in Omani society occurred at such a rapid pace largely because they were enacted from the "top down," by a governmental system whose constitution places a priority on the well-being of all its people—a system in which the question of succession to the throne is now on the forefront of many people's minds.

TRANSFORMING EDUCATION

Upon his accession to the throne, Sultan Qaboos instituted a massive campaign designed to transform Oman's educational system. The young leader was determined "to break the chains of ignorance," declaring that, "the important thing is that there should be education, even under the shadow of trees."[1] From his earliest days in power, Sultan Qaboos called on his people to join together to create a national renaissance,[2] pointing to education—including education for women—as the number-one priority. Tapping into Islamic precedent, the sultan reminded Omanis of the imperative attributed to the Prophet Muhammad that "the acquisition of knowledge is compulsory for every Muslim, whether male or female."[3]

Education Pre-Renaissance

In 1970 there were only three primary schools in the entire country, with a total enrollment of nine hundred students. The first *saidiyyah* school, a government-funded institution restricted to boys, was opened in Muscat in 1929. It was followed by two others, in Mutrah and Salalah. In addition to these government schools, there were Qur'anic schools in most neighborhoods that were attended by girls as well as boys. Finally, there were private schools for boys in addition to some foreign-run schools in the capital region.[4]

Prior to 1970, formal education in Oman, aside from indigenous religious schools, was largely initiated by foreigners. Eloise Bosch, an American teacher who spent decades in Oman with her husband, Dr. Donald Bosch, an iconic medical figure in the country, credits US volunteers with launching a variety of educational initiatives at that time, not only in Oman but throughout the Middle East.[5] Although many of the first American teachers and healthcare workers arrived in Oman under the auspices of church-affiliated organizations in the United States, their "mission," as guests in the sultanate, was confined to bettering the welfare of its citizens. Nomenclature notwithstanding, proselytizing was expressly forbidden.

The "Freed Slave School" is widely considered to have been the first private, non-Qur'anic school in Oman. It was founded in Muscat at the turn of the twentieth century by Rev. Peter Zwemer, the younger brother of Rev. Samuel Zwemer, an early member of the American Mission in Oman.

Its origins are evocative of a movie script. According to historical accounts, in 1896, as eighteen Swahili-speaking East African boys were being transported to lives of servitude, their seagoing vessel was intercepted by the British frigate *HMS Lapwing*. Upon learning of this event, Peter Zwemer applied to the British Consul in Muscat for guardianship of the boys. In his own words, "Feeling duty-bound to undertake this unsought but promising task, I signed a bond to provide for their support and training until of age."[6]

In time, the "Freed Slave School" would be known by different names, including the Mission School and the Peter Zwemer Memorial School. Educating boys in both English and Arabic for more than ninety years, this school grew into a respected institution, credited with finding employment for virtually all of its graduates.

In 1947 Rev. Jay Kapenga and his wife, Marjory (Midge), of the United States, assumed responsibility for the Peter Zwemer Memorial School. Years later, their daughter, Margaret Kapenga, a former secretary to the late King Hussein of Jordan, became its principal, managing its administrative affairs. As the only coeducational institution in Oman, the school, housing a maximum of sixty pupils, offered bilingual instruction in Arabic and English from kindergarten to sixth grade.

The legacy of the Mission School, or the Peter Zwemer Memorial School, was formidable. In Eloise Bosch's assessment, "the importance of the Freed Slave School cannot be underestimated because it was the inception of an educational programme that ultimately educated hundreds, if not thousands, of Omani boys and girls,"[7] many of whom are counted today among the most distinguished citizens of Oman. Given the current narrative of US activity in the region, characterized largely by exploits of a military, combative nature, it is especially important to remember this chapter of American idealism "at its best." After almost a century in service to the people of Oman, the school closed in 1987, signaling the end of an era of privately controlled education—only to be replaced by an unprecedented national effort of gargantuan proportions.

Post-1970 Initiatives

From the year 1970 onward, education emerged as the cornerstone of the country's ambitious national development policy. Sultan Qaboos announced bold measures, setting goals designed to ensure that all members of Omani society, regardless of age or location, had equal access to education. As if to emphasize the seriousness of this objective, he established the Ministry of Education, along with three other national ministries, during the first year of his reign.

Government School Construction

With the government shouldering the expense, no effort was spared to construct schools throughout the country, even providing transportation for students in the remotest locales. Within the first year of the Omani renaissance, the government had completed sixteen schools, attended by 7,000 students; by 1972, the number had expanded to forty-five schools with an enrollment of 15,000.

Except for those few Omanis who could read Qur'anic texts, illiteracy was widespread when Sultan Qaboos assumed power. Throughout the 1970s, as Omani youngsters by the tens of thousands attended schools, most of them for the first time, older generations were also invited to join in the nationwide educational initiative. Mandating that employers allow workers leave time from their jobs, the Ministry of Education set up a program of evening classes for adults, again providing transportation, where possible.

The country's leadership prioritized the need not only for education at all levels, including education in academic and technical subjects, but also for vocational training. Within two years of assuming power, Sultan Qaboos announced the establishment of a vocational training program in Muscat in the hope of ultimately replacing a labor force largely imported from other countries with one composed primarily of Omani nationals.

By the mid-1990s, with completion of the goal of nationwide school construction in sight, the Ministry of Education began to shift its emphasis from "bricks and mortar" toward reviewing curricula and raising the qualitative standards of education in the country, introducing reforms designed to meet the needs of Omanis in a twenty-first-century globalized world. Today, these efforts are continually being reviewed and assessed, particularly in the context of a growing—and expectant—youthful population.

In 1996 Sultan Qaboos announced the Basic Law (also called the Basic Statute of the State), which serves as the country's constitution. Article 13, "Cultural Principles," deals specifically with matters relating to education. The importance it places on education is unambiguous:

• Education is a cornerstone for the progress of the Society which the State fosters and endeavours to disseminate and make accessible to all.
• Education aims to raise and develop the general cultural standard, promote scientific thought, kindle the spirit of research, respond to the requirements of economic and social plans, build a generation that is physically and morally strong, which takes pride in its Nation, Country, and heritage and preserves its achievements.
• The state shall provide public education, work to combat illiteracy and encourage the establishment of private schools and institutes under its supervision and in accordance with the provision of the Law.[8]

Private and International Institutions

During the past four decades, the expansion of public education in Oman has been accompanied by the growth of private alternatives for both Omanis and resident foreign nationals. Serving to complement the government's efforts in the education sector, there are currently some 454 private schools in the sultanate, among which 40 are international schools.[9] Expatriates from many countries, including the United Kingdom, the United States, India, and Pakistan, among others, have established institutions that cater to the many diverse communities that reside in Oman.

These initiatives were supported during the earliest years of the Omani renaissance. In 1971 Sultan Qaboos announced his support for an educational institution designed "to provide a high standard of British education for English-speaking children."[10] Established by royal decree, the British School Muscat bears the distinction of being the only private, not-for-profit school in the sultanate to have been founded in this manner. The school lives on today as an outstanding institution, offering instruction to girls and boys of various nationalities and abilities from ages three to eighteen.

During the school's fortieth-anniversary celebration in 2013, the Prince of Wales and the Duchess of Cornwall visited the British School Muscat. In 2003, during a previous visit commemorating the school's thirtieth anniversary, Prince Charles hailed it as "one of the leading schools in the Middle East."[11] With an enrollment of approximately a thousand students, this institution continues to serve as testimony to the "the strong and enduring relationship between the UK and Oman."[12]

Efforts to serve the growing expatriate community in the capital region were enhanced in 1987 with the establishment of the American British Academy (ABA), a private, coeducational, international school offering a kindergarten through grade twelve English-language curriculum for students from more than sixty countries. With a strong emphasis on cultural diversity, the ABA, an International Baccalaureate (IB) World School[13] offering diplomas at three grade levels, is accredited in both Europe and the United States.

Another alternative for the children of Muscat's growing English-speaking community is the American International School of Muscat (TAISM), an academic success story that underscores the long history of cooperation between the United States and Oman. On land donated by Sultan Qaboos, TAISM, a private institution in the capital city, provides instruction from kindergarten to grade twelve, pursuing "academic excellence for students in the international community through an American-based education that develops ethical, responsible, and globally-conscious life-long learners."

Within the city limits of Muscat lies the Sultan's School, a premier coeducational institution, founded by Sultan Qaboos in 1977. More than 1,200 students from prekindergarten to grade twelve receive a bilingual education in English and Arabic, meeting the highest international standards. Whether pursuing an IB diploma or participating in the Model United Nations program, students at the Sultan's School, as in all Omani schools, are required to devote substantial time and effort toward community-service projects while they prepare for careers in medicine, international business, law, and engineering. This institution is just another example of many that serve to complement the public sector's mission to provide education of the highest quality.

Higher Education

Just as primary and secondary education is available to all Omanis, so, too, is higher education. Admission to the nation's colleges and universities is free and available to all citizens, regardless of gender, religion, ethnicity, or family income. In 2010 women comprised the majority of students at the undergraduate level (at 68 percent), with their graduation rates exceeding those of their male cohorts.[14]

There are currently fifty-four colleges and universities throughout the sultanate,[15] divided almost equally between public and private institutions. In addition to Oman's premier national university, there are nineteen private colleges and seven private universities in various governorates throughout the country, offering a range of certificate, diploma, BA, MA, and PhD programs. In 2011–2012, more than 47,000 students from every corner of the sultanate were enrolled in these institutions.[16] Several teacher-training colleges, technology colleges, as well as institutes for vocational training, education, health, banking, and industry serve to further address the requisite needs of a rapidly modernizing country committed to full engagement in the world of the twenty-first century.

Approximately seven thousand government-funded scholarships are available to promising young Omanis for study within the country;[17] eligible recipients include individuals who qualify for "social welfare" and "low income" grants. In addition to government subsidies, additional scholarship monies are available through companies in the private sector.

In recent years, the *relevance* of education to the continued success of the expressed national enterprise has been a recurring theme in Oman. In an effort to prepare the younger generation for meaningful employment, an additional thousand scholarships have been mandated for graduate study in scientific disciplines deemed essential to meet the demands of the Omani labor market.[18]

Similarly, as Omanis prepare to assume their place in an increasingly difficult and competitive global environment, English-language proficiency has emerged as an educational priority at all levels, especially in the fields of international business and commerce. To meet this challenge, before beginning the normal four-year course of study toward an undergraduate degree, students entering the nation's universities are required to devote a full year to a "foundation program" focusing on mastery of English as well as information technology skills.

Sultan Qaboos University and Others. The sprawling campus of Sultan Qaboos University (SQU), situated on the outskirts of the capital city of Muscat, represents, in many ways, the embodiment of the leadership's vision for education in Oman. In 1986, with Oman's basic primary and secondary educational infrastructure firmly in place, SQU, a coeducational institution devoted to "the intellectual and cognitive development of the Omani individual,"[19] opened its doors to an expectant nation. At its opening ceremony, Sultan Qaboos declared, "We live in an age of science and education. Education and work are our only means of progress and development within the context of our Islamic civilisation."[20]

Consisting of nine colleges—including Arts and Social Sciences, Education, Economics and Political Science, Nursing, Law, Medicine and Health Sciences, Science, Agriculture and Marine Sciences, and Engineering—SQU has a highly selective admissions process, based primarily on academic merit. With a current enrollment of approximately 15,500 students, SQU grants both undergraduate and graduate degrees in wide-ranging areas of specialization. Following royal decree, at least 50 percent of students enrolled at the national university must be women. Today women represent more than half of all undergraduates and account for 35 percent of students at the graduate level, where they can choose from thirty PhD programs.[21] Internationally recognized for its high standards, the university collaborates with scholars from around the globe, partnering with colleagues through joint research efforts, academic conferences, and seminars, both at home and abroad.

On the occasion of the university's first commencement in 1990, its royal namesake congratulated the new graduates, reminding them of their responsibilities toward "the progress and welfare of our country." Recalling Oman's rich legacy of seafaring and international commerce, Oman's ruler made an important announcement, confirming a widely anticipated expansion of the university's academic program. Once again using tradition as the springboard for modernization, Sultan Qaboos introduced a major new college within the university:

> Inspired by the prominent historic role Omanis have played in international commerce over the centuries—when Omani traders used to carry their goods to the four corners of the earth and exchange them with people of other nationalities . . . we have ordered that a College of Commerce and Economics be set up and ready to receive students in 1993.[22]

Even as a twentieth-century school within a modern university, the College of Commerce and Economics provided yet another link in the unbroken chain of Oman's rich history and culture.

While many public colleges and universities have been added to the list of outstanding schools in Oman, SQU continues to stand as the country's flagship institution, playing a leading role in the country's comprehensive program of education and human resource development. Ever cognizant of

---

What a Difference Three Decades Makes

After an absence of more than three decades, I found myself strolling around the magnificent campus of Sultan Qaboos University, awed by its beautiful sandstone buildings, impressive courtyards, and lush gardens. With its seven colleges and state-of-the-art facilities, it might well be a modern American or European university, save for the traditional, and distinctively Omani, attire everywhere in sight. In every direction, the campus is abuzz with activity, as young women and men—the latest gadgets in hand—carry on lively discussions with friends as they walk easily, confidently—perhaps to their next class, to the library, or to another meeting with friends. Digging into the deepest recesses of my memory, I vividly recall images of the past—irrepressible snapshots of yesteryear. Where are the girls and boys I saw thirty years ago, who were tutored in tents or under trees while school buildings were being erected for the very first time? Could some of them, perhaps, have become parents of the self-assured men and women who are free to pursue their dreams at SQU today?

how far education had come in Oman in a relatively short period of time, a reflective Sultan Qaboos told the graduating class of 2000, "You . . . may not remember that time when there were schools in tents."[23]

Bridging the Cultural Divide. Qaboos bin Said's personal history—including his study in England and his international travel—combined with his unwavering commitment to education and intercultural dialogue has led to several bold initiatives aimed at bridging the perceived cultural divide between Islam and the West. Among these, of course, is the requirement that Omani university students gain proficiency in English and information technology before they begin their four-year program of study, demonstrating a resolve to participate effectively in a competitive global environment.

A further initiative is the sultan's commitment to broadening his students' educational perspectives through study abroad. Currently, the Ministry of Higher Education awards more than 3,200 scholarships annually for overseas study.[24] The most popular destinations for students are the United Kingdom, Australia, New Zealand, and India, with the percentage of Omani students furthering their education in the United States having declined in recent years. More than half of all Omanis studying abroad are women. Business administration is the most popular major, followed by engineering and information technology.

In contrast to the prevailing pattern within many developing countries, however, Omani nationals who pursue their education in foreign countries invariably return to their homeland after earning their degrees. Perhaps it is their strong cultural ties that lead them to return home. In any event, they hope to find employment in Oman to suit their new skills in a wide variety of fields.

Most significant, perhaps, in bridging the cultural divide, are the academic chairs for the study of Arab and Islamic civilization that the Ministry of Higher Education oversees at some sixteen leading universities around the world. These include seven academic chairs in the name of Sultan Qaboos, including, in the United States, those at Georgetown University (where Oman has also supported the Center for Contemporary Arab Studies), Harvard University, and the College of William and Mary. In the United Kingdom, this distinction has been awarded to the Universities of Oxford and Cambridge. In addition, academic chairs in the name of the sultan of Oman have been awarded in Melbourne, Australia; Utrecht, the Netherlands; Beijing, China; Tokyo, Japan; and Lahore, Pakistan, among others. In large part, these endowed chairs represent the sultan's vision to direct his country's resources toward furthering cultural exchange, promoting dialogue among people of diverse backgrounds, and establishing enduring ties of friendship.

Beyond Recognition

Educational opportunities available to Oman's citizens have expanded beyond recognition. Even the most casual observer cannot but marvel at the profound changes that have occurred in this sector since 1970. Children born into poverty, some of whom were born in caves (as in the case of one high-level university administrator who was interviewed for this book), have gone on to earn PhDs from both Omani and international institutions, acceding to levels of professional achievement that would have been unthinkable fifty years ago. In November 2010, the United Nations Development Programme reported that Oman had experienced the fastest progress of any country in the Human Development Index between 1970 and 2010, with a quadrupling of gross school enrollment and literacy rates.[25]

By 2012, almost a thousand government schools in Oman served more than half a million male and female students.[26] To illustrate the importance the government places on education and training, expenditures for 2014 were earmarked at an incredible US$3.38 billion, or 11 percent of the total budget,[27] a 25 percent increase, in real terms, over the previous year.[28]

For women in Oman, the transformation in education has been particularly noteworthy. In 1970 few girls could even enroll in school; today, female literacy from ages fifteen to twenty-four is on par with that of males, at roughly 98 percent, even in the farthest reaches of the country. Although Oman was the last of the Gulf Cooperation Council (GCC) countries to initiate universal education, its young women today are at the forefront among their neighbors.

In 2004 the sultan appointed a woman, Rawya bint Sa'ud al-Busaidia, to head the Ministry of Higher Education. This marked the first time a women was chosen to head a ministry in the sultanate, a milestone of considerable importance, particularly because of the significance of her mandate. Of additional note is the fact that the Oxford-educated scholar holds the distinction of being the first female cabinet minister to have been appointed in any of the countries of the GCC.

TRANSFORMING HEALTHCARE

Until the accession of Qaboos bin Said to the throne in 1970, public health efforts in Oman were largely initiated by foreign nationals—first by the British, and later, to a substantial degree, by citizens of the United States. Lacking neither talent nor dedication, these committed individuals labored under arduous conditions, often without the most basic of medical necessities— even electricity. When Sultan Qaboos assumed authority in 1970, he made healthcare, the second of his "twin pillars," a national priority, promising that it would undergo the kinds of reforms that would similarly transform education in the sultanate.

Healthcare Pre-Renaissance

Until the late 1950s, nationally funded and managed healthcare efforts were limited to a few widely scattered government dispensaries and health centers in a few major cities of the coastal and interior regions. One of the greatest obstacles to the development of healthcare in Oman was the absence of electricity. The government installation of a large generator in Riyam Bay in 1961 was hailed as a landmark event, marking the first time that the public would have access, albeit on a limited scale, to electricity.

The discovery of oil in 1964 gave rise to a new twenty-bed hospital in the capital region, constructed by the national oil company, Petroleum Development Oman. Although an encouraging step forward, this facility was not open to the public, its services being restricted to the employees and families of the company.

These isolated, and relatively modest, improvements did little to address the critical needs of the vast majority of the population. In the period before 1970, high rates of infant mortality and deaths from otherwise preventable diseases were the norm. Omanis could expect to live, on average, for only forty-nine years.

With little being done by the public sector, the healthcare void was filled to a considerable extent by volunteers from abroad. Despite the limits to what they could accomplish, their tireless efforts transformed tens of thousands of lives. The example and dedication of these foreign doctors and nurses and their local colleagues, often under the most trying conditions, served to forge a bond of friendship between the peoples of these far-flung, and seemingly disparate, nations that would continue through today.

During much of the nineteenth century, before Americans arrived to assist in the establishment and operation of health centers and clinics, the British government organized a small contingent of medical personnel in Muscat, primarily for the purpose of screening the crews and passengers on steamers bound for Muscat harbor, looking for symptoms of disease and pestilence. By 1875, Lt. Col. A. S. G. Jayakar of the Indian Medical Service was assigned to Oman's capital city as British Agency Surgeon, a post in which he served with distinction until 1900.

According to available records, the first hospital to be constructed in Oman was funded by the United Kingdom. The Muscat Charitable Hospital, founded in 1910, and located near the British Consulate, was a small, but positive, step toward addressing the healthcare needs of residents in the capital city. Containing a mere fifteen beds, it provided additional outpatient services for the local population.

During the first six decades of the twentieth century, American citizens, many of whom were affiliated with the Dutch Reformed Church, traveled to Oman, both as teachers and as medical workers. Given the near-total absence of governmental medical facilities during this period, the assistance provided to the people of Oman by these foreign guests, at least in the capital region, had a measurable impact on the welfare of many. Looking back on those early days, Donald Luidens reports that these humanitarian efforts, while admirable, were also fraught with a certain element of danger:

> Pioneer missionary Samuel Zwemer lost a beloved brother and two young daughters to the tropical sun and attendant diseases; medical missionaries Drs.

Sharon and Marion Thoms and Christine Bennett succumbed; Rev. Henry Bilkert was killed in the desert by disgruntled nomads; and others were unable to weather the blistering heat, often returning to the United States in broken spirits and bodies.[29]

Yet, countless people, both foreign and Omani, contributed selflessly for many years in pursuit of these altruistic endeavors. Many names are lost to history. But the efforts of a few, such as those mentioned here, are recorded, and their stories bear witness to an established pattern of friendship and cooperation, particularly between Oman and the United States.

In 1891–1892, Samuel Zwemer, whose pioneering efforts in the field of education have been noted previously, visited Muscat. He was received by the sultan himself, Faysal bin Turki (r. 1888–1913). After the two men agreed on the need for foreign medical assistance in Oman, Zwemer appealed to the American Mission in New York, which responded by dispatching several volunteers from the United States to begin the work of the "Arabian Mission in Oman." Its stated purpose was to assist in both education and healthcare in the sultanate.[30] Included in this early wave of volunteers was Zwemer's brother, Peter.

According to the late Dr. Donald Bosch, who would later become an iconic figure in the medical history of Oman, medicine "was the best medium with which to reduce suspicion and hostility, opening the doors of friendship and mutual respect." During those early years in the field, the traditional courtesy and kindness of Omanis, inherent within the "ideology of politeness" (see chapter 1), was a considerable blessing as foreign workers and volunteers labored under the most challenging of conditions. Bosch commented frequently on the "innate hospitality of the Omani people," which led to enduring friendships, particularly among peoples of vastly different cultural backgrounds:

> Virtually every person who had visited Oman expressed the same experience. One might expect that local residents would hesitate to invite strangers, especially strangers who did not speak their language, into their homes. But Omanis would invariably ask foreigners to sit with them, and, in a short time, something to eat would appear. If the family had no available food, someone would rush to a neighbor to procure a tin of fruit or some kind of sweet. The social status of the individual Omani seemed to make no difference, poor people as well as wealthier persons, were equally hospitable.[31]

The first sustained American effort toward improving healthcare in the sultanate was undertaken by a woman. Opening a clinic in Muscat in 1904, Elizabeth DePree Cantine, a trained nurse "rightly regarded as the mother of modern medicine in Oman"[32] was, in the words of Dr. Bosch, "the first in a long line of medical personnel who literally gave their lives for the sick men, women, and children of Oman."[33] Her tireless efforts resulted in the establishment of the Mission Hospital that would serve the needs of the people of Oman for generations.

American efforts toward improving healthcare in Oman continued after Cantine's departure. She was immediately succeeded by Sharon Thoms and his wife, May, both physicians. Renting a house by the sea in Mutrah, near Muscat, they reportedly treated ten thousand cases in the first year. In this conservative society, May Thoms's medical training was a tremendous asset because Omani women were far more comfortable receiving treatment from someone of their own gender. The Thomses are credited with the founding of the second hospital of record in Oman: in 1910, the Assaada Women's Hospital opened in Mutrah. Operated and managed by the American Mission in Muscat, it was staffed by a team of qualified nurses.

In 1927 Dr. Paul Wilberforce Harrison, another in the long list of legendary medical expatriates, arrived in Oman for the first of what would be two "tours of duty." Although he was duly impressed by the "friendliness and tolerance" of its people, he observed that they suffered from extreme poverty, contributing, no doubt, to their "very low tolerance to every form of disease."[34]

During a second tenure in the country from 1932 to 1939, Dr. Harrison, accompanied by his second wife, Anna Bilkert Harrison, and their young family, was charged with overseeing the administration of a new hospital in Mutrah.[35] Years later, his son, Timothy, would recall with vivid imagery this unforgettable period of his life, when as a five-year-old, he would observe, from his vantage point high atop the hospital wall, the endless procession of camel caravans traveling to or from Oman's rugged interior:

> Until you have lain on your tummy and watched it, a camel caravan arriving from the desert interior is hard to imagine. Two or three hundred camels, single file, loaded, moving fast, beautifully graceful, would go by. No motor cars, absolutely noiseless. It was awe inspiring. There were no riders on the freight camels, but each carried six or seven heavy, invariably burlap sacks . . . filled with dates on their way to foreign markets from gardens as much as seventy miles away.[36]

Following the Harrisons' departure, Dr. Wells Thoms arrived in Oman, following in the footsteps of his parents. In his invaluable commentary on this period, Donald Bosch noted that the new ruler of Oman, Said bin Taymur, and Wells Thoms had known each other as boys. This boded well for a supportive and amicable relationship, for "the new Sultan was ready to assist the Mission when possible."[37]

Throughout the years, the indefatigable efforts of the Americans in Oman continued. In a chapter titled "Unknown Oman," the American archeologist Wendell Phillips, describing his 1952 visit to Muscat, recalled with unreserved admiration their dedication and commitment toward improving the health of the Omani people:

> In the spirit of the miracle of Calvary, the doctor [Wells Thoms] and his charming wife, Beth, aided by their locally trained staff, treat more than twelve

thousand patients a year on an annual budget of around $20,000. Certainly few endeavors anywhere in the world can approach this record of worthwhile dollar expenditure.[38]

In the period before 1970, trachoma, a debilitating eye disease that if left untreated almost certainly leads to blindness, was endemic in Oman. With the help of his dedicated staff, Dr. Thoms performed thousands of surgeries to correct the condition, restoring the gift of sight to countless Omanis. One observer reflected, "If there ever was a tradition of love and service in one family it was in the Thoms family. Sharon, Wells, and for a time, even son Peter, all gave themselves to Oman and its people over a total period of some sixty years."[39]

By the 1950s, the American Mission Hospital in Mutrah[40] had grown into a hundred-bed facility. With its reputation secure, it was the largest employer in the country, second only to the army, performing a staggering ten to twelve surgeries each day.

It was during this period, in 1955, that Donald Bosch, an American physician, and his wife, Eloise, a teacher, arrived in Oman at the behest of the Reformed Church of America, to lend their hearts, skills, and considerable energies to the daunting task of addressing the healthcare needs of a people and a country that they and their three children would grow to love. Traveling from Iraq—where they had studied Arabic—via Bahrain, Dr. Bosch recalled that the customs officer in Muscat declined to inspect the family's luggage, "saying that anyone coming to Oman from the same organization as the American Mission was certain to be honest and trustworthy; therefore, no need to examine their belongings."[41] An auspicious welcome, to be sure.

After being received cordially by Sultan Said bin Taymur at the royal palace in Muscat, Dr. Bosch lost no time in joining Dr. Thoms in his important work. Following the latter's retirement in 1970, Dr. Bosch became the Mission Hospital's chief medical officer, acceding, in short order, to a similar position at Khoula Hospital. By this time, the Mission Hospital in Mutrah had a partner in the thirty-five-bed Women's Hospital in Muscat. Both facilities were staffed almost exclusively by Omanis.

The role of Omani nurses and assistants in assuming ever-greater responsibility for the welfare of their fellow citizens would prove to be a vital factor in the eventual transformation of healthcare delivery systems in the sultanate. In 1958 Anne DeYoung, a veteran missionary and the "matron" of the Mission Hospital, started a nursing school within that facility with the intention not only of improving the quality of care but also of "Omanizing" the hospital staff by training local citizens to serve their fellow countrymen. Initially, all the nursing students were men. Ever sensitive to cultural considerations, they were joined, eventually, by local women. In order to better communicate with the hospital's patients, DeYoung authored a handbook designed to assist nurses from America and elsewhere in the use of "hospital Arabic."

For nearly half a century, while her husband practiced medicine, Eloise Bosch, trained as a teacher, taught at the American Mission School in

Muscat. When the need arose, which it often did, she served at her husband's side. In the couple's poignant memoir recalling life in Oman in the 1950s and 1960s, she recalls the profile of the average patient who entered the doors of the Mission Hospital:

> We generally assumed that each patient had five diseases before he came to the hospital complaining of yet another problem. The five diseases were malaria, trachoma (an eye disease), intestinal parasites, malnutrition, and anemia. But what brought the patient to the hospital was usually something else, such as a broken bone, a serious burn, pneumonia, meningitis, tetanus, strangulated hernias, obstructed labor, intestinal obstruction, serious trauma such as camel bites or fishing accidents.[42]

Another eyewitness, Pauline Searle, who was employed at the Mission Hospital for a time in the late 1960s, paints a sobering picture of the work environment in the healthcare sector:

> The conditions were unbelievable to anyone used to hospitals anywhere else. Goats roamed the corridors, even appearing at the theatre door on occasion, people were everywhere—cooking meals in the corridors, their children under foot, or sleeping in odd corners. Patients were often two to a bed. . . . Above all, the death toll was high, largely because the patients from the interior had been forced to travel, often for days, over appalling roads where they existed at all, to come for help. To see them arrive was heartbreaking.[43]

Harkening back to this same era, Dr. Bosch recalls conditions in the Mission Hospital operating room:

> Managing a hospital without electricity was a major challenge. . . . We utilized car batteries to power two standing lamps. These worked well but, of course, the batteries needed frequent replacement. The instrument we found to be most useful was the ordinary three or four cell flashlight, torch. One person was responsible to hold the flashlight and keep it focused on the operative sight. Because of the absence of electricity and, therefore, the absence of air-conditioning, it was necessary to have one person standing behind the surgeon continuously wiping the surgeon's forehead to prevent sweat drops from contaminating the wound.[44]

Nevertheless they persevered, because for decades, whatever standard of care they could provide was all that was available to the people of Oman. But with the ascension of Qaboos bin Said to the throne, this was about to change—dramatically. Following the formation of the Ministry of Health in 1971, the American Mission voluntarily turned over its hospital and medical facilities to the Omani government, "with the idea that expatriate personnel would henceforth work as part of government programs, not as members of private hospitals."[45] Omani staffers, particularly those who had assisted the foreigners for so many years, were uniquely positioned to assume new positions of responsibility in this critical area of national need.

Profile: Pioneers of Healthcare

In 1972 Sultan Qaboos conferred upon Donald T. Bosch, MD, the Order of Oman, the highest honor that can be awarded to a civilian, marking the first time a tribute of this magnitude had been bestowed on a US citizen. In addition to recognizing an exceptional individual, this tribute said much about the culture from which it sprang. On the one hand, a Western observer noted, "It says much for Oman, a strict Muslim country, that one of the first people they honoured under the new regime was a Christian missionary";[46] on the other hand, this unprecedented royal accolade reflects the spirit of Oman itself, an inclusive culture in which a person is recognized for his or her individual virtues, regardless of race, religion, or ethnicity.

Until his retirement in 1983, Dr. Bosch remained involved in the transfer of medical functions to the Omanis, assisting the new Ministry of Health in assuming the operation of the mission hospitals. In gratitude for the couple's years of unbroken service to the people of Oman, Sultan Qaboos granted Donald and Eloise Bosch Omani nationality, providing them with a comfortable seaside home near the capital in which to enjoy their retirement years.

The legacy of Donald and Eloise Bosch endures even today. Having heard of their contributions to the citizens of Oman, I found it difficult to contain my excitement at being invited, in 2006, to meet these two inspiring humanitarians at their home in Haramel, near the capital city. As the gentle doctor and his gracious wife warmly welcomed a small delegation of US citizens into their spacious seaside residence, precious photos, memorabilia, and expressions of appreciation earned from their many years of service in the sultanate were everywhere in evidence.

While our hosts, quintessential "ambassadors of goodwill," answered a barrage of questions with grace and patience, we were struck by their peaceful demeanor and self-effacing manner. As they spoke, we were filled with awe and deep respect. The Rotarian motto "service above self" never seemed so apt. To this unsuspecting audience, "Don" Bosch appeared more excited about sharing information about his other recognized passion, the collection and identification of the seashells of Oman and eastern Arabia, proudly exhibiting a specimen of one of the most beautiful species, which had been named in honor of his wife— *Punctada eloisae*.[47]

How gratifying, we mused, it must be for these two pioneers, who arrived in the sultanate during an era when operating by flashlight was the norm, to reflect on the astonishing developments that have catapulted their beloved Oman into modernity over the course of a very few years.[48]

Post-1970 Initiatives

Against the tableau of inadequate healthcare, high infant and maternal mortality, and abbreviated life spans, one can only imagine the excitement that gripped the nation in July 1970, when news of the accession of Sultan Qaboos swept through the land. Reflecting on the significance of that historic moment, Eloise Bosch wrote, "His Majesty, Sultan Qaboos bin Said came to power and since then Oman, moving steadily on the road to progress, has never looked back. . . . We looked forward to a new government with new policies"[49]

Care for All

And, indeed, the ruler of Oman *has* fulfilled his promises, arguably, far beyond what anyone might have imagined when, as a relatively unknown, twenty-nine-year-old, he ascended to the throne, promising to transform his country. Today, healthcare in the sultanate is universal and virtually free to all citizens. This is enshrined in the law of the land. According to Oman's constitution, the Basic Statute of the State (also known as the Basic Law), first issued in 1996 and amended in 2011, "The State guarantees aid for the Citizen and his family in cases of emergency, sickness, disability, and old age, is responsible for public health and the means of prevention and treatment of diseases and epidemics, and endeavors to provide healthcare for every Citizen" (Ch. 2, Art. 12).

Oman has a total of 66 hospitals, both public and private, featuring state-of-the-art medical technology. Among the public hospitals, forty-nine are the responsibility of the Ministry of Health while five are owned and operated by other governmental institutions, including Sultan Qaboos University, the Sultan's Armed Forces, and the Royal Oman Police.[50] Health centers, "polyclinics," and smaller, local hospitals exceed 226,000 in number,[51] dotting the landscape in cities, towns, and villages throughout the land, providing an integrated, three-tiered network of local, district, and regional health facilities. Even in the most remote areas, Omani citizens are served by mobile health units, dispatched at government expense. Furthermore, in the unlikely event that a serious medical condition requires treatment in a foreign country, the expenses associated with that contingency are covered by Oman's Ministry of Health.

Women and families have been particular beneficiaries of the government's largesse. Combined with the strides women have made in the education and employment sectors, the successful administration of family planning programs has reduced the country's traditionally high birth rate. As Omani women continue to achieve higher levels of education and enter the workforce in unprecedented numbers, the initial age of childbearing is correspondingly delayed. At the same time, traditional attitudes regarding large family size are being reevaluated in Oman, just as they are in rapidly urbanizing societies the world over.

A further indication of the success of Oman's medical expansion is the country's foray into medical tourism. In 2012 *Arabian Business* magazine reported plans to construct a massive state-of-the-art medical facility in Salalah, in the southern governorate of Dhofar. At an anticipated cost of US$1 billion, the "International Medical City in Oman," the first of its kind in the country, will feature a 530-bed regional hospital, in addition to an organ transplant and rehabilitation center, a diagnostic center, and a health-care education complex.[52] Amid great expectations, this project is being billed as "the landmark integrated healthcare development project in the MENA [Middle East/North Africa] region"[53] and as a "first-class health-care hub for both the local community and the international health tourism market."[54]

Outstanding Achievement
The World Health Organization (WHO), which has provided technical sup-port to the sultanate since 1974, has recognized Oman's Ministry of Health for "outstanding achievement," citing the government's sound health poli-cies and strategies for rapid, dramatic changes in health and mortality in the past four decades, reflecting a health transition similar to what is observable in developed countries.[55]

In 2000, the last year in which the WHO ranked the healthcare systems of individual countries, Oman was ranked the eighth best in the world. The average life expectancy for Omanis has increased by twenty-seven years—from forty-nine years in 1970 to more than seventy-six years today.[56] Within less than two generations, improvements in healthcare delivery services have dramatically reduced infant and childhood mortality levels. In four decades, the infant mortality rate has dropped to less than one-tenth of its former level and the under-five mortality rate has dropped fourteenfold.[57] The WHO points out that "such patterns reflect one of the fastest declines in under-five mortality ever recorded globally."[58] The dramatic expansion of healthcare services in the sultanate within two generations is testimony, once again, of the determination of the national leadership to remake Oman into a symbol of hope for both citizens and visitors.

Renaissance in Perspective: Kumzar

For this longtime observer of Oman's extraordinary, but deliberate, journey toward modernity, a chance visit to one of the most remote corners of the sultanate provided dramatic confirmation of the impact of the national goal of extending education and health services through-out the land.

Governorate of Musandam, January 2006: Stirring from a restful sleep, in the early morning hours on the deck of our dhow, our senses were awakened by the enticing aromas wafting from the hull below. Plying the choppy waters around the Strait of Hormuz, weaving in and around the Omani "fjords" rising dramatically from the sea, our cook,

Muhammad, making ingenious use of a small gas stove in the galley below, had prepared for all the "ancient mariners" on board a sumptuous, multicourse breakfast of eggs, turkey sausage, and fried tomatoes, accompanied by breads, fresh fruits, coffee, and tea.

Thus fortified, we headed for the remote fishing village of Kumzar, the farthest outpost in Musandam, the northernmost governorate of Oman. Separated from the rest of the country by the United Arab Emirates and located a mere thirty-five miles from Iran, across the Strait of Hormuz, the people of Kumzar, a distant outpost of dramatic beauty, have long interacted with many other cultures. Their unique language attests to this fact; it combines Arabic and Farsi, the language of ancient Persia (modern-day Iran), with hints of Hindi, Baluchi, and even Portuguese.

As we waded ashore to reach this ancient settlement ringed by forbidding mountains, children waited eagerly to greet us. There, against that rocky and barren landscape, devoid of the usual amenities of modern life, stood a school building and a health center, testimony to the determination of the national government to extend education and healthcare to all citizens, even in the farthest reaches of the land.

Young Kumzaris of both sexes greeted us, eager to engage their foreign visitors in conversation—perhaps, even, to practice their rudimentary English. Attired as scouts, or sporting their school uniforms and backpacks, they rushed to inquire about our nationality as well as our impressions of their country. At one point, a member of our delegation produced an American-style football. While this was an object considerably less familiar to them than the omnipresent soccer ball, the young and playful Omani children eagerly awaited their turn to throw it, having fun and trying to master this foreign curiosity.

Boarding our vessel for the return voyage to Khasab, capital of the Musandam governorate, from which we would return to our own homes in the United States, we waved goodbye to our young friends onshore. As that remote community gradually faded from view, I could not help but marvel at the changes that had transformed Oman since my first visit some three decades earlier. Here, at the farthest reaches of the sultan's realm, youngsters could look to a future that would have been inconceivable to their grandparents. Their future, brimming with promise and opportunity, underscores the essence of the new Oman.

WOMEN IN OMAN

The Omani renaissance, beginning in 1970, ushered in an era of unprecedented hope and optimism for all people—women and men—of this diverse and ancient land. Signaling a new day, Qaboos bin Said sought to mobilize *all* citizens, asserting that "women and men are companions." Referring to women as "half of Oman's potential" or using the metaphor of women as representing one of the two wings of a bird needed to launch a modern state, the sultan quickly emerged as the country's leading advocate for women's empowerment, in both word and deed. In 1994, at the opening of the second term of the *Majlis al-Shura* (Consultative Council), the elected lower house of Oman's parliament, Qaboos called "upon Omani women everywhere, in the villages, and in the cities, in both urban and bedu communities, in the hills and mountains, to roll up their sleeves and contribute to the process of economic and social development—everyone, according to their capabilities, experience, skills and their position in life." Explaining that "the country needs every pair of hands for the progress of its development, stability, and prosperity," he added, "We call upon Omani women to shoulder this vital role in the community, and we are confident that they will respond to this call."[59]

There can be no doubt that Sultan Qaboos values women and considers them essential to Oman's future. As he put it, "If the energy, capability, and enthusiasm of women were excluded from a country's active life, then that country would be depriving itself of 50 percent of its genius." As a result, today as in centuries past, women in Oman serve at the center of the family order while simultaneously exploring exciting new opportunities. Herein lies another link between tradition and modernity in this uniquely progressive land.

Stereotypes Unmasked

An all-too-common assumption, embraced especially by Westerners, holds that the societies of the Middle East are inherently misogynistic, holding females in virtual bondage, suppressing their freedoms and stifling their vast potential. Regrettably, this "broad brush" approach views the peoples and cultures of a diverse region in monolithic terms. To a large extent, this intractable stereotype of "women in the Orient" gained considerable momentum during the nineteenth and twentieth centuries from the writings and essays of foreign, particularly male, travelers whose pronouncements concerning Arab and Muslim women were drawn, for the most part, from their limited observations of women in the *public sphere* alone. Rarely did the nineteenth and early twentieth-century Western European male, while traveling through the "exotic Orient," en route most likely to the Holy Land, venture into the *private sphere* of homes and communities where gender roles were, and are, far more dynamic and circumspect than those they might have observed on the streets of Cairo, Damascus, Baghdad—or Muscat.[60]

Contrary to these deeply entrenched stereotypes, the lives of women in the Middle East are not confined to the domestic realm, serving as mothers and housewives; for, although those roles are highly valued within Arab, Islamic, and, indeed, most traditional cultures in the Middle East—a region that is neither static nor homogeneous—women are increasingly active in public life, studying, working, shopping (and even driving) alongside their male counterparts. This dynamism, particularly in the context of gender roles, is exemplified in the Sultanate of Oman.

Women have played a vital role in the social and economic life of Omani society for centuries; their participation has been critical to its stability and continuity. Throughout that country's history of maritime activity and global economic pursuits, Omani women have been called, routinely, to assume practical control of their households. Particularly during periods of the prolonged absence of men, who may have been engaged in trade and commerce, or, perhaps, even in overseeing national security interests abroad, the responsibility for family welfare and finances—that is, within a larger tribal context—would have fallen on the shoulders of women.

In the nineteenth and early twentieth centuries, when many Omani men left Arabia for more lucrative work in East Africa, sending remittances to their families back home, women were left to assume a greater share of family responsibilities. Labor-driven migration continues, even to this day, as *bedu* men leave their remote settlements in the interior to find seasonal employment—harvesting dates, for example—along the coastal regions. During these periods, the well-being of their families falls to the women.

Islam and Women

It might come as a surprise to some in the West that the message of Islam in seventh-century Arabia, as revealed to the Prophet Muhammad, measurably raised the status of women. Economic freedom, including the right to property and gainful employment, is guaranteed by the Qur'an. Unfortunately, throughout the centuries, and even in the present day, these rights and freedoms have often been overlooked or ignored, particularly in heavily paternalistic societies.

Here, however, the disconnect lies not with Islam *the religion*, but rather with *tradition*; for, while the Qur'an enhanced the economic position of women, local traditions, often requiring women to remain within the confines of the home—that is, within the private sphere—made it difficult, if not impossible, for them to exercise their legitimate economic rights, particularly in the public sphere. It is through the lens of history *and* tradition therefore that "the role of women in Islam" might be better appreciated.

Drawing on history, the late Salma al-Lamki, a former professor at Sultan Qaboos University and a member of the *Majlis al-Dawla* (State Council), the appointed upper house of Oman's parliament, wrote that Sultan Qaboos's exhortations for women's public participation are entirely consistent with tradition, firmly rooted in Islamic precedent. Citing Khadija, the wife and "soul partner" of the Prophet Muhammad, who was an independent and successful businesswoman in her own right, al-Lamki posits, "I believe that this modern-day legacy, generated by today's Omani women, as well as other Arab and Muslim women, is a legacy which has, ironically, come full circle . . . from the earliest scriptures and traditions of *Sitina Khadija*."[61]

Oman's own history reveals many examples of prominent women who gained fame on the battlefield, in the religious schools, and in the halls of power. Foremost among them was the legendary Queen Shamsa, who ruled pre-Islamic Oman during the peak of its copper production. When foreign forces threatened to invade her domain and seize control of that highly valued ancient commodity, Shamsa formed an alliance with Sargon, the Mesopotamian ruler of Akkad, demonstrating impressive political and diplomatic acumen.[62]

With the accession of Qaboos bin Said to the throne, girls were guaranteed universal access to education for the first time in modern Omani history. Buttressed by a faith tradition that sees acquiring knowledge as an obligation for both men and women, the leader of the Omani renaissance signaled a new dawn for women in his country, encouraging them to mobilize and to participate actively in all aspects of their nation's emergence into the modern age.

Post-1970 Progress

Persuaded by Sultan Qaboos's commitment to a model of *inclusive* national development and even inspired, perhaps, by their own authentic religious tradition, women in Oman have heeded the call to exercise their right not only to acquire an education but also to pursue professions, engage in civil society, and participate in associations. Encouraged to be equal partners in Oman's march toward modernization, women have enthusiastically responded to the myriad range of possibilities currently available.

The progress of Omani women is reflected not only in steadily increasing employment figures but also in the variety of fields in which they serve. In addition to maintaining their traditional role as mothers and homemakers, women today are involved in all areas of life and at all levels, seeking, and securing, a wide range of jobs, from supermarket checkout assistants to government ministers, as well as serving as doctors, dentists, teachers, bankers, executives, and entrepreneurs. To a great extent, the "glass ceiling" for Omani women, particularly for those who have had the benefit of education, has been shattered.

Consistent with global trends, the greatest employment opportunities for women in Oman are within the government. Current figures suggest that women comprise 40 percent of the public sector work force. This is more than evident at the nation's airports, where female officers serve alongside men at baggage handling and security checks. They have joined the Armed Forces as well as the Royal Oman Police, with one even having attained the rank of Lieutenant Colonel.

In government, women are represented at the highest levels, serving in both houses of the nation's parliamentary body, the *Majlis Oman* (Council of Oman), as cabinet ministers, and within the foreign service and diplomatic corps. A particularly striking example of Omani female representation abroad is exemplified by a capable and dynamic "sister team" serving currently in the United States. Appointed by Sultan Qaboos in 2005, Hunaina Sultan al-Mughairy was the first Arab woman to serve as an ambassador to the United States. A trained economist and indefatigable campaigner for the US-Omani Free Trade Agreement, passed by Congress in 2006, al-Mughairy was joined in 2011 in the United States by her sister, Lyutha Sultan al-Mughairy, appointed by the sultan to serve as the Omani ambassador to the United Nations.

Legal Rights and Protections

The Basic Statute of the State (Basic Law), announced by Sultan Qaboos in 1996, which serves as Oman's constitution, expressly prohibits discrimination based on gender. Article 17 states, "All citizens are equal before the law and share the same rights and public duties. There is no distinction between them on the ground of gender, origin, color, language, religion, sect, domicile, or social status."[63]

The parameters of family and personal status law are critical to ensuring freedom to women. Drawing on the tenets of Islamic law (*shari'ah*), the sultan of Oman issued, in Royal Decree 97/32, the following prescriptions, guaranteeing women a balanced and equitable relationship with men, based on fairness and justice:[64]

- *It is a man's duty to support his wife, even if she is wealthy* [Art. 37 and Art. 49].
- *It is a woman's right to keep her maiden [family] name after marriage* [Art. 37].
- *It is a woman's right to manage her private property* [Art. 37].
- *It is a woman's right to initiate divorce in accordance with the marriage contract* [Art. 82].
- *It is a woman's right to determine dowry [mahr]*[65] *amount* [Art. 23].

In 2008 an amendment to the Land Law in Oman extended to women, like men, the right to purchase and hold property, without any discrimination. Given that a leading feminist writer of the Arab Islamic world, Leila Ahmed, asserted that the right to own property is one of the greatest privileges that Islam, historically, extended to women, it should come as little surprise that this revision in Oman's law was heralded as a significant step toward furthering female empowerment.

In both the public and private sectors, worker assurances are comprehensive and generous. Women are entitled to subsidized maternity leave and to "equal pay for equal work." Gender discrimination in the workplace is strictly prohibited. The national social security system provides old-age pensions as well as disability, medical, and survivorship benefits to all employed citizens. Male workers are eligible for retirement at age sixty, while women can retire at fifty-five.

The Ministry of Social Development remains committed to monitoring and supporting the needs of families, with particular emphasis on women,

providing services and supporting programs that foster greater empowerment and advancement. It oversees the needs of the Oman Women's Association (OWA), a vast network of almost ten thousand volunteers with sixty
local chapters, extending to communities in every corner of the country.[66]
Dedicated to empowering the women of Oman, the OWA offers a range of
services and programs focusing on child welfare, information technology,
financial and economic literacy, health and nutrition, and cultural and social
awareness. Informal counseling and legal advice relating to domestic issues
is available at many of its regional centers, further advancing the organization's goals.

In 2008 the United Nations Population Fund reported that Oman was
"one of the most advanced countries in the Gulf region as far as women's
rights are concerned." In addition to having made great strides in education,
Omani women, since 1970, "have been working in various fields and actively
participate in the national development process."[67]

The national recognition due the women of the sultanate was formalized
in 2010 with the announcement that the government would set aside October 17 of each year for the annual observance of Omani Women's Day. On
this day, representatives at the highest level of government come together to
honor women throughout the land for their tenacity and achievement.

Beyond the Cultural Veneer

Through their example, Omani women defy the usual Western stereotype
of the "Eastern woman"; more important, they stand as models for their
counterparts throughout the wider region. It is immediately evident even
to the most casual observer that while women may opt to dress conserva-
tively, favoring modest, traditional attire (as do their male counterparts),
their potential and ambitions are far from suppressed. Contrary to deeply
entrenched stereotypes of Arabian women, the women of this country excel
in school, follow their dreams, run their own businesses, drive to the office,
and are a vital part of every aspect of their country's modern life.

In terms of participation, women in the Omani renaissance play an integral role in their country's success in the twenty-first century as they have
in centuries past, albeit, *then*, in a far less measurable and public fashion.
With far greater opportunities and options, they are today at the forefront of
national life, in the workplace and in the polling place, working side by side
with their male counterparts.

Putting this remarkable transformation in perspective, particularly from
the experience of modern Western history, it is noteworthy that in the case
of Oman, the inspiration—indeed, the catalyst—for women's empowerment
has come from the top, rather than from the "masses." The initiative to cast
Omani women into the national limelight originated with the head of state
himself, Qaboos bin Said. It has been observed that in the Gulf region, the
impetus for social and, to a great extent, political change "takes place when
rulers and the ruling elite decide in favor of it."[68] This top-down dynamic is

observable in some of Oman's neighboring states as well; although, in the terms of integrating women into the development process, Oman is one of the most progressive examples in the area.

Consistent with other modernizing trends over the last four decades, the evolving role of women and the subtle redefinition of gender relations in Oman are also culturally authentic, reflecting the country's deeply religious, predominantly Ibahdi tradition, which is both moderate and dynamic. "So far most changes concerning gender relations have been accommodated and absorbed into the existing traditional social patterns. Changes . . . have not posed a challenge to religious authority but have gained approval and acceptance through their grounding in religious doctrine."[69] To emphasize this point, Holliday points out that during the earliest years of Oman's renaissance, the Grand Mufti, the highest religious official in the land, was the only religious leader in the Gulf to give his blessing to the inclusion of women in the political process.[70]

Reflecting on his country's remarkable transformation in this and other arenas, Sultan Qaboos observed, "We are making progress, but quietly. Slowly. I believe in evolution . . . and not a sudden evolution. But the progress we have made is irreversible." Indeed.

From total exclusion to genuine empowerment in just over four decades, females have achieved parity with males across the land—*at least according to law*. In today's Oman, personal status laws guarantee females equal rights in both education and employment. The mechanisms are in place; it remains for all members of society, including women, to take their place among the new generation of empowered Omani citizens.

GOVERNANCE AND PARTICIPATION

With the objective of "democratization" frequently dominating the conversation among global policymakers, particularly in the context of the modern Middle East, a word about the evolution of political culture in the new Oman is in order. Omani political culture is highly nuanced. Although this might come as a surprise to some, the government of Oman is managed and regulated in a manner that is uniquely "democratic"—a term that, while bandied about loosely, continues to elude definition. For while the sultan is, unquestionably, the primary legislator and policymaker in his country, an "absolute monarch" in the strictest sense, Qaboos bin Said *does not* rule absolutely.

In Oman, the monarch's power is constrained by Islamic law (*shari'ah*), by tradition, and through the practice of "consultation and consensus," concepts that are central to the process of determining leadership in the Islamic community, whether on the local, regional, or national scale. The head of state is assisted by a trusted cadre of advisers, ministers, and technocrats whose counsel is sought, considered, and weighed routinely before royal decrees are announced and laws are enacted. And, then, there is *tradition*—as relevant now as it has been in generations past.

Consultation and Consensus

In many ways, the evolution of institution building and democratization in Oman stands out as a radical departure from comparable historical experiments in many Western nations; for example, while the idealistic revolutionaries of the United States and France sought to overturn the established order in favor of new, yet untested, institutions, the modern leadership of the sultanate has drawn heavily on tradition—incorporating venerable cultural prescriptions into a new paradigm in an effort to blend *the old with the new*. Included among these historic considerations are the important Islamic notion of *consultation* and *consensus*, the relatively egalitarian culture of Ibadhism, and the venerable authority of tribal organization as personified in the person of the sultan. Together they combine to form a unique, but culturally authentic, "road map" for political modernization.

Central to political culture in Oman are the interconnected ideas of *shura* (consultation) and *ijma'* (consensus), combining to invite participation by many, regardless of their station in life. To a significant degree, this particularly egalitarian notion is, in itself, inherent to the wider Islamic system of jurisprudence in which the Qur'an, followed by *hadith* (traditions and sayings of the Prophet Muhammad) and *ijma'*, combine to form the corpus of *shari'ah*. These characteristics are central to the institution of the *majlis*, or "council," which has historically been part of the decision-making process in Oman, in the tribes and even in the villages. *Consensus* is at the heart of all things Omani.

Jeremy Jones suggests that in Oman's political culture, the notion of *shura* carries far greater resonance than it does within other political systems in the Islamic Middle East. This is due, in large part, to Oman's predominant Ibadhi tradition. It is here, ensconced within this unique cultural milieu, that *shura* is so deeply ingrained in decision making. *Shura* culture "is where Oman works out its political development. *It is a tradition which is designed to permit change*" (italics mine).[71] This tradition, designed to *legitimize* change, is inherently dynamic and, as such, is indispensable to the success of any society, particularly one such as Oman's, with the seemingly insurmountable obstacles that faced its leadership in 1970.

Jones maintains that the philosophy and rationale for consensual decision making are clear and, arguably, inherently democratic: "Decisions agreed upon by all on the basis of a consensus reached through participatory consultation," he argues, "are likely both to be better decisions because more thought by more people has gone into them than decisions taken by one person alone, and to stand more chance of being effectively implemented."[72]

Role of the Sultan

The current sultan of Oman, Qaboos bin Said, a direct descendant of Imam Ahmad bin Said, founder of the venerable Al Bu Said dynasty, is by definition the "absolute ruler" of the Sultanate of Oman. The monarch is both the chief of state and the head of government, the sole ruler of the country. He rules by decree. He is the prime minister and commander-in-chief of the Armed Forces. He holds the portfolios of the minister of defense, the minister of finance, and the minister of foreign affairs and serves as the chairman of the central bank.

Unlike other hereditary dynasties throughout the world and, in particular, throughout the neighboring Gulf countries, there is no *ruling family* in Oman. The sultan alone rules. There is, however, the royal family—even two, if one includes the Zanzibari members, some of whom sit among the royals at official functions. The assignation "royal" (as in "royal family") is restricted to those and *only those* who are directly descended from the line of Sultan Turki bin Said (r. 1871–1888). Even with that designation, their function remains strictly limited to that of a supporting or advisory role vis-à-vis the head of state. This distinction between *ruling* and *royal* might, at first glance, appear to be a purely semantic exercise; it is, however, essential if one is to understand the nuances of power, authority, and, as will be made clear, protocols for succession in the Omani political mosaic.

EVOLUTION OF POLITICAL CHANGE

While the celebrated narratives surrounding the birth of the US and French republics, in 1776 and 1798, respectively, recall how representative governments arose as a result of popular sentiment and mass uprisings "from below," the evolution of political power and *democratization* in the modern Middle East and, in particular, within the various monarchies of the Arabian peninsula is far more nuanced, reflecting centuries of culture and tradition. In most cases, in the modern era—and at least until the present time— societal transformation in these countries has been initiated by the rulers, whose imprimatur serves to legitimize changes in direction.

This pattern of political evolution in Oman is one that might well strike observers, particularly Western observers, as a deviation from the norm. In Oman and, for that matter, in many of its neighboring states, organic, institutional change is initiated for the most part *from above*, rather than from the ranks of the *proletariat*. For many on the outside, particularly for those who are unaware of the traditions and cultural mores of this region, this apparently topsy-turvy, top-down paradigm of reform and modernization appears "irregular," standing as it does in stark contrast to the historical narrative of democratizing experiences of the United States, France, and, most recently, Eastern Europe. If for this reason alone, an explanation of the structure and dynamics of Omani society is instructive.

Creating the State Apparatus

From the moment of his accession to power in 1970, Sultan Qaboos introduced initiatives designed to provide ever-greater political representation for the diverse elements of Omani society, but always "in a number of stages, in

direct response to the demands of each successive stage of national development."[73] He achieved this by appointing members of Oman's various tribal,
ethnic, and regional groups to the Council of Ministers, an executive body
that functions effectively as the sultan's cabinet.

In 1981 the sultan established the *Majlis al-Istishari* (State Consultative
Council). In a characteristically evolutionary approach to the development of
Omani institutions, he envisaged the creation of this body as "the first step
aimed at providing greater opportunities of participation for our citizens."[74]
Three years later, in 1984, the council held its first session, initially with
forty-five appointed members.

In 1990, as he marked the twentieth anniversary of his reign, Qaboos bin
Said announced that the State Consultative Council would be replaced by
an *elected Majlis al-Shura* (Consultative Council), designed as a "pioneering
experiment and a strong solid building block of the institution-based state
we are striving to consolidate."[75] From a historical perspective, the establishment of this institution was a milestone in the modern political history of
Oman, representing the first in a series of measures designed to pave the way
for a parliamentary system of government. At the same time, this precedent
drew on tradition, seeking the participation of those whose would *best represent* their constituents. The people were eager to participate: "The *walis*
invited local *sheikhs*, notables, village elders and scholars to elect persons who
were literate, articulate and capable of contributing to this process."[76] In
the words of Sultan Qaboos, this historic initiative marked "a further step
on the road of participation which will serve the aspirations and ambitions
of the citizens throughout Oman."[77] Today the *Majlis al-Shura* draws its
representatives from each of Oman's sixty-one provinces.[78]

While sharing with his countrymen his rationale behind this historic
announcement—as he does frequently—Qaboos bin Said revealed his particularly unique approach toward modernization. Referring to the establishment of an *elected* body, he issued a statement that, perhaps, best summarizes
his philosophy of Oman's evolution toward modern statehood:

> This step is taken in accordance with the principles of our glorious Islamic
> Law. . . . It is also in accordance with our established tradition to work con-
> scientiously and gradually at a pace which suits the life of our country. We
> should be open to the experiments of others to enrich the Omani experiment
> without imitation for the sake of imitation.[79]

The marriage of established tradition and modernization, "without imitation
for the sake of imitation," would continue to be the hallmark of the Omani
renaissance for years to come.

Basic Statute of the State

The Basic Statute of the State, the cornerstone of Oman's legal system,
was introduced in 1995 on the twenty-fifth anniversary of Sultan Qaboos's

accession to the throne. The country's first written constitution, the Basic Statute, or Basic Law, is, by any measure, a milestone in the evolution of the modern Omani state.

According to the Basic Law, the system of government in the sultanate is hereditary, enshrined in the person of the *sultan*, a direct male descendant of Turki bin Said, whose lineage has a direct bearing on the procedures for royal succession (discussed in detail below). The sultan, serving in a dual role as both chief of state and prime minister, remains the primary legislator in the land. Presiding over a Council of Ministers, who assist in recommending and implementing national policy, the sultan is also the supreme commander of the Armed Forces and is, charged with implementing national policies, promulgating laws, and appointing judges.

Among the most noteworthy provisions of the Basic Law are those featured in Chapter 3, "Public Rights and Duties," which states that "all citizens are equal before the law" (Art. 17). Oman's constitution guarantees a comprehensive range of human rights, including personal freedoms and civil rights. It forbids discrimination based on "gender, origin, color, language, religion, sect, domicile, or social status." It addresses the social duties that govern the relationship between the citizen and the state and, importantly, defines a political culture based on the rule of law, including equality before the law, innocence until proven guilty, the right of habeas corpus, and the right to legal representation.

Although Islam is recognized as Oman's state religion, the Basic Law affirms the rights of others to follow their own religious traditions, including the "freedom to practice religious rites in accordance with recognized customs . . . provided that it does not disrupt the public order or contradict with morals" (Ch. 3, Art. 28), meaning accepted standards of behavior.

The sovereignty of law is the basis of government in Oman. The state guarantees the independence of the judiciary (Ch. 6, Art. 60) and makes interference in lawsuits or "matters of justice" crimes punishable by law (Ch. 6, Art. 61). Building on earlier precedents, the Civil Transactions Law, announced by royal decree in 2013, represents the most important Omani legislation to date because it firmly established the "sovereignty of the law and implementation of the 'state of institutions.'"[80]

In the context of national political development, perhaps the most significant provision of the Basic Law is the establishment of a bicameral parliament, supplanting previous initiatives. Membership in the upper house, the *Majlis al-Dawla* (State Council), is by appointment of the sultan. During its fifth (2011–2015) term, this body had eighty-four members, fifteen of whom were women. The lower chamber, the *Majlis al-Shura* (Consultative Council), is a representative body,[81] elected, since 2003, by universal suffrage. It members serve renewable four-year terms. During its seventh term (also, 2011–2015), it also had eighty-four members, among whom only *one* was a woman—a somewhat disappointing electoral result that will be examined below.

Together, these two bodies comprise the *Majlis Oman* (Council of Oman). A member of the Arab Inter-Parliamentary Union, the *Majlis Oman* resembles, in several respects, the British parliamentary model. Its powers—and, in particular, those entrusted to its lower, elected chamber, the *Majlis al-Shura*—have been enhanced substantially as Oman's political institutions have evolved (see below, "Revisions to the Basic Law").

Leadership by Example

In 2003 universal suffrage became the law of the land in the new Oman as Sultan Qaboos extended to all males and females over the age of twenty-one the right to engage in the political processes of the state. Put into comparative historical perspective, this is a privilege that was not achieved by women in the United States until almost 150 years after that nation's founding.

As with most of the major reforms and development programs in the new Oman, this decree was not the result of a popular groundswell of "feminist" activity throughout the land but instead was the initiative of the head of state. It is worth noting that in the case of advocating for women's rights and

---

Women in Office

I can attest personally to the difficulties Omani women face as they aspire to win a "seat at the table" in the arena of public affairs. During the most recent round of elections to the *Majlis al-Shura* in October 2011, only seventy-seven of the more than a thousand candidates vying for the eighty-four seats in the elected chamber were women. Visiting the sultanate at that time, I was struck by billboards featuring female candidates displayed prominently throughout the capital region. Expectations ran high. Days before the elections, a leading newspaper, noting that only twenty-one women had run for office during the last round of voting in 2007 (with none having being elected), wondered, "Will women make it to the Majlis Al Shura this time?"[82]

At 76 percent, the turnout of registered voters (45 percent of whom were women) was impressive—enviable, in fact, by the standards of many industrialized countries. Yet, in spite of high hopes, only one female candidate was elected to serve in the highest representative body in the land—the first to be elected since 2004. "Disappointing Result for Women," declared a headline on October 17, the day following the announcement of electoral results. Ironically, that day coincided with the national day set aside to observe the importance of women's roles in modern Oman. "It would have been great to have celebrated 'Omani Woman's Day' with four or five women elected. I really thought this was going to be a historical election in terms of women, but sadly it was not," lamented a schoolteacher.[83]

asserting the importance of their role in national development, the sultan of Oman leads by example.

Beginning in the 1990s, as the campaign for universal education in Oman had produced a new generation of female graduates, Sultan Qaboos appointed women to positions of power and authority, first to the State Council and then to cabinet positions and high-profile ambassadorial posts in foreign capitals. These appointments reflect a greater strategy designed to prepare the populace to assume ever-greater responsibility. Advocating the full participation of women in the country's development—a remarkable, if pragmatic, policy—remains an estimable challenge, especially in this deeply traditional, conservative society. In many respects, Qaboos bin Said is ahead of the cultural "curve."

Revisions to the Basic Law

In October 2011, in the wake of the "Arab Spring," which rocked the Middle East, certain provisions of the Basic Law were amended for the first time, underscoring, according to government sources, "the importance of full public participation in the country's overall development"[84] and paving the way for greater communication, accountability, and transparency at all levels within the context of national decision making.

The most significant changes relate to redefining the role of the *Majlis Oman*, the country's bi-cameral parliament, vis-à-vis the Council of Ministers (the sultan's cabinet). Particularly noteworthy is the expanded profile of the *Majlis al-Shura*, whose members are elected directly by the citizens. Under the 2011 amendments, the *Majlis Oman* is granted wider legislative and regulatory powers. Among them is the right to amend, as well as the obligation to approve, all laws proposed by the Council of Ministers before they are submitted to the sultan.

For the first time in the modern history of the state, the *Majlis al-Shura* has the prerogative to propose laws on its own initiative. In addition, before being submitted to the sultan for his consideration, the annual budget of the state, as well as all development projects, must be submitted by the Council of Ministers first to the *Majlis al-Shura* and then to the *Majlis al-Dawla* for review, discussion, and recommendations.

Finally, underscoring accountability in public office, the revision of the Basic Law grants members of the *Majlis al-Shura* the right to challenge any minister suspected of wrongdoing under the law.

Municipal Councils

In a 2011 royal decree, Sultan Qaboos announced the creation of "municipal councils" in each of the eleven governorates (*muhafadhat*) in the country. Signaling a further step in the evolution of popular political representation and decentralized rule in Oman, 192 council members are elected from each of the sixty-one districts (*wilayat*) in those governorates. The introduction of municipal councils is significant because it marks "the beginning of a new stage of popular participation and represent[s] a further step toward integrating different sections of society with government institutions," complementing the role of the *Shura* Council in preparing and prioritizing future development plans.[85]

Although their role is purely advisory, the function of council members is to provide opinions and recommendations on the development of infrastructural systems and services within their respective districts. In addition to their elected members, the municipal councils are composed of high-ranking representatives of government ministries, including, but not limited to, those responsible for water, education, health, housing, and social development. The first elections of the municipal councils were held in December 2012. Voter turnout was greater than 50 percent.[86]

The movement toward political participation and inclusion in Oman, while still evolving, is progressing at a rate that surely surpasses that of other developed societies during their own early evolutionary experience. Considering the virtual absence of modern political institutions in his father's day, Sultan Qaboos's introduction of a bicameral parliament, the municipal councils, and the attendant rights and privileges he has extended to his citizens underscores his determination to usher his country into a modern, yet culturally authentic, age.

Succession to the Throne

Over the years, it has been my experience that at some point during virtually every discussion of Oman's extraordinary climb into modernity, the inevitable question of succession is raised. Typically, this subject is broached respectfully, even with a certain degree of hesitation, because for many who have either been inspired or directly affected by Oman's renaissance, the prospect of losing its current leader, Sultan Qaboos, is daunting.

Indeed from July, 2014, to March, 2015, this question became a very real subject of concern. During this period of eight months, Qaboos bin Said was absent from Oman while undergoing medical treatment in Germany for an undisclosed illness. Rampant speculation over the identity of the sultan's likely successor and, more important, concerns over how a transition would affect the stability of the nation, were widespread—with foreign bloggers and pundits, in particular, suggesting some of the most worrisome scenarios.

Yet it came to pass that, on March 23, 2015, Qaboos bin Said returned to Oman, a moment for which all his countrymen had longed. Spontaneous celebrations swept through the country as Omanis from every corner of the land rejoiced at the news. The sultan, it was reported, was in good health.

And while the news of the sultan's return and apparent recovery was greeted with great jubilation amidst prayers of thanksgiving, the Omanis who were interviewed for this book maintain that the reported collective angst over Oman's future after Qaboos was overstated. As one confided, "His Majesty the Sultan has spent the last forty-five years creating a state with institutions. His prolonged absence in Germany provided an opportunity by which to measure the success of these institutions. They performed well. We are headed in the right direction. That is more important than who the next sultan will be. . . . I am confident and always optimistic."[87] To a great extent this measure of confidence can be attributed to Sultan Qaboos's track record of strategic planning at every level. It is far from surprising that a framework for a peaceful transition of power was already in place.

In 1976 Qaboos bin Said married his cousin, Sayyidah[88] Nawwal (also known as "Kamile") bint Tariq. The marriage ended in divorce, producing no children. The question of succession is, however, made clear in the Basic Law of 1996, later amended in 2011.

According to Chapter 1 ("The State and the System of Governance"), Article 6, of the Basic Law, "Within three days of the throne falling vacant," the Royal Family Council, composed of male members of the royal family over forty years of age, will meet and agree on a successor who must be the son of an Omani father and an Omani mother.

In the event that the Royal Family Council is unable to agree on a candidate, the choice of a "Sultan for the Country" will fall to the Defense Council, together with the chairperson of the *Majlis al-Dawla*, the chairperson of the *Majlis al-Shura*, and the chairperson of the Supreme Court[89] along with two of his most senior deputies. This group "shall instate the person designated by His Majesty the Sultan in his letter to the Royal Family Council."[90]

Therefore, the Royal Family Council will have the first option of selecting a successor. If they fail to arrive at a consensus within three days of the death and burial of the reigning monarch, Sultan Qaboos's personal choice, sealed in an envelope, copies of which are held in Muscat and Salalah, will be revealed.

DEMOCRACY IN ACTION: A CROSS-CULTURAL PERSPECTIVE

While many in the West tend to interpret *democracy* somewhat legalistically—that is to say, strictly in terms of laws and elections—blithely dismissing monarchies as inherently *undemocratic* and, therefore, targets of enlightenment and even benevolent interference (read "regime change"), this is at best a myopic vision. Robert Kaplan cautions that "the future of American power necessitates an understanding of other people's historical experiences, not just its own."[91]

In the Middle East, every monarchy—including Morocco, Jordan, and the six Gulf Cooperation Council members—has enjoyed a long history of amicable relations with the United States. They continue to maintain friendly bilateral relations, economically and politically, even cooperating in the global fight against terror and extremism. At the same time, they are, in their own way, and *at their own pace*, gradually developing political institutions that are moving toward greater popular participation and increased transparency. Kaplan points out that "in some societies, particularly in the Middle

East, democracy is a matter of informal consultation between ruler and ruled, rather than an official process."[92] This is a cultural dynamic that, regrettably, is lost to many outside observers.

This is nowhere more apparent than in Oman, where "Omani-style" democracy, while not a carbon copy of the experience in any Western society, is evolving at a slow, but deliberate and irreversible, pace. The mere introduction of a wide array of personal freedoms combined with the implementation of political institutions that are increasingly responsive to citizens—initiatives that have emanated from *within* and *from the top*—portend favorably for the future. After more than four decades in power, Qaboos bin Said is democratizing his country incrementally rather than suddenly in the hope that a campaign of social awareness and political enfranchisement will lead to increased civic responsibility and national stability.

The acclaimed author Jan Morris, who first visited the sultanate in 1965 only to return fifty years later, is quick to caution outside observers that "this is a highly intelligent, highly realistic Islamic sultanate, and it knows better than any impertinent foreigner how best to interpret its past and arrange its future."[93]

REFLECTIONS

When Qaboos bin Said assumed the mantle of leadership in July of 1970, he inherited a country whose potential for advancement was matched only by the extent of its backwardness. A once vibrant, flourishing society, Oman had become a global recluse plagued by few opportunities for education and limited healthcare—and those, provided largely by foreign emigrés.

Making education and healthcare the twin pillars of his reform, the sultan addressed them with characteristic vigor. For the first time, public schools opened their doors to both girls and boys. Today, with more than a thousand government schools and almost half that number of private schools, the lofty goals that were announced in 1970 to a likely dubious, but still hopeful, audience have surely been realized, if not surpassed.

In addition to the great strides that Oman has made in educating its citizens at home, the importance of education as a means to promote dialogue and understanding among peoples of diverse backgrounds has been manifested in the creation of "study abroad" scholarships and endowed chairs at leading academic institutions around the world. In its own way, this, too, is peculiarly Omani, given the country's formidable history as a maritime power, interacting with peoples of various cultures and traditions.

Today healthcare in Oman is at a level comparable to that of many twenty-first-century developed nations. Cited by the WHO for "outstanding achievement," Oman has seen average life expectancy increase by almost thirty years since 1970. With hundreds of hospitals and clinics throughout the land, medical care is free and available to all citizens. A major "medical city" will further enhance Oman's national health portfolio, not only for its citizens but also for foreign visitors, foreshadowing a dimension of the sultanate's growing and diversified economy: medical tourism.

In order to build a vibrant, civil society in Oman, Sultan Qaboos insisted on the need to integrate women into the modernization process from his first days in office, calling on all Omanis—specifically *women*, as well as men—to join in this new and formidable national endeavor. Notwithstanding the "Orientalist" stereotype of the "Eastern woman," Omani women, by virtue of their history and culture, exemplify the vision of strong and proactive women. It is against this backdrop that Qaboos bin Said exhorts all citizens to participate to the fullest extent in their nation's modernizing efforts.

In contemporary Western parlance, Oman's head of state has "walked the walk." Sultan Qaboos has written into the Basic Law multiple provisions ensuring the rights and freedoms of women—*all in compliance with Islamic, Shari'ah law.* He has appointed women to positions of great responsibility—in his own cabinet, in the diplomatic corps, and in the upper, appointed house of the Omani bicameral parliament. As a result of these efforts, women in today's Oman are assuming roles that would have been unimaginable even two generations ago.

Yet, while the message, at least from the head of state, is clear, a residual reluctance remains, in this deeply conservative society, to fully endorse women's efforts to enter the public sphere. For some, in Oman *and elsewhere*, this transition represents a departure from traditionally prescribed (and patriarchal) models.

Concluding this chapter on civil society in Oman is an examination of governance and institution building. During the more than four-decade reign of a leader whose family has ruled Oman since 1744, representative institutions have been introduced where virtually none had existed previously.

Significantly, Oman's leadership draws on *tradition* for its inspiration, inviting leaders of traditional, tribal communities to participate in the formulation and execution of plans for local and national development. The venerable observance of *shura* (consultation), the historic bedrock of the Omani political dynamic, has evolved as the pool of citizens invited into public discourse has grown—from a select group of males whose role was purely advisory, to a broad cross-section of citizens, both male and female, representing a wide socioeconomic and geographic field.

This new crop of representatives, especially those in the "lower," elected house of the national parliamentary body, as well as those chosen by the people to serve in the municipal councils, has enhanced the government's ability to serve its citizens in a responsive—and responsible—manner. The 2011 amendments to the 1996 Basic Law have expanded the powers of elected representatives while, at the same time, setting into place new mechanisms for increased transparency and accountability at all levels.

As Oman's institutions are evolving, they are doing so deliberately, evolutionarily. Qaboos bin Said, the architect of modern Oman, understands both the history and traditions of his people. In the opinion of Robert Kaplan, "there is really no ruler in the Middle East quite like Sultan Qabus. . . . He has institutionalized his rule through the building of well-functioning ministries, advanced the status of women, built schools throughout the interior, [and] worked to protect the environment."[94] He has pursued a vision for the Omani renaissance that has unfolded gradually, peacefully. He had inspired millions to dream large dreams. In this respect, he has been successful.

CHAPTER 5

CONSTRUCTING A MODERN ECONOMY

Given the appalling social and economic conditions that existed in Oman in 1970, the progress that has been accomplished in a relatively short period of time is by any measure, both quantitatively and qualitatively, extraordinary. This was recognized in 2010 by the United Nations Development Programme (UNDP), which reported that between 1970 and 2010 Oman had the fastest progress of any country in the Human Development Index (HDI), with a quadrupling of gross enrollment and literacy rates and a twenty-seven-year increase in life expectancy.[1]

In 2011 the HDI report ranked Oman nineteeth in the world among 185 member states, evaluating not only education and health criteria but also standards of living and quality of life.[2] In 1970 per capita gross domestic product (GDP) in Oman stood at US$371, but by 2013 it had soared to an impressive US$21,929.[3] This extraordinary record of achievement would not have been possible without the income from hydrocarbon production, which continues to account for the bulk of national revenues.[4] Most observers would point out further that the measurable improvements in the lives of Omanis would also not have been possible but for the vision and largesse of the country's leader, who has systematically distributed this bounty throughout the land through comprehensive social and economic programs—not only in education and healthcare, as we have seen—but also in infrastructure, recreation, tourism, and the arts—transporting Oman into the modern age, yet all the while preserving Oman's ties to its rich culture and history.

POWERING A SUSTAINABLE ECONOMY

As is the case in neighboring countries in the Persian Gulf region, oil is the primary source of natural mineral wealth in Oman. During the early years of Sultan Qaboos's reign, the global price of crude oil increased dramatically (from US$2/barrel in 1971 to US$35/barrel in 1980). Throughout the last four decades, escalating global oil prices and new natural gas discoveries

have led to an unprecedented level of economic development in the sultanate, fueling rapid growth, contributing to budget surpluses, and maintaining
low levels of inflation.[5]

Although the export of oil initially fueled Oman's economic boom, limited reserves make oil inadequate to maintain the economy for the long term.
Consequently, its leadership has had to look to other sources to power a sustainable economy. Oman's eighth five-year development plan (2011–2015),
announced in November 2010, targets the creation of jobs for Omanis,
expansion of the private sector's role, encouragement of foreign investment,
and economic diversification. Together, these initiatives have created the
conditions necessary to sustain a post-oil economy well into the twenty-first
century.

Oil and Natural Gas: Fueling Development

While oil is the mainstay of the sultanate's economy today, its debut on the
Omani stage was painfully slow in coming, particularly in comparison with
discoveries by Oman's Gulf neighbors. In 1937 Sultan Said bin Taymur,
the father of the current ruler, granted a seventy-five-year concession and
exclusive exploration rights to the Iraq Petroleum Company (IPC), which,
in turn, established a subsidiary, Petroleum Development (Oman and Dhofar) Ltd., to begin the search for this precious commodity. IPC had four
major shareholders, each with an interest of 23.75 percent, including Royal
Dutch/Shell group, Anglo-Persian Company, Compagnie Française des
Pétroles, and Near East Development Company, with a fifth, Partex, holding a 5 percent share.[6] The history of this quest is legendary, particularly for
those who had searched relentlessly, enduring repeated disappointments for
so long. Its final discovery must have seemed miraculous.

Oil was first discovered in Yibal in 1962 and in the following two years was
discovered in the fields of Natih and Fahud. Following the construction of a
power plant at Fahud, extraction in commercially viable quantities began. In
1967, thirty years after the first concession was signed, the first tanker, filled
with more than half a million barrels of Omani oil, left the sultanate, bound
for foreign shores.

In subsequent decades, as more fields have been uncovered in both the
central and southern regions of Oman, additional pipelines have been called
into service. The country's two refineries, in Mina' al-Fahal and Sohar, which
opened in 1982 and 2007, respectively, have helped to satisfy demand.

Over time, the share of Petroleum Development Oman's investment in
the country's oil industry increased. Registered as a limited liability company,
today it oversees more than 70 percent of the country's crude oil production,
estimated at 945,000 barrels per day in 2013,[7] and nearly all of its natural gas
supply. The government of Oman, working through the Ministry of Oil and
Gas, is its major shareholder, with a 60 percent interest. Royal Dutch Shell
maintains a one-third interest, with the French companies Total and Partex
holding shares in the single digits.[8]

Currently, more than 90 percent of Oman's oil is shipped to emerging markets in the Far East. China, the largest importer of Middle Eastern oil, is the biggest consumer of Omani crude, purchasing nearly 60 percent, followed, in descending order, by Japan, Taiwan, Thailand, India, Singapore, and South Korea.[9]

When invited, Oman declined to join the Organization of Petroleum Exporting Countries (OPEC) cartel, electing to attend meetings with observer status alone. Not only was this decision consistent with the country's unwavering policy of independence, but it freed the sultanate from OPEC's quota restrictions, enabling it to continue to produce and export oil commensurate with its own perceived national interests.

Although Oman's revenues from oil exports have continued to increase in recent years,[10] the sultanate is a relatively modest producer of this highly coveted hydrocarbon, with oil fields that are smaller and more widely scattered than those of its neighbors. Moreover, Oman's harsh and often rugged terrain makes extraction difficult and therefore expensive, with the result that producing a barrel of oil in Oman costs seven times what it does in Saudi Arabia.

In addition to the relative expense of bringing oil to market, Oman's proven reserves, estimated at between 5 billion and 5.5 billion barrels,[11] are nowhere as extensive as those of its neighbors are. Some forecasters predict the depletion of this coveted resource within a decade or two. A refrain often heard in Muscat is that there are "only eighteen years of reserves left"; but, since this refrain continues to be repeated year after year, there is the possibility that improved drilling and extraction techniques may mean that petroleum reserves in Oman, while undoubtedly finite, may last a little longer than originally predicted.

Although Oman cannot count on oil to provide for its needs indefinitely, liquefied natural gas (LNG) holds great promise for the country's economic future. Current industrial development plans in Oman are focusing increasingly on natural gas resources, first discovered in major quantities in the center of the country in 1991. Oman's LNG processing plant is located in Qalhat, site of an ancient city north of the port of Sur. As a clean energy source, natural gas is used in water desalination and in industry; moreover, it is a principal ingredient in the production of petrochemicals and fertilizers, two important emerging industries in the sultanate.

Current estimates of proven gas reserves are substantial, at approximately thirty trillion cubic feet.[12] They are projected to grow even further. The hope is that in the future, with new discoveries, the contribution of the gas sector to the national economy will grow substantially, gradually eclipsing that of the oil sector. Current estimates project that by 2020, revenues from liquid natural gas will reach 10 percent, providing additional revenue for the country's ongoing development programs.

As Omanis pursue expanded economic opportunities abroad, they are looking beyond the Gulf region and, in particular, to the Indian Ocean basin, a region with which they are well acquainted, by virtue of their maritime history. Discussions are under way to construct an India-Iran-Oman "energy triangle," whereby Iran would transfer its substantial reserves of natural gas to an Omani LNG facility that would, in turn, convert the gas into LNG for use by Omanis to fuel growing domestic power needs and large-scale industrial projects.

In addition, plans are proceeding to develop an undersea pipeline connecting India and Oman for the distribution of Iranian natural gas.[13] A collaborative project of this nature would be virtually inconceivable for any other country within the Gulf Cooperation Council (GCC); yet, given the sultanate's amicable relations with both countries, especially with Iran, a venture of this sort—one that would ultimately serve the populations of all countries involved—could well become reality.

"Omanization": Expanding the Omani Workforce

Currently, with the lowest average age in the GCC,[14] fully half of Oman's citizens are under the age of twenty-five.[15] According to the International Labor Office in Geneva, more than thirty thousand young Omanis, including growing numbers of new graduates, enter the job market each year,[16] eager to earn money, marry, and start families. Providing meaningful employment for this segment of the population, a necessity for ensuring sustainable economic growth, has become a priority not only for Oman but for other countries in the region as well.

This demographic phenomenon, combined with the prospects of decreased oil revenues in the sultanate, has inspired a national initiative known as "Omanization," designed to limit the country's dependence on expatriate workers and diversify the nation's economy, reducing its reliance on hydrocarbon extraction and production.[17] In a 1990 address to the Oman Chamber of Commerce and Industry, Sultan Qaboos, in characteristic fashion, took a long-term view of the nation's economic welfare: "Omanization is a fundamental and vital prerequisite without which we cannot secure the cherished honourable standard of living for the coming generations."[18]

Although the proportion of Oman's expatriate labor force—most of which is drawn from South Asia or Southeast Asia—does not begin to approach that of its Gulf neighbors to the north, the sultanate is seeking, nonetheless, to reduce its foreign labor pool, which stood at 44 percent of the total labor market in 2014,[19] even further by creating jobs and attracting young Omanis, including women, into the workforce. Toward this end, it is actively encouraging all citizens, through education and training centers, to invest personally in contributing to their country's future in a variety of sectors.

In particular, the Omani government is emphasizing training in information technology, business management, and English. Government encouragement and support of entrepreneurship and private initiatives, particularly in utilities and communications, have succeeded beyond expectations. In this context, there have been some noteworthy successes.

The economist Herman Franssen has pointed to one example, citing the impressive achievement of Petroleum Development Oman (PDO) in moving toward the Omanization of its workforce, with an increase in Omani employees from a previous 30 percent to between 70 and 80 percent.[20] PDO has spearheaded an In-Country Value program designed to award contracts to Omani companies, place Omani workers, and provide job-specific educational opportunities for students. Since 2011, when Sultan Qaboos initiated a National Objectives Program to increase employment, PDO has provided 10,000 job and training opportunities for Omani workers, including 5,700 such opportunities in 2013 alone.[21]

And in the water and electricity sectors, the percentage of Omani workers has been steadily increasing according to a Ministry of Manpower requirement. By 2019, Omanization is expected to extend to all administrative, technical, and management positions in those sectors.[22]

Partnership with the Private Sector

For more than four decades, Oman has been emphatic in its support of the private sector. The private sector is perceived as "the main engine of the national economy." It enjoys many freedoms and legal protections as its contribution as a percentage of the country's GDP continues to grow.

Private-sector growth has stood out as a priority for the government since the early years of the Omani renaissance. Addressing the country's *Majlis al-Shura* in 1988, the sultan was clear:

> We are planning to encourage the private sector to increase investments in the industrial projects . . . [to] create new job opportunities. Omanis should take the initiative and play a substantial role in all fields. . . . No one should shun the jobs of his father and forefathers, or hesitate to make use of job opportunities in the private sector on the pretext that he holds an academic degree and that he should have a Government job.[23]

In 1995 Oman's leader emphasized that the private sector, with its emphasis on free enterprise and competition, forms the "backbone" of all modern economies, adding that Islam "recognizes and respects private ownerships [*sic*] and urges . . . individuals to work" because accumulated wealth offers opportunities to others through employment and charity.[24] At the opening of the Annual Session of the *Majlis Oman* in 2006, he added, "We are . . . pleased to see that there is a growing willingness to take jobs in a range of different fields. We hope this indicates an increasing awareness among all members of the community of the importance of work, whatever its nature."[25]

Yet, challenges do remain. For while the government has set quotas for Omanization in key industries, some employers, faced with rapidly escalating minimum-wage requirements for citizens, find it more cost-effective to hire foreign workers. In February 2011, Omani nationals employed in the private sector received a minimum monthly wage increase of 43 percent, the equivalent of US$520. In February 2013, the Council of Ministers announced a further increase, by more than 60 percent, in the minimum gross salary for citizens working in the private sector, raising the monthly minimum wage to the equivalent of US$844.[26] For some private entrepreneurs, these guidelines are daunting, particularly in a labor market in which nonnationals are prepared to work for lower salaries.

A Sound Investment

For entrepreneurs and international businesspeople alike, the Sultanate of Oman has proven to be a sound investment choice for a number of reasons, foremost among which is the government's vigorous endorsement of a privatization policy that extends to all sectors of the economy, including utilities and ports.

The country has enjoyed an untarnished record of political stability combined with a record of impressive economic growth for more than four decades, making investments safe and the business climate appealing. Its currency, the Omani riyal, is pegged to the US dollar. With the lowest inflation rate in the GCC, hovering at between 1.2 percent[27] and 1.5 percent[28] in the summer of 2014, Oman is the envy of many economies, particularly its Gulf area neighbors.[29]

A member of the World Trade Organization since 2000, Oman is one of only five countries in the Middle East (in addition to Morocco, Jordan, Bahrain, and Israel) to enjoy a Free Trade Agreement (FTA) with the United States. Signed by Congress in 2006 and enacted three years later, this privileged arrangement is enjoyed by only twenty nations of the world. Prior to receiving this recognition, the sultanate reviewed its labor laws, introducing several reforms, among which was granting private-sector workers the right to form trade unions.

Oman boasts a regulatory framework that is one of the most business friendly in the Gulf region. It includes comprehensive and far-reaching economic incentives, including tax and duty exemptions, no personal income tax, no foreign-exchange controls, and interest-free long-term loans for tourism and industrial projects. Foreign investors are allowed to own up to 100 percent of the projects they initiate.[30] These incentives, combined with the expansion of a robust private sector that has developed a variety of businesses producing manufactured goods for export, make Oman a compelling destination for the international investor.

In the areas of "rule of law" and property rights, the sultanate again scores well. The World Bank has ranked Oman among the top countries in the GCC on the Rule of Law Index, while the *World Economic Forum Global Competitiveness Report* of 2010–2011 also gave Oman a high grade on the protection of property and the enforcement of intellectual property rights.[31] And, finally, Oman's extraordinary location, strategically positioned as it is at the crossroads of international trade and commerce since time immemorial, makes it an attractive destination for business and investment.

In October 2013, the US ambassador to Oman, Greta C. Holtz, accompanied a delegation of more than forty senior Omani officials and executives to three major cities in the United States to promote bilateral trade and investment opportunities. According to Ambassador Holtz, the Omani "road show" exceeded expectations in building business partnerships and opening investment opportunities.[32] Recalling the venerable history of economic relations between the United States and Oman dating back to the late eighteenth century, the senior American official not only emphasized the obvious benefits that Oman has derived from membership in the FTA alliance but also pointed out to US business representatives the rewards of investing in a dynamic economy within a stable political environment. According to Holtz, the advantages to both partners have been substantial:

> Since the implementation of the FTA, Omani exports to the United States have increased by 60 per cent and US exports to Oman increased by over 26 per cent. Thirty-five new US companies have registered in Oman since 2009, nearly 50 per cent of the total registered US companies since 1982. Foreign direct investment by Americans in Oman has increased by 12 per cent since 2009 despite a severe global recession, and overall trade between Oman and the United States has increased by 50 per cent.[33]

Today, as in the past, trade and commerce, a bond shared by both Oman and the United States, has successfully strengthened bilateral ties between these two nations while, at the same time, contributing to the prosperity of each.

Economic Diversification

Characteristic of Qaboos bin Said and his style of governance is the long lens through which he views his nation's progress. "Vision 2020," the sultan's blueprint for long-term growth and sustainable development, was unveiled in 1995. At the core of this plan was the government's commitment to diversify the national economy by reducing the contribution of the oil sector to the gross domestic product. Specifically, "Vision 2020" envisages a "post-oil economy" with an emphasis on the importance of diversification—highlighting, in particular, the development of the tourism, manufacturing, and real estate sectors.

With hydrocarbon production expected to continue in the future, albeit at lower levels, "Vision 2020" calls for additional investment in the extraction of copper (for which Oman was renowned in ancient times), zinc, and bauxite, along with increased production of aluminum, plastics, petrochemicals, and fertilizer.

The development of a diversified economy is designed to ensure a stable economic future for Omanis. In particular, it is hoped that infusions of private and foreign investment will contribute to greater employment opportunities for the country's burgeoning youthful population. With an eye toward moving the sultanate's economic performance in the direction of "a steady, significant acceleration of non-oil activities," the Omani Center for Investment Promotion and Export Development was developed to lead the way in promoting a variety of non-oil export products originating in Oman. These products range from steel, cement, and fine ceramic tiles to fiber-optic and electrical cables, from industrial packaging materials, furniture, fertilizer, and world-famous perfume to premium dates and deep-sea fish.

Building on the "Vision 2020" agenda, in 2013 Oman's Supreme Council for Planning established guidelines for the country's economic well-being further into the future. Under the banner "Oman 2040," the guidelines address the period from 2021 to 2040, seeking ways to ensure maximum diversification by identifying and expanding the country's available opportunities and resources as well as by prioritizing industrial and infrastructural development.[34]

INFRASTRUCTURE FOR THE TWENTY-FIRST CENTURY

When Qaboos bin Said took the reins of state in 1970, he inherited a country that seemed more a part of the eighteenth century than it did a part of the twentieth. With only six miles of paved road and no newspapers, let alone radios or television, Omani citizens were virtually cut off from one another and from the rest of the world. Lacking electricity and even municipal water systems, Omanis were deprived of the basic necessities of modern life. Among Sultan Qaboos's priorities was to construct a functioning national infrastructure so he could bring this once-vital country into the modern world.

Improving the nation's infrastructure was necessary not only to improve the day-to-day lives of the Omani people but also to allow the kind of economic diversification that would enable Oman to remain competitive in the wake of the eventual and inevitable decline of the country's petroleum reserves. Initial profits from petroleum exports enabled the government to invite consultants, international organizations, and corporations to the sultanate to design plans for massive infrastructure projects: New technology was made available to ensure the sustainability of agriculture and fisheries, two staples of the Omani economy. The widespread construction and expansion of roads, bridges, railways, ports, and airports began in earnest. Proposals for public housing, a national electric grid, a telecommunication system, and the reliable delivery of potable water were also put into effect. Once these elements were in place, the Omani government set up mechanisms to support them and to ensure their continued, efficient operation.

Agriculture and Water Delivery

In 1970, Oman was a desperately poor country, its people surviving on a subsistence economy, barely eking out a living from the land and from the sea. Almost immediately, the new government's attention turned to supporting agriculture and fishing, the two sectors that had served the Omani people since time immemorial.

The proportion of arable land to the total land area in Oman was estimated in 2011 at 1 percent.[35] Historically, large-scale agricultural land has been confined primarily to two areas of the country, Batinah and Dhofar. The first is the 150-mile-long Batinah corridor, long regarded as the country's "bread basket," stretching from the capital region of Muscat northwest along the coast of the Sea of Oman. The rich alluvial soil and fresh, subterranean water flowing from the nearby Hajar Mountains provide ideal conditions for the cultivation of a great variety of crops, chief among them dates. Further inland, in the governorate of Dakhiliyah, a great variety of crops are cultivated in the large farms surrounding Nizwa and the Jabal al-Akhdar. The second area of arable land is the far slimmer, but equally important, 50-mile-long stretch in the southern governorate of Dhofar, where a more tropical climate yields abundant harvests of bananas and coconuts.

While limes, tomatoes, potatoes, onions, and alfalfa are grown in abundance in Oman, the date palm (*Phoenix dactylifera*) is by far the most important crop, accounting for over half of the total area under cultivation. With more than 250 varieties,[36] dates represent the largest share of the country's agricultural exports. Known throughout Arabia as the "Tree of Life," the date palm is a food source without equal. Enjoyed abroad as a prized delicacy, the amazingly versatile date is deeply ingrained in the pattern of daily life and etiquette in Oman, proffered to guests in homes, offices, and businesses as a gesture of welcome, and enjoyed during the holy month of Ramadan to break the daily fast. The government launched a new "Million Date Palm Project" in 2009 in several of the country's governorates to support the growth and expansion of this important symbol of Oman's history and heritage, valued today as it was in the past.

As unprecedented revenues from the export of oil and gas began to infuse the national treasury, the government had the means to introduce new, modern, and increasingly more efficient techniques to boost the productivity of farmers. Chief among these were water development projects that focused not only on maintaining and developing traditional water resources (that is, *falaj* systems) but also on developing new strategies, including promoting public conservation awareness, constructing recharge dams,[37] and building water desalination plants.

The construction of desalination plants, first introduced in the 1970s at al-Ghubrah Power and Desalination Plant in Muscat, is expected to increase in the foreseeable future. As new industries and tourism-related projects develop, the demand for water will grow, and with it, concern about the depletion of groundwater resources. Alternative sources of water—in this case, from the sea—are being developed in four national "zones": Muscat, Sohar, al-Sharqiyah, and Dhofar.[38] In 2014 the *Times of Oman* reported that the state-owned Oman Power and Water Procurement Company, the exclusive buyer of power and desalinated water from independent producers, will more than double the desalination capacity of independent water projects within the next six years,[39] ensuring that supply will satisfy demand into the future.

Acknowledging the importance of farming in Oman, Sultan Qaboos declared 1988 the "Year of Agriculture." The eighth five-year development plan (2011–2015) includes a variety of programs aimed to boost productivity through the introduction of improved plant strains, enhanced technical support, and more efficient irrigation techniques. Today, with approximately 175,000 acres under cultivation, agriculture employs some 12 percent of the country's labor force and accounts for nearly 22 percent of Oman's non-oil exports.[40] As a result of sustained efforts, including those designed to diversify agricultural products, Oman continues its march toward the goal of food self-sufficiency.

Fisheries

With an extensive coastline, skirting both the Sea of Oman and the Arabian Sea, the sea has been an integral part of the collective consciousness of most Omanis—in ancient as well as in modern times. Today, fishing and its associated activities remain an important source of income for large numbers of citizens, providing employment for more than 48,000 people.[41] Fish is integral to the diet of the Omani people, even among the tribal people of the interior desert regions, where it is salted and dried for use year-round.

In 1987 Sultan Qaboos, emphasizing "that the traditional occupations of our fishermen shall be preserved and nourished, and their interests protected," announced the formation of the Oman Fisheries Company to support the industry and its markets, both domestically and abroad.[42] Most recently, Oman's Ministry of Agriculture and Fisheries announced plans to establish aquaculture projects throughout the sultanate to promote commercial fish farming. In addition, the government is providing infrastructural support for nineteen existing fishing harbors and an additional six, scheduled to be built under the current five-year development plan, complete with landing and storage facilities.[43]

With substantial reserves, aquaculture projects, improved harbors, and storage facilities, the country's fishing sector is expected to serve, as it has throughout the country's history, as an indispensable feature of the Omani cultural milieu. Taking their rightful place in the twenty-first century, Oman's "farmers of the sea" will contribute substantially to the continued growth of the national economy while, at the same time, honoring a cherished tradition.

Ports: The Channels of Trade

Mindful of Oman's proud and glorious past as a nation of merchants and seafarers, the Omani renaissance has not only resurrected many ancient ports along its 1,100 miles of coastline but also constructed new facilities in order to maintain a competitive edge in the modern global market. The current five-year development plan has allocated more than US$2.5 billion for investments in myriad projects in the ports sector, all of which are designed to boost the economy and encourage non-oil sectors to play a greater role in the diversification program.[44]

Port Sultan Qaboos
Port Sultan Qaboos, Oman's principle deepwater port, is located in Mutrah, the sister city to Muscat. For centuries, Mutrah has served as the commercial hub of the capital region, welcoming ships carrying both cargo and visitors to Oman's shores. In recent years, as activity in the sector of high-end tourism has risen, Port Sultan Qaboos has become an increasingly popular destination for international visitors; in recognition of its outstanding services to cruise-ship passengers, it earned the coveted Most Responsive Port award from London's *Cruise Insight* magazine in 2012.[45]

Given the dramatic increase in the number of tourists arriving in Oman aboard luxury liners, the Ministry of Transport and Communications, together with the Ministry of Tourism, collaborated between 2011 and 2012 on a proposal to transform Port Sultan Qaboos into a "fully-fledged tourist hub" while diverting commercial as well as import and export activities to Sohar Industrial Port to the west of the capital city.

Approved in 2013, this massive project, now well under way, not only will entail the construction of new infrastructure in Sohar to accommodate the substantial increase in commercial vessels and cargo formerly destined for the capital but also will necessitate construction of many new facilities in Mutrah to better accommodate the rapidly increasing numbers of tourists arriving and departing on international vessels.

The designation of Port Sultan Qaboos as a tourist hub is an ideal place from which to experience the sultanate for the first time. Setting foot on Omani soil, visitors can stroll along the "corniche," the picturesque coastal boulevard in Mutrah, delighting in the ambience of the place. Winding through the historic *suq* (bazaar), a popular destination among foreigners and locals alike, visitors will revel in the visual and sensory beauty of the place, featuring spices, gold, frankincense, and—yes—even myrrh.

Port Sohar
The government's decision to redirect all commercial import and export operations to Sohar will revive the historic role of this important port. Lying along the western reaches of Oman's long coastline, Sohar is reputed to have been the home of the legendary Sinbad, the sailor of Omar Khayyam's *One Thousand and One Nights*. Its geostrategic importance is immense, lying, as it does, outside the Strait of Hormuz and the politically charged waters of the Persian Gulf.

Since 1999, work has been under way in Port Sohar on what is likely to be one of the world's largest port development projects. Proceeding in stages, and at the enormous expense of a projected US$15 billion, this maritime and industrial center, supported in part with private investments from US companies, will feature twenty-one jetties, with depths ranging from fifty to eighty feet. Equipped to handle a staggering capacity of up to three million containers annually, it will have the potential to expand further, to accommodate an additional three million containers each year.[46]

Port Salalah

Lying almost equidistant between the Indian subcontinent and the Red Sea, Port Salalah is ideally suited—today as in yesteryear—as a global transshipment point. Resurrecting its role as entrepôt of the ancient world when Salalah was at the center of the lucrative frankincense trade, this strategically located hub in Oman's southernmost Dhofar governorate is today a major container port and maritime destination, continually expanding to provide transshipment services to more than 1,500 vessels annually for some of the largest container terminal companies in the world.

As private and public investors join together to raise Salalah's profile in the economic sector, constructing railways and pipelines from the desert to the sea, this ancient port will reemerge as a center of the Indian Ocean maritime market. While other major ports within the boundaries of the Persian Gulf might vie for dominance in international shipping, the ports of Oman, such as those in Sohar and Salalah, lie outside the vulnerable Strait of Hormuz. This direct line to markets in the emerging markets of China and India provides the sultanate with a distinct advantage relative to its neighbors. The result is that "Oman, a beacon of stability, is being configured as the Gulf countries' alternative link to the outer world."[47]

Duqm Port

Arguably one of the most ambitious and far-sighted projects undertaken recently in Oman is the multibillion-dollar project centered around the port of Duqm, in the central coastal governorate of Wusta. This ambitious scheme, designed to further transform Oman into a major commercial destination and world-class business hub, represents the epitome of a diverse, integrated economy.

In Duqm, a massive new city is being born, ideally located along the coastline of the Arabian Sea midway between Muscat and Salalah. Building on Oman's seafaring history, Duqm features a new port with fishery facilities, a refinery, an industrial zone, and—to accommodate maritime traffic—extensive dry-dock facilities and a large container terminal. For ease of access and egress, a massive international airport will also service the area.

Having awarded the design contract to a US-based international architectural firm, the government of Oman and its partners envisage Duqm as an innovative and sustainable "socioindustrial model," expected to house approximately a hundred thousand people, by the year 2025.[48] One writer for the *Times of Oman* could hardly contain his excitement in 2013 when describing this unprecedented enterprise:

> The Port of Duqm project would position Oman as the leading international logistics and petrochemical hub, connecting Asia with Western and African markets. Duqm enjoys a strong politico-economic location. It boasts a

world-class infrastructure, several specialized business zones for petrochemicals, logistics, aquaculture, manufacturing, services, and tourism, as well as an investor friendly business framework.[49]

Within Oman's stable political environment, healthy economy, and investor-friendly climate boasting specialized business zones—for petrochemicals, aquaculture, manufacturing, services, and tourism—it is anticipated that the continued enhancements to Duqm's facilities will draw international businesses to Oman, connecting the sultanate with markets in Asia, Africa, and the West[50]—*in the future as in the past.*

Land Transportation: Roads and Railways

Compared with the mere 6 miles of paved roads in Oman when Qaboos bin Said took the throne in 1970, Oman's massive construction efforts have resulted in more than 37,420 miles (60,240 km) of roadways, half of which—or almost 19,000 miles—are paved. Of those roads, more than 1,200 miles (1,943 km) are expressways (see figure 5.1 to view early efforts to develop a national roadway system in Oman).[51]

One of the most important new infrastructural systems under way in Oman is the construction of a nationwide railway system, the Oman National Railway. Billed as "the latest and final component of the country's overland transport system," construction on the first of nine segments of the

Figure 5.1   In the early days of Oman's modern renaissance, road construction was a priority
Photo by author (1974).

Muscat Revisited

After an absence of more than thirty years, my return to Oman in 2006 was an extraordinary experience. Muscat, in particular, was barely recognizable. Its transformation from the capital of Arabia's poorest country to one of its most progressive was staggering. New shopping centers and malls, luxury hotels, fast-food emporia, schools, clinics, hospitals, and even an immense athletic stadium dotted the landscape. It had become a thoroughly modern city.

In the new Oman, endless miles of paved roads, highways, and interchanges, flanked with tiers of breathtaking foliage and flowering shrubbery, had been constructed as if overnight. This country, with barely six miles of paved road in 1970, had progressed to the point where "rush hour" in today's Muscat sorely tests the patience of local drivers—both men and women.

However, while the improvements in infrastructure and public services were staggering, the essence of the place had remained, somehow, intact; for, as dramatic as Oman's modernization efforts were, the essential character of the country—and its citizens—seemed unaffected. There was evidence everywhere that development in this country was being undertaken with thought and care, reflecting a proud history and enduring culture.

Today, while Oman's march into modernity remains firmly on course, the country's paradigm for modernization is very much in line with its own sense of aesthetics. Having opted out of the regional race for record-breaking postmodern glass and steel skyscrapers, Muscat, whose skyline is largely devoid of tall buildings, provides "as picturesque and pristine a vision of fairy-tale white castles as any romantic could hope for."[53]

rail system, expected to begin in 2015, will extend more than 105 miles (170 km), from Sohar to al-Buraymi.[52]

Oman's national rail system, carrying both freight and passenger traffic, is expected to begin operations in 2018. In the first phase, it will move freight from Sohar to Muscat, then on to the new port at Duqm, before ending in Salalah, effectively uniting Oman's coastal regions. Eventually, the country's rail system will connect to those of the other countries in the GCC, boosting commerce and tourism not only within the country but also between the sultanate and its neighbors.

Air Transport

No country could expect to compete on an international scale without a state-of-the-art air transport system. As Oman has experienced rapid growth in its population as well as in both tourism and trade, its air transport sector has expanded to keep pace. Oman Air, the national carrier with a current fleet of thirty aircraft, operates direct flights connecting Muscat with major international cities in addition to serving domestic passengers flying to Salalah, Khasab, Duqm, and major petroleum installations. Two major projects merit special mention: one in Muscat and the other in Salalah.

Bayt al-Falaj Airport, originally built in 1929 with only a dirt runway for military purposes, was expanded somewhat with the help of the British in the 1960s to enable it to handle a few civilian flights. In 1970 Sultan Qaboos, aware of the serious inadequacies of that antiquated facility, began construction of Seeb Airport, which is now Muscat International Airport. The new airport, which opened on December 23, 1973, had accommodated some 87,000 passengers by the end of its first year.[54] By the end of 2013, the number of passengers passing through Muscat International per year had skyrocketed to an astonishing 8.31 *million*, combined with more than 102,000 tons of freight.[55]

A new Muscat International Airport, construction of which was begun in 2005 at a reported cost of US$1.8 billion, is expected to double the capacity of the capital city's existing airport upon its completion. During the first phase of construction, it will feature facilities capable of accommodating twelve million passengers and larger aircraft. By the end of this massive endeavor, extending over the course of four stages, passenger capacity at Muscat International Airport is expected to reach an astonishing forty-eight million per year—more passengers than San Francisco International Airport handled in 2013.[56]

The expansion of the nation's second biggest airport, in Salalah, in the southern governorate of Dhofar, will be an economic boon to a historic region of the country that serves as a rapidly growing business and tourist destination. When completed, the Salalah Airport, which experienced more than a doubling of its passenger capacity between 2011 and 2012, will provide service to two million passengers per year and will expand to accommodate up to six million travelers annually.[57]

Electricity

Under the reign of Said bin Taymur, the government of Oman had only two electric generators—one to serve a small part of Muscat and the other to serve the sultan's palace in Salalah. By the year 2012, the sultanate was producing more than twenty billion kilowatt-hours of electricity—*1,500 times* the electricity it produced in 1971. In a land where doctors only fifty years ago had to resort to candlelight to perform surgical procedures, Oman now ranks seventeenth in the world in electrical production, with electricity available to approximately 98 percent of the country.[58]

Generated primarily from natural gas, electricity in Oman is distributed for the most part by two networks, the Main Interconnected System (MIS) and the Salalah System. The MIS, the larger of the two, covers most of the northern areas of the country, while the Salalah System covers the most of the southern portion. The Rural Areas Electricity Company (RAECO) uses diesel generators to provide electricity to areas not served by either network. Oman is also a member of the grid interconnection system of the GCC, which allows for the transfer of electricity between the member countries.

As part of its efforts to develop a post-oil economy, Oman is investing in renewable sources of electricity, particularly solar power and wind. RAECO is currently planning solar projects in 'Ibri, al-Sharqiyah, al-Mudaybi, and Dhofar as well as a 50-megawatt wind farm expected to go online in Dhofar in 2017.[59]

Information Technology

Before 1970, the Omani people were as isolated by the lack of a nationwide communication infrastructure as they were by the absence of other developments in the sultanate. Within a week of assuming power in 1970, Sultan Qaboos set out to correct that situation, creating Radio Sultanate of Oman, first broadcasting from a small station in Bayt al-Falaj, near Muscat, and the following year from a second station, in Salalah. Three private radio stations were added to the mix in 2007.

A government-controlled television station soon joined the radio stations, broadcasting from Muscat beginning in November 1974. By the end of 2011, four free (nonsubscription) television stations were broadcasting from Muscat, one of which is privately owned. Although some of Oman's broadcasters are monitored by the state, Article 31 of the Basic Law guarantees freedom of the press.

By 2012, 94 percent of Omani households had televisions, there were 305,000 telephone landlines in the country, and more than 5.2 million people had cell phones.[60] And by 2013, 84 percent of households had computers, and 66.5 percent had access to the Internet.[61] Cell phones and sophisticated mobile devices are ubiquitous in Oman, permeating every corner of the country. First-time visitors to the sultanate, often laboring under stereotypical images of desert dwellers living lives bereft of modern conveniences, are invariably struck by the incongruity of seeing villagers in the most remote regions—and even their Bedouin neighbors—dressed in traditional Omani attire while reaching effortlessly for the latest smartphone or computerized device.

CULTURAL EXCHANGE—AND PRESERVATION

While Qaboos bin Said has steered Oman solidly in the direction of modernization, including extending universal education and healthcare to his people, expanding the nation's economic base, and building a world-class infrastructure, he has done so, always, with an eye toward integrating with the larger world while, at the same, time preserving Oman's rich heritage.

A crucial part of this effort is Oman's focus on tourism, including the development of a world-class hospitality industry, as well as an emphasis on both ecotourism and cultural tourism. Consistent with these projects is Sultan Qaboos's commitment to preserve Oman's precious historical and religious sites and to pass on to future generations of Omanis an appreciation and continuation of the ancient Omani trades and crafts that are at the center of their cultural identity.

Focus on Tourism

The centerpiece of Oman's economic diversification efforts is tourism. Consistently ranked by a world-renowned think tank as one of the most peaceful countries in the world,[62] in which random violent crime of any kind is "extremely rare,"[63] Oman is justifiably regarded as a prominent emerging market, attracting international attention not only as a promising venue for investment but also as a preferred tourist destination. The sultanate's favorable location, geographical diversity, and stable political climate, combined with the warmth and hospitality of its people, bode well for its success in this market.

As home to four United Nations Educational, Scientific, and Cultural Organization (UNESCO) World Heritage Sites,[64] Oman is undoubtedly "one of the undiscovered treasures of the planet."[65] It has the ability to transport even the most seasoned international visitor back in time. One besotted visitor put it succinctly: "Oman offers an accessible, widely unspoiled slice of Arabia for casual travelers and destination trophy-hunters alike."[66]

Oman was selected by the ministers of the twenty-two Arab states as the Arab Tourism Capital for 2012, the same year that Muscat was ranked second (after London) out of the ten best cities in the world to visit by the *Lonely Planet*, an internationally renowned tourism and travel website. This came as no surprise to a journalist from England's *Daily Telegraph* who had already lauded Oman's efforts in this area, writing that "the country which had done the most to 'give tourism a good name in the Middle East, is undoubtedly Oman.'"[67] Hailing Oman as one of the "best places to go in 2015," the *New York Times* dubbed the sultanate "the Middle East's best kept secret," where staggering peaks in the dramatic landscape come from mountains not skyscrapers.[68]

The Omani people have been well known for their hospitality to visitors for centuries, but the sultanate had neither a tourism market nor even a single hotel before Qaboos bin Said came to power in the 1970s. Since that time, the development of tourism and the proliferation of hotel accommodations have been nothing short of astonishing. Today, of course, there are scores of five-star hotels and world-class resorts from which to choose throughout Oman, with amenities and services equal to and superior to many other vaunted establishments around the globe.

Within less than four decades, the country's progress in developing the hospitality industry has been impressive. The government has taken great pains not only to construct hotels and provide related services but also to restore and maintain many of Oman's natural and historical treasures.

Destination Oman

I can recall vividly—and, admittedly, with a twinge of nostalgia—my first visit to the sultanate in 1974, as a member of an international delegation invited to assist the new national government in setting goals and establishing specific development programs. Our delegation was escorted to the one, and only, modern hotel in the capital—a brand-new, if fairly Spartan, and as-yet-unfinished complex near the old airport. By the standards of Oman in the 1970s, al-Falaj Hotel was the epitome of luxury.

Never mind that this establishment, the first in a long line of world-class luxury hotels to follow, was still in the throes of construction. Never mind that the bed linens, still sealed in their factory-made wrappings, had to be extricated from their plastic cases for first use or that the provision of ice cubes—a valued, if disparaged, necessity for Western guests—required herculean efforts of persuasion.

Conventional "creature comforts" notwithstanding, the experience of being in such a place, a land of great beauty and friendly people brimming with optimism, was simply enchanting. Writing home to my family, I declared, "This is an exotic land, unlike any I have visited before. Its people have perfected politeness to an art form. Their hospitality and openness are disarming. What's more, they believe that their future will be bright. I am so lucky to have had this opportunity."

Investments in both tourism and heritage, taken together, have resulted in an exceptional combination, ensuring not only that "people will come" but also that, when they do, Oman will not disappoint.

Established in 2004, Oman's Ministry of Tourism is charged with developing this important sector of the economy. Under the current five-year plan, the number of tourists visiting the sultanate is projected to reach 2.5 million by 2015. In order to satisfy this demand, the government has partnered with a number of international companies to develop ambitious development projects, each competing to attract the growing high-end market in both tourism and real estate.

Many projects have been completed or are well under way. To the uninitiated, first-time visitor, Oman offers a wide variety of experiences, each unmistakably "Omani," reflecting the country's unique landscape and cultural heritage while, at the same time, satisfying the modern traveler's desire for comfort and modern amenities. One may choose to relax in the luxurious accommodations of one of the many five-star resorts along the sea, or escape to a desert camp to be lulled asleep amidst a vast stillness, under a spectacular display of stars.

Exotic, friendly, and brimming with adventure, the sultanate offers a surprising and welcome alternative to the average tourist destination. And

Modern Luxury in an Ancient Land

The construction of hotels and luxury resorts in Oman continues to be a major focus of the country's efforts toward economic diversity. As travel magazines, newspapers, and blogs continue to heap accolades on Oman as a top international tourist destination, the pace of construction of high-end tourist accommodations, while unprecedented, is challenged by increasingly high demand. And while many investors are expanding hotel options within centers of major urban growth, others are looking to draw visitors to more remote areas of natural beauty.

From the perspective of someone who experienced the challenges of travel in Oman at the beginning of the country's modern renaissance, I should like to offer a small sample—while by no means intended to be all-inclusive—of a few of the best-known and exquisitely appointed hostelries in the country.

Al-Bustan Palace Hotel, commissioned by Sultan Qaboos himself, situated in a beautiful and secluded bay near Oman's capital city, was built in 1985. Recently refurbished, this seaside hotel is luxurious without being gaudy. Al-Bustan's grand atrium features a 130-foot-high domed roof set off by a five-ton crystal chandelier. A popular venue for high-level conferences, this impressive facility offers international guests and dignitaries the finest in Omani hospitality. Prominently displayed at the center of a roundabout outside the hotel's gates is the "Sohar," the eighty-seven-foot, handcrafted dhow built in 1980 and navigated to China by the British historian Tim Severin, to honor 'Abdullah bin Gasm's ninth-century journey—a powerful reminder of Oman's illustrious past.

The Shangri-La Barr al-Jissah Resort and Spa, on the outskirts of Muscat, a sprawling complex in a dramatic setting, commanding stunning views of both mountains and sea, is another world-class accommodation. Offering exquisite service complemented by a wide variety of outdoor activities and sumptuous cuisines, this world-class hostelry guarantees a relaxing, and indulgent, respite for guests of all ages.

The Wave is one of the most impressive and ambitious resort complex projects in the country, attracting investors from around the world. Built on reclaimed land at an estimated cost of US$805 million, the Wave stretches along twelve miles of pristine beachfront west of Muscat. Featuring three luxury hotels, a spa, a conference center, a marina, and a yacht club, the resort contains more than four thousand residential units, including villas. Oman's first Professional Golfers' Association (PGA) links-style[69] golf course, designed by the famed Australian pro Greg Norman, boasts commanding views of the Sea of Oman.

For a refreshing, calming change of pace, the Chedi Muscat hotel exudes a kind of minimalist elegance and Zen-like quality. Located a short distance from the hustle and bustle of the capital, it offers superb lodging, dining, and spa accommodations amid tranquil water gardens. These are only some of many, equally memorable hotels from which to choose in the capital region alone. For the twenty-first-century visitor to Oman, whether pursuing business or pleasure, or simply wandering in search of adventure, myriad opportunities and endless choices await, both within the capital city and beyond.

while the breathtaking mountains, fascinating caves, magnificent beaches, and alluring deserts combine to make Oman a prized destination, it is perhaps the people who are its greatest treasure. They are gracious, generous, and respectful of others. The result is a cultural experience that is unrivaled. Exploring Oman with his family, one American tourist remarked, "How a land so harsh and forbidding can produce a people so welcoming is a wonder in itself, . . . more grand, possibly, than the mountains, the deserts and the beaches. I prayed the hospitality would survive."[70]

Ecotourism and Environmental Stewardship

While Oman's cultural diversity and historic structures are national sources of pride and strength, the sultanate's ecological diversity is a source of wonder, especially for first-time visitors. Against a backdrop of stunning landscapes and breathtaking vistas, forbidding deserts and lush oases, dramatic mountain ranges and spectacular fjords, the lure of Oman as a popular travel destination is unmistakable.

From the earliest days of his rule, Sultan Qaboos has prided himself on preserving his country's natural beauty as well as celebrating its heritage: "We must cherish and preserve this beautiful land that God has given us and protect it from wanton destruction."[71] Through his initiatives, he has amply demonstrated his resolve.

Respect for the environment is integral to the government's agenda. In a country ruled by an enlightened, urbane leader, it should come as no surprise that Oman was the first Arab state to establish a ministry whose sole responsibility was the environment.[72] Every two years, since 1991, the Sultan Qaboos Prize for Environmental Protection has been awarded by UNESCO in recognition of significant achievements in environmental management, biodiversity conservation, and sustainable food production. Inspired by the sultan's commitment to the natural world, this award, one of the most prestigious international prizes for ecological achievement, demonstrates the high regard that Oman's leader places on the world's most pressing environmental issues.

Recognizing the importance of his country's ecology, as well as the need to develop effective national strategies for its preservation, Oman's leader has placed a premium on the role of stewardship, frequently emphasizing the need to devote greater attention to environmental protection, "a responsibility that knows no political boundaries,"[73] by elevating it to the level of a national duty "to be undertaken by each citizen."[74] In 1991 Sultan Qaboos reminded the members of the *Majlis al-Shura* of their responsibility, saying, "We give a high priority to the conservation of the environment and its protection from pollution. . . . Environmental conservation is a vital matter and should receive the attention it deserves."[75]

Within the framework of Oman's national strategy toward economic diversification—and its particular emphasis on tourism—the potential for lucrative ecotourism, one of the fastest-growing niches in the international market, is nowhere more compelling than at Ra's al-Hadd, the country's easternmost point.

Jutting into the Arabian Sea, approximately a hundred miles south of the capital, Muscat, Ra's al-Hadd is renowned as a pristine nature reserve and site of turtle-nesting beaches. Currently, plans are under way to develop this exceptionally beautiful area into a prime tourist destination, complete with its own airport. The vision for Ra's al-Hadd includes beachfront amenities, ecotourism resort complexes, luxury hotels, villas, and chalets as well as sports clubs and marinas.

In addition to development projects like Ra's al-Hadd, sportsmen and outdoorsmen of every stripe will delight in the variety of options available throughout the country. Along the long coastline, white, sandy beaches framed by palm groves invite visitors from distant lands to relax and recharge under the warm Omani sun. For the more ambitious souls among them, there is fishing, snorkeling, sailing, scuba diving, and the ever-popular activity of dolphin spotting.

It will likely come as a surprise to golfing aficionados that in this unique corner of Arabia they can work to lower their handicaps at a number of world-class courses designed by some of the most recognizable names in the sport. Cyclists, including mountain bikers, will find challenging terrains and spectacular vistas an ideal combination. The Tour of Oman, launched in 2010, has become a highly anticipated annual event for cyclists the world over.

For the outdoor adventurer, or merely the thrill seeker, mountain climbing in the rugged Hajar Mountains or along the cliffs overlooking the Musandam peninsula will furnish memories to last a lifetime. Spelunkers can explore the recesses of al-Hoota Cave complex, marveling at the blind fish in a subterranean lake, or go further afield to the *Majlis al-Jinn* ("meeting place of the spirits") in the Hajar Mountains, reportedly the world's second-largest cave system.

Cultural Tourism

From Musandam in the north to Dhofar in the south, Oman provides visitors, both domestic and foreign, with innumerable opportunities to appreciate not only the ancient history, traditions, and customs of this enchanting land but also its evolution into the modern era. There are far too many to list, but included below are a few of the sites that are certain to enrich appreciation of the sultanate's remarkable history and culture. Complete descriptions of Oman's vast range of cultural experiences—including museums, festivals, forts, and castles, to name a few—are available at the Ministry of Tourism website, http://www.omantourism.gov.om/wps/portal/mot/tourism/oman/home.

Museums

The Omani government has constructed an impressive array of museums to showcase everything from the sultanate's maritime history to its modern art, from its priceless artifacts to its traditional dress. Each museum represents the ever-present effort of the sultanate to preserve its cultural heritage in a distinctly modern form.

Museum of the Land of Frankincense. Given the profound historical importance of Dhofar in the context of international trade and commerce in the ancient world and, indeed, well into the modern age, the importance of the Museum of the Land of Frankincense cannot be overstated. Here, in the southernmost governorate of Oman, in the heart of a historic area recognized in the year 2000 as a UNESCO World Heritage Site, lies one of the most prominent historical museums in the country.

Under the auspices of the Office of the Adviser to His Majesty the Sultan for Cultural Affairs, the Museum of the Land of Frankincense was opened to the public in 2007. Located at al-Baleed Archaeological Park in Salalah, the site was chosen by UNESCO because of its considerable historical and cultural significance. Al-Baleed, on the coast of the Arabian Sea, is important not only because of its location in this fabled region of the frankincense tree but also because it is believed by archaeologists to contain important remnants of two settlements: one, an early Islamic city, and the other, a community dating to the Bronze Age.

The Museum of the Land of Frankincense is especially noteworthy because of its emphasis on both historical and cultural features of the sultanate's evolution. It is divided into two halls: the first focuses on the history of Oman, presenting a narrative of Oman's journey through the ages, complemented by an exhibition of relevant archaeological artifacts; the second is devoted to the theme of Oman's indelible maritime heritage, featuring models of seafaring vessels across the ages. The Museum of the Land of Frankincense is a transformative experience, bringing to life Oman's glorious legacy in its many manifestations.[76]

Sultan's Armed Forces Museum. In the capital of Muscat, a visit to the Sultan's Armed Forces Museum at Bayt al-Falaj is indispensable for understanding the major events in Oman's illustrious history. Built in 1845 as a summer residence for the legendary sultan Said bin Sultan (r. 1807–1856), the location of this impressive whitewashed nineteenth-century fort was carefully chosen; it commands a strategic plain, protecting Muscat as well as all land routes between the interior and the capital city. In 1915 a battle fought on the hills above this fort by the sultan's forces proved critical for the continued rule of the Al Bu Saids, effectively ensuring their future hegemony in and around the capital region.[77]

Bayt al-Falaj was inaugurated as the Sultan's Armed Forces Museum in 1988 by Sultan Qaboos in his capacity as supreme commander of the Armed Forces. Well-maintained and informative displays, including a collection of historical weapons and uniforms, make this museum a treasure trove of the military and political history of Oman. As its name would suggest, there is a reliable *falaj*, or channel of pure water, on the site.

Bayt al-Baranda. Located in a beautifully restored historic building, formerly the headquarters of the British Consul in the capital city, Bayt al-Baranda is one of Muscat's newest and most impressive state-of-the-art museums. A modern facility appealing to visitors of all ages, particularly with its inviting interactive features, Bayt al-Baranda serves as an excellent starting point from which to learn about Oman's past. Attractive displays highlight the country's geological evolution and cultural history from prehistoric times to the present, including a history of human settlements and lifestyles, both past and present.

Bayt al-Zubayr. In the heart of the old city of Muscat lies "the house that became a museum." Bayt al-Zubayr, a priceless repository of culture and history, takes its name from the prominent merchant family that has dwelled within the walls of this impressive edifice since 1914. Opening its door to the public in 1998, this private museum features the Zubayr family's priceless collection of historical photographs and Omani artifacts, including irreplaceable antique silver jewelry, exhibitions of Omani firearms and swords, and a valuable collection of iconic daggers (*khanjars*). On display are examples of traditional male and female attire, as well as handmade objects and household items reflecting the history of domestic life in Oman. This exciting complex of four buildings, including a research library, is further enhanced by a garden featuring a *barasti* (palm frond) hut, a *falaj* (water distribution) system, and a *suq* (market).

Bayt Muzna Gallery. Located just steps away from *Bayt al-Zubayr* is the Bayt Muzna Gallery. Ensconced in a royal residence of bygone days, constructed in traditional fashion around an open central courtyard, Bayt Muzna, the inspiration of the US-born wife of a prominent Omani, is dedicated to showcasing the art of Oman and the Arab world, including painting, sculpture, and photography.

Ghalya's Museum of Modern Art. Nestled beyond the hustle and bustle of the Mutrah *suq* in Muscat's capital region stands a series of low, seemingly innocuous buildings, once marked for demolition. Here, along the corniche, or "coastal road," in full view of the scenic harbor, is Ghalya's Museum of Modern Art, the dream project of an exceedingly urbane and visionary woman, Sayyidah Ghalya bint Fahr bin Taymur Al Said.

Opened in 2011, Ghalya's Museum transports visitors to an era in the lives of Omanis immediately preceding the transformative period in Oman's modern history, affectionately known as "the blessed renaissance." In addition to a clothing museum and a "minimalist" art gallery intended to showcase local and international artists, this innovative enterprise contains reproductions of rooms representing those in typical Omani homes from the period 1950 to 1975, telling "the stories of the Omanis and their deeply rooted heritage, customs, and traditions."

The Oman Natural History Museum. Located within the Ministry of Heritage and Culture complex in Muscat, this museum, opened in 1985, highlights the rich diversity of Oman's flora and fauna. In addition to lush botanical gardens, Oman's Natural History Museum features attractive displays of indigenous mammals, insects, and birds. It contains fossils from both land and sea, including extinct mammals and the preserved specimens of exotic animals of Arabia, including leopards, gazelles, red foxes, ibexes, and flamingoes, as well as the Caracal lynx, the oryx, the Arabian wolf, and a variety of birds, reptiles, and seashells.

A popular feature of the museum is the whale room, housing the massive skeleton of a sperm whale that washed up on the Omani coastline in the 1980s.

The Oman Children's Museum. Established by the Ministry of Heritage and Culture as the first science museum in Oman, the Oman's Children's Museum, located near Qurum Nature Park in Muscat, was dedicated on November 17, 1990, by Sultan Qaboos bin Said. The museum features forty-five permanent exhibits and interactive displays. Some fifty thousand visitors experience its wonders every year.

National Museum. A highly anticipated addition to the cultural landscape in Oman is the National Museum. Announced by royal decree in 2013, the new museum, under the supervision of the Ministry of Heritage and Culture, is currently under construction in Muscat, near al-'Alam Palace, one of the royal residences. Ambitious in scope, this undertaking showcases Omani antiquities dating back nearly six thousand years while, at the same time, offering visitors the opportunity to view many of the country's more recent treasures, artifacts, and cultural traditions.

Festivals
Oman's many local and regional festivals are sources of delight for residents and tourists alike. Among the most highly anticipated and well attended every year are the Muscat Festival and the Salalah Tourism Festival.

Muscat Festival. Featured each winter in the nation's capital, the Muscat Festival, held over the course of a month, serves to showcase the country's businesses, commercial interests, and touristic attractions. More important, perhaps, are the cultural attractions featuring artists and artisans, craftspeople, and tradesmen not only from every part of Oman but also from many foreign countries as well, making it a true venue of shared traditions. Men, women, and "children of all ages" and backgrounds gather at this joyful event, with more than 1.5 million attending in 2012.[78] Food and entertainment, parades and fireworks, and even fashion shows, combine to create a relaxed and festive atmosphere. With musicians, dancers, artists, and craftspeople from so many countries celebrating their respective cultural traditions, the spirit is unmistakably evocative, albeit on a smaller scale, of a World's Fair—ever consistent with the spirit of cosmopolitanism that is integral to the Omani national experience.

Salalah Tourism Festival. Oman's second biggest city is home to the Salalah Tourism Festival, an event that draws visitors from every corner of the sultanate, the GCC states, and beyond. This popular event is scheduled to coincide with the *khareef* (monsoon) season, which extends from June 21 to September 21 each year, a period of exceptional beauty, when the surrounding mountains are bathed in lush greenery, as gentle rains cool the evening air—thereby earning the governorate of Dhofar the reputation of being one of the best summer destinations in an otherwise-sweltering Middle East.

   As with other successful events of this nature, the tourism festival in Salalah has wide appeal, with games, rides, food, and crafts. Famous for being the "Perfume Capital of Arabia," Dhofar is fast becoming one of the most popular tourist destinations in the region. The combination of many archaeological sites, natural beauty, and now a successful annual cultural event has been important in drawing attention, as well as investment, to this southern, historic corner of Oman.

Forts and Castles

Over the centuries, more than five hundred forts, watchtowers, and castles have been located strategically on hills and mountains throughout Oman to protect the country's villages and seaports. In recognition of Oman's unique national heritage, many of these structures are being restored, methodically and lovingly, to their original splendor. They serve as a source of pride for its citizens and a dazzling reminder to visitors of Oman's glorious past.

Bahla Fort. Bahla is the traditional capital of the powerful Bani Nebhan (*al-Nabahinah*) dynasty, which ruled over this area of the current Dakhiliyah governorate from the twelfth to the fifteenth century. To protect against invaders, Bahla was surrounded in ancient times by a 7.5-mile (12 km) wall, much of which stands today.

The largest fort in Oman, the Bahla Fort is built on a stone foundation, its walls and towers constructed of mud brick. Recognized as a UNESCO World Heritage Site, it was reopened recently after several years of rigorous restoration.

Nizwa Fort. Also located deep within the Omani heartland, in the region of Dakhiliyah, lies the fortified city of Nizwa, ancient capital of the interior, one of the largest cities in the sultanate and the historic bastion of the Ibadhi faith tradition.

In 630 CE, Nizwa was visited by an emissary of the Prophet Muhammad, persuading its ruling family to convert to Islam. From that point on, it has held the distinction of being the religious center of the country. As its fame grew, it attracted such notables as the renowned medieval traveler and chronicler, Ibn Battuta, who, in the fourteenth century, sang the praises of this fabled city with its "beautiful bazaars . . . [with] mosques . . . large and scrupulously clean."

Dating from 1652 to 1660 CE, the Nizwa Fort stands as testimony to the power and prestige of the Ya'rubid imam Sultan bin Sayf I (r. 1649–1679). The highlight of this impressive structure, built over a period of twelve years on an underlying structure that dates to the twelfth century CE, is an impressive circular drum tower, measuring more than 150 feet (45.72 m) in diameter and 150 feet in height. From the narrow platform perched high atop the interior of the tower, the surrounding oases and mountains are clearly visible. Recently renovated, the Nizwa Fort stands today, proud and impregnable again (see figure 5.2 for two views of the interior tower of the Nizwa Fort, before and after renovation).

The Nizwa Fort is surrounded by a *suq* (traditional marketplace) where locals trade in traditional and imported merchandise like vegetables, fruits, meat, fish, dates, spices, and handicrafts. Each Friday morning unfolds as a noisy procession of livestock, from sheep and goats to camels, at the auction block adjacent to the *suq*, await their reassignment to new owners.

Jabrin Fort and Castle. Following the death in 1679 of Imam Sultan bin Sayf, who liberated Oman from Portuguese control, his son Bal'arab bin Sultan was elected to be his successor. Regrettably, long-simmering sibling rivalry and bitter disagreements surfaced almost immediately as Sayf bin Sultan, the brother of the new imam-designate, challenged his sibling's authority.

Bal'arab was, by all accounts, a gentle man who "loved peace and rejected war, . . . [who] encouraged scholars and poets and showered them with gifts."[79] Rather than challenge his brother head on, he withdrew to the town of Jabrin, where he built "an elegant country home." Jabrin Fort and Castle was a magnificent engineering feat in its day, projecting an aura of both strength and delicacy. Within the walls of this serene residence, adorned with fine carvings and decorated ceilings, the son of the legendary founder of the

A

B

Figure 5.2   Two views of a national treasure, the tower in the fort at Nizwa: *A*, in 1974, before restoration, and *B*, in 2012, after restoration

Photos by author.

Ya'rubid dynasty withdrew, bombarded and besieged, while his brother Sayf bin Sultan vied for power and authority over the land.

Bal'arab bin Sultan remained cloistered in this magnificent fortress until his death under mysterious circumstances in 1692. Following Bal'arab's death, his brother Sayf immediately assumed the power he had sought for so long, presiding over Oman until 1711.

Sohar Fort. A wide variety of historic sites regularly draws visitors to Sohar, the capital of the verdant agricultural Batinah region west of Muscat. The most prominent feature of this historic city is the Sohar Fort. Built between the thirteenth and fourteenth centuries CE by commanders of the Strait of Hormuz, the fort had numerous escape tunnels, which were used to obtain reinforcements and supplies during sieges. One of these secret tunnels stretched 193 miles (310 km) to the fort at Rustaq, one of the former capitals of Oman.

Rustaq Fort. The history of Oman, shaped by a succession of cultures, comes alive in Rustaq, a rural oasis village nestled in the foothills of the Hajar Mountains. The fort is located on a site originally controlled by Persian invaders. Although construction of this building began in the thirteenth century, it was subsequently rebuilt and modified, gaining national prominence when the first Ya'rubid imam, Nasr bin Murshid (r. 1624–1649), made Rustaq his capital.

Built primarily for the purposes of defense, the fort at Rustaq is a structure of magnificent proportions. The immense complex encompasses an area of over one square kilometer. Accented by four towers, it is built on three levels, containing separate houses and reception areas, storage facilities, a prison, an armory, and a mosque.

There are strategically placed "murder holes" over several doorways leading to the exterior, openings into which scalding date syrup (predating, perhaps, modern-day napalm) could be poured over unsuspecting intruders. While the Rustaq Fort features its own private *falaj*, a well was added as a contingency, in the event that the *falaj* became blocked or contaminated by aggressors. Rustaq is the burial place of Ahmad bin Said Al Bu Said, founder of the Al Bu Said dynasty, which bears his name.

Nakhl Fortress. The impressive fortress at Nakhl, dramatically positioned on a hillock above a town of the same name, lies at the edge of the Jabal al-Akhdar Mountain in northwest Oman, in the Batinah governorate. Restored in recent years, this building, believed to have originated in pre-Islamic Oman, has an aura of its own, majestically perched high above a verdant oasis and nestled within massive stone outcroppings. Whether exploring its many battlements or climbing to the heights of its formidable watchtowers, visitors are rewarded with breathtaking views of the large *wadi* (riverbed) and palm orchards below.

Khasab Castle. In the north of Oman lies Khasab, Musandam's provincial capital. This region is inhabited by members of the Shihuh tribe, whose language is quite distinct from that of other Omanis. At Tawi, near the town's center, prehistoric petroglyphs, or rock drawings, depict boats, houses, animals (including elephants), and men on horseback, attesting to ancient settlements and interaction with diverse cultures.[80] Older still are perfectly preserved sea fossils embedded on the sides of the Jabal Harim Mountain, thousands of feet above the sea, testimony to the seismic activity from a distant, perhaps Jurassic, era.

The castle at Khasab, painstakingly renovated by Oman's Ministry of Heritage and Culture, is a visual feast. The building, constructed around a large preexisting central tower, served as a Portuguese garrison until 1644. During the second half of the seventeenth century, the complex was renovated by Sayf bin Sultan. The Al Bu Said dynasty continued to use the castle in following centuries to protect the coast, which is adjacent to the strategic Strait of Hormuz.

Taqah Castle. In the southernmost Omani governorate of Dhofar lies the small fishing village of Taqah. Here is the ancestral home and final resting place of Sultan Qaboos's mother, Mazoon bint Ahmad al-Mashani, who died on August 12, 1992.

In the center of this charming community is the Taqah Castle, a small, but elegant, nineteenth-century treasure, built as a private residence for Shaykh 'Ali bin Timman al-Mashani. During the reign of Sultan Taymur bin Faysal (r. 1913–1932), it served as an administrative center and a residence for local *walis* (provincial governors). Restored and refurbished in 1992 to reflect the rich historic legacy of a glorious bygone era, the castle stands as yet another example of the government's program to preserve national treasures, reminding its citizens of their rich national heritage.

Mirbat Castle. Within the governorate of Dhofar, in the heart of the land of frankincense, lies the port of Mirbat. At its center is a nineteenth-century castle that has served historically to defend the city while providing a residence and administrative center for the local *wali*.

During the protracted insurrection in Dhofar in the 1960s, the well-documented and fiercely fought battle at Mirbat Castle was a milestone in the conflict. Both the town and port were saved, as pro-government forces, using conventional tactics, successfully defended the fortress from rebel forces. In 1991 the government began renovations on the site, which officially opened to the public on the occasion of the "Year of Omani Heritage" in 1994.[81]

The Royal Opera House Muscat

Sultan Qaboos's most recent effort to place Oman at the forefront of the world stage is the creation of the Royal Opera House Muscat, one of the most important cultural achievements of the Omani renaissance. "We have reached a moment in the long history of our nation," he explained, "when it is time to embrace the concept of world culture and take part in its development on a wider scale. It is in this spirit that we have established the Royal Opera House Muscat for the people of Oman and for humanity at large." But for Sultan Qaboos, the Royal Opera House was a contribution not only to world culture but also to a dialogue that transcends division: "We have no doubt that the Royal Opera House Muscat will contribute to the expansion of world heritage in its noble ideals of peace, harmony and understanding among all people, as they share meaningful and deeply felt legacies through the performing arts."

The idea of the Royal Opera House was envisaged years ago. In 2004 an international design competition was announced, with the goal of constructing a building that would be both functional and reflective of local history and culture. Following plans submitted by a British company, construction began in 2007 on an expansive twenty-acre site near the shoreline of the Sea of Oman. The site was developed over a period of four years, to include not only a massive building complex of more than 275,000 square feet but also elegant gardens, elaborate water features, retail facilities, and parking.

The building's design is timeless and classically Islamic, reflecting the country's proud heritage. Consisting of eight floors, three below ground and five above, its imposing "desert rose" stone exterior, with towering pillars and grand colonnades, is reminiscent of Omani forts. Its inviting interior of indigenous limestone and gleaming white travertine marble is embellished with delicate, finely carved wooden screens and elaborate panels highlighted in gold leaf.

From its exquisite design, to its outstanding materials and workmanship, to its cutting-edge technology, there are a number of features that distinguish this venue. Among them is a major mechanical innovation that enables the physical shape and seating capacity of the auditorium to change in order to meet the different acoustical demands of operatic, theatrical, and concert events—all without compromising the elegance and architectural integrity of the space. A fifty-ton pipe organ (with more than 4,500 pipes), handcrafted in Germany for this magnificent theater, can also be moved, to suit demand. Finally, touchscreens on each seatback allow patrons to select subtitles in a variety of languages, enabling even neophytes to explore new art forms. In addition to being a cultural landmark in the Middle East and, particularly, in the Gulf region, it is, in terms of technical facilities, arguably the best of its kind in the world today.

During its first season, sold-out audiences enjoyed a cavalcade of international artists, including celebrated soprano Renée Fleming, tenor Andrea Bocelli, world-renowned cellist Yo-Yo Ma with the London Philharmonic Orchestra, and American trumpeter Wynton Marsalis performing with the Jazz at Lincoln Center Orchestra. Whether experiencing Bizet's enduring opera *Carmen* or the world-famous Mariinsky Ballet of St. Petersburg (Russia) dancing to Tchaikovsky's immortal "Swan Lake," audiences would be transformed in this magnificent center for the performing arts.

Throughout the following seasons, this temple of culture continues to draw regional and international stars to Oman for the enjoyment of audiences from across a broad spectrum of societies, both local and foreign.

An Opening Night to Remember

In September 2011, I opened a note that casually crossed my desk. I read it first with a measure of disbelief, then with surprise, and finally, with elation:

> *Under the Patronage of*
> *His Majesty Sultan Qaboos Bin Said*
> *The Diwan of the Royal Court, Royal Protocol, The Palace-Muscat*
> *Has the pleasure of inviting you*
> *To attend the opening of the Royal Opera House in Muscat,*
> *on October 12, 2011*

Although I had followed closely for many years the inspiring record of Oman's emergence from isolation to modernity, I could never have imagined attending the much-heralded inauguration of this highly anticipated project.

On the appointed evening of October 12, a stream of international guests departed from our luxury hotel. As we approached the Royal Opera House complex, the sight was breathtaking—a white building of gargantuan proportions, bathed in floodlights adjusted to accentuate the finest details of its rich Islamic architectural design.

As the intoxicating aroma of frankincense wafted seductively through the grand foyer of the majestic Royal Opera House Muscat, this seasoned traveler to the Middle East was transformed, recalling a time, many years earlier, when this remote, backward, and relatively unknown land on the fringes of the Arabian Peninsula was beginning to awaken from decades of isolation and stagnation.

Proffering our official, engraved invitations embellished with the royal coat of arms, we proceeded into the main foyer of the opera house. It was a storybook vision of glistening marble and warm wood tones that, on this historic occasion, was further accentuated by a wide runner of red plush carpet adorning the grand staircase, designed to guide His Majesty Sultan Qaboos bin Said to the royal box. The massive reception area was electric with anticipation.

What a truly historic turning point this was. As scores of distinguished guests, from both East and West, resplendent in national attire and formal dress, filed into this elegant venue, it was abundantly clear that something very special was at hand.

Escorted by gloved attendants to our sumptuously upholstered seats appointed in red fabric emblazoned with gold embroidery, we awaited the arrival of the country's ruler. As the distinguished heir to one of the oldest royal dynasties in the world approached his box, the expectant audience sprang to its feet. With a lingering wave and warm smile, he graciously acknowledged the crowd. The Royal Guard of Oman then played the Omani national anthem.

In preparation for this historic event, the Royal Opera House Muscat commissioned the legendary Italian film and stage director Franco Zeffirelli (*Romeo and Juliet*, *Taming of the Shrew*) to design the sets for a lavish production of Giacomo Puccini's *Turandot*, an opera and love story of monumental proportions. Under the baton of the Spanish tenor and legendary impresario Plácido Domingo, a chorus of international stars, accompanied by the Italian orchestra Fondazione Arena di Verona, performed Puccini's final masterpiece for the first time in the Middle East.

It was dazzling! The extravagant sets, elaborate costumes, and elegantly expressed emotions of this timeless paean to love were enchanting. Amid this splendor—with the elegant Zeffirelli holding court in a nearby seat, with Maestro Domingo totally enraptured by his music, and with the sultan of Oman clearly visible in the royal box—the term "out-of-body experience" can only begin to express the sensation that this writer and others felt on that magical and historic evening in Muscat. It was grand. It was personal. But, most significant, the debut of the Royal Opera House underscored the resolve of the ruler of one relatively small, little-known country to reach across international borders to achieve dialogue through the arts.

The 2011–2012 inaugural season of the Royal Opera House Muscat was off to an auspicious start. For this lifetime student of the Middle East and admirer of the sultanate's remarkable renaissance, October 12, 2011, would forever stand as "an Arabian night to remember."

Religious Heritage: The Sultan Qaboos Grand Mosque

The Islamic faith and, in particular, the Ibadhi tradition within that faith, remains as important to the identity of twenty-first-century Omanis as it has throughout the past fourteen centuries. Qaboos bin Said, who has steered his country into the modern age, possesses a scholar's knowledge of Islam, finding its tenets to be not only relevant but also inspiring as he guides Oman's caravan of development.

The Sultan Qaboos Grand Mosque is a palpable source of pride for Omanis and, for that matter, other Muslims. Following a royal decree in 1992, the palace announced an international design competition for this project. The site was carefully chosen—within the Bawshar district outside of Muscat, at the intersection of several highways—connecting the capital city with road-ways linking the interior and coastal towns. Built as a witness to the enduring faith of both monarch and citizenry, the mosque was dedicated by its name-sake in 2001 in these words:

> We have set ourselves to make this blessed Mosque a center of culture and thought; to contribute to the rebirth of [our] Islamic heritage; . . . to highlight and project the civilised values of the Islamic nation and to update its means and ways of tackling its affairs and find solutions in a way that preserves its purity of origin and values.[82]

The entire complex has an ethereal quality to it. Five minarets represent the pillars of Islam. The central minaret soars triumphantly 328 feet (91.5 m) into the sky. Inspired by traditional Islamic design, vaulted arches, graceful arcades, intricately carved wooden panels and screens, and a series of marble-tiled courtyards lend a feeling of elegance and serenity to this monument to the faith. Arcades and colonnades featuring colorful mosaics evocative of the *ummah*, or the global community of Muslims, remind awestruck visitors of the extraordinary appeal that this faith tradition has held for peoples of every continent.

Built from 300,000 tons of Indian sandstone, the massive main prayer hall, a square 245 feet (75 m) on each side, is capped by a central dome rising 165 feet (50 m) above ground. Capable of accommodating 6,500 worship-pers, this impressive space is illuminated by thirty-five immense chandeliers of brilliant Swarovski crystal.

An extraordinary feature of the interior is a fine handmade Persian carpet, crafted as a single piece, covering the entire floor of the main prayer hall. Six hundred skilled women labored for four years to weave this exquisitely detailed, twenty-one-ton masterpiece. Incorporating geometric, floral, and arabesque themes, it consists of a staggering 1.7 billion hand-tied knots. Its beauty is overwhelming.

Whether by day, when the gleaming white marble of the exterior daz-zles the eye in the sunlight, or by night, when the golden ribbed dome and graceful minarets illuminate the skyline for miles around, the Sultan Qaboos Grand Mosque is a magnificent achievement, serving as an iconic image of "Oman's place in a cultural and artistic continuum stretching thousands of miles in each direction."[83] At the same time, credit for this extraordinary complex must certainly be given to its namesake, a leader who has inspired the modern renaissance of Omani talent and achievement.

The Sultan Qaboos Grand Mosque is a stunning architectural achieve-ment of historic and magnificent proportions. Standing as a religious center-piece for Omanis, most of whom adhere to the Islamic faith, it remains the largest integrated mosque complex in the country. This magnificent com-pound serves as more than a place of worship, functioning also as a meet-ing and gathering place. During certain times of day, the library, offices, and magnificent gardens are open to the general public. It is serene, a place of peace. "Though it is a mosque and religious complex, the tone is clearly one of inclusion. The world is welcomed. It is the spirit of the ocean more than of the desert."[84]

Roots of a Dynasty: The Village of Adam

Deep within the Dakhiliyah governorate of Oman stands the *wilayah* of Adam, the birthplace of the founder of the royal dynasty that rules Oman to this day. It was here, in a remote village on the desert's edge, within reach of Nizwa, the religious capital of the interior, that Imam Ahmad bin Said Al Bu Said was born in 1710.

While most of Adam's residents have long since abandoned the ancient quarter in favor of more commodious dwellings outside its crumbling walls, its original buildings remain. Here is a storybook scene, evocative of a movie set, frozen in time (see figure 5.3). Entering through the old gates, one navigates carefully through an inscrutable warren of winding paths flanked by multistoried buildings, through arched doorways and painted metal doors, to behold rooms with painted ceilings, recessed niches, and even colored graffiti scribbled by residents that have long since passed.

The first home of the leader whose name would be immortalized in the annals of history, and whose family would uphold Oman's sovereignty and independence, stands to this day. It is likely for this reason and for the potential wealth of historical information intrinsic to such a site that the Omani

Figure 5.3 Village of Adam, ancestral birthplace of the Al Bu Said dynasty
Photo by author (2012).

government instructed the Ministry of Heritage and Culture to undertake a massive restoration project in the old quarter. Following modern techniques while, at the same time, using original materials such as mud brick, wherever possible, the restoration of Adam will add substantially to the inventory of heritage sites in the sultanate.

Traditional Handicrafts

On the occasion of the tenth National Day, in 1980, Sultan Qaboos declared, "We must . . . foster and safeguard our traditional industries so that our cultural heritage is handed on intact to generations to come."[85] As the sultan of Oman regularly reminds his countrymen, particularly youth, traditional work, such as handicrafts, "which some wrongly regard as beneath them," represents service to the country of the highest order.[86]

Traditional, often painstaking, endeavors, such as those that involve working the land or sailing the sea in search of food, caring for animals, or making simple household articles, are valued and encouraged in the new Oman. In 1986 Sultan Qaboos reminded Omanis that "we are proud of our heritage." He called on them "not to desert the traditional professions upon which our old society stood, especially the . . . handicrafts which all play an important role in developing our motherland."[87]

In 2003 Sultan Qaboos established the Public Authority for Craft Industries, charging it with the responsibility of nurturing traditional crafts through conservation and awareness, as well as through instruction and exhibition. Perhaps an indication of the importance of this governmental body is that its chair has been given the rank of "minister," equivalent in status to the others in the sultan's Council of Ministers.

The importance that the current government attaches to traditional crafts such as these—even as it moves wholeheartedly toward modernization— was underscored in practical terms when, during a visit to Bahla in 2013, Sultan Qaboos announced the establishment of the Ajyal College of Traditional Industries. As a major center of heritage, as well as "one of the most important cities in Oman," Bahla "was a logical choice for this new center that would be charged with training the next generation of young men and women in the production of traditional handicrafts."[88]

Today's Frankincense: Marketing a Tradition

A somewhat unique, and charming, caveat in the ongoing saga of Oman's march toward development and economic diversification—but always with an eye on the past—is the creation and marketing of an intoxicating fragrance that blends modernization with tradition. While the global appetite for burning frankincense has declined steadily during the last several centuries, this uniquely fragrant resin is still valued and widely used in homes, businesses, and offices throughout the sultanate. The surviving frankincense trees in Oman's southern governorate of Dhofar, while far fewer in number,

Oman's Craft Heritage

Oman's commitment to preserving its traditional crafts is immediately apparent to anyone traveling throughout the sultanate. The legendary "pit-weavers," in the village of al-Akhdar, for example, are renowned throughout the land. With looms positioned at ground level, elderly weavers, often with young apprentices at their side, adroitly create cloth of rich colors and traditional designs, positioned in pits dug below ground level, allowing greater mobility for themselves and for the trea-dles. On the sidelines, others are dying yarn, dipping it in a mixture of deep blue indigo before hanging it in the sun to dry (see figure 5.4 for a view of traditional Omani weavers in al-Akhdar).

Figure 5.4   Workshop for traditional Omani weavers, village of al-Akhdar
Photo by author (2006).

In nearby Bahla, whose massive, recently restored fort is celebrated as a UNESCO World Heritage Site, potters can be observed creating a rich array of bowls and urns with great dexterity, effortlessly demonstrating a craft as old and revered as the history of settled populations the world over.

are rigorously protected, making them ever-more precious. The tree's amber resin may be said to have reinvented itself for today's global market through the imagination and efforts of an enterprising Omani in 1983. Inspired by the alluring, seductive scent produced by frankincense, especially when blended with other precious natural oils and essences, an idea was born to resurrect the great Arabian art of perfumery with a distinctively Omani "twist."

Guy Robert, a legendary French *parfumier*, was charged with the task of creating the world's "most valuable perfume." Putting his heart and soul into this effort, the result was the creation of a unique and intoxicating fragrance blending, among 120 other essences, not only the highest-quality variety of silver frankincense from Dhofar but also myrrh and a rare variety of rose, the "Omani rock rose," grown on the slopes of the remote Jabal al-Akhdar Mountains of the north. The resulting fragrance, Amouage Gold, an opulent combination of rare and expensive oils, soon generated worldwide attention that continues to this day.

Today, on the outskirts of Oman's capital, Muscat, Amouage is blended in a perfumery and then bottled in exquisite, hand-finished crystal flacons topped with gilded caps. International visitors flock to a showroom where they are invited to enjoy traditional Arab hospitality while sampling this transcendent Omani fragrance, which in Robert's words, represents the "symphony" and "crowning glory" of his career.

REFLECTIONS

With the basic national infrastructure in place and the educational and healthcare needs of the population assured, the twenty-first century has ushered in an era of exciting opportunities and unprecedented economic growth in Oman. Since the accession of Sultan Qaboos to the throne in 1970, ambitious national projects have been fueled in large part by revenues from oil exports. And while the hydrocarbon sector has been enhanced by the introduction of liquefied natural gas, Oman's relatively modest reserves are not sufficient to sustain the economy in perpetuity.

In this context, a national strategy for long-term growth, announced by the ruler in 1995, had, at its core, an ambitious program of economic diversification to reduce the country's dependence on oil. As new enterprises have come on board, many of which are inspired by Oman's own history of international trade and commerce, investments have grown substantially, with the private sector emerging as the dominant force, moving the economy to new and unprecedented levels of growth. In a country characterized by political stability and friendly people, Oman's favorable tax laws and investment regulations have made the sultanate an increasingly attractive climate for business, both local and foreign.

Inasmuch as a healthy and sustainable economy is dependent upon meaningful employment of its citizens, a major focus of the country's current national strategy calls for the "Omanization" of the labor force, replacing expatriate labor with Omani workers. In addition to traditional academic education, this national mandate has given rise to technical and vocational training. Most important, perhaps, it requires an understanding and willingness of citizens to engage in all fields of endeavor and at all levels. In this regard, Sultan Qaboos has been persuasive.

Among the earliest sectors of the economy targeted for development were the traditional areas of agriculture and fishing. The Omani government has taken bold measures to ensure that infrastructural systems are maintained and improved while, at the same time, establishing new national projects to support and enhance these venerable livelihoods.

As Oman's twenty-first-century economy continues to diversify, with ambitious projects planned or under way, the government is investing heavily in new and expanded infrastructure. Drawing on its enviable geostrategic location and venerable seafaring tradition, historic ports are being expanded and modernized while, in one very impressive case, a new port facility, with the potential to revolutionize maritime trade and commerce in the Indian Ocean region, is being unveiled. Improvements are also being made to roads and railways, air transport, electricity production, and communications technology.

The greater part of this section focuses on cultural exchange and preservation, the most prominent example of which is tourism, a sector that, in terms of new economic growth, is fast outpacing almost all others in Oman. A country of immense natural beauty and diversity, pleasant climate, rich history, political stability, and what is, perhaps, the greatest national treasure of all—warm and friendly people—Oman is quickly becoming one of the most desirable tourist destinations on earth.

Appealing to a largely high-end market, the options for visitors are endless, in terms of both accommodations and activities. From world-class hotels, to luxury resorts, to planned communities, or even remote desert camps, tourists can explore mountains, deserts, and seas; climb through castles and forts; survey the rich artifacts in museums; attend the opera; hear a symphony; engage in a variety of sporting activities; or simply wander leisurely through a maze of ancient *suqs* in search of hidden treasure.

Included in this section is a description of the Royal Opera House Muscat—along with a personal account of the opening night of this cultural masterpiece. Inspired by his vast knowledge and keen appreciation of music, Sultan Qaboos bin Said inaugurated this spectacular venue for the performing arts in 2011 as a gift to the people of Oman. More than an exquisite and inspiring structure, the Royal Opera House Muscat is an important symbol, representing both Oman's long history of cosmopolitanism and the power of music and dance to bring people of widely diverse cultures together. In so many ways, this is the embodiment of the modern Omani renaissance.

Under the heading of cultural exchange and preservation, I have included "religious heritage," for Oman is a country that reveres its own faith tradition while, at the same time, respecting others. The quintessential symbol of Omani spirituality is a massive mosque complex in the capital city, envisaged by and constructed under the watchful eye of its leader. The Sultan Qaboos Grand Mosque, an exquisite monument to faith in terms of form, style, and substance, bears witness to the living tradition that guides the people of this land.

In keeping with Qaboos bin Said's conviction to modernize his country without abandoning its valued heritage and cherished culture, the government has supported the preservation and expansion of the traditional crafts that make Oman unique. Toward this end, the sultan has created a "public authority" to oversee every aspect of the country's craft industry, not only to ensure its sustained viability but also to attract a new generation of Omanis to engage in these traditional pursuits. Toward this end, he recently announced plans to create a college for this purpose in a historic craft center.

In addition to supporting private initiatives, the government has spearheaded many public programs designed to honor its national heritage. Similarly, scores of private citizens have looked to Oman's past for inspiration. One such story, told here, recalls the phenomenal international success of a product borne of an idea blending history with fragrance. It is a uniquely Omani tale.

CHAPTER 6

FOREIGN RELATIONS: A POLICY OF MUTUAL RESPECT

Oman's geostrategic location, its extensive maritime history, and its particular blend of religious and societal attitudes have, to a considerable extent, shaped the sultanate's relationships with other countries, both within the Gulf region and beyond. Viewed through the lens of history and culture, the independent foreign policy forged during the reign of Sultan Qaboos bin Said is wholly consistent with Oman's past.

Throughout its history, Oman has suffered the oppression of foreign aggression, felt the sanctity of its sovereignty challenged, and stood firm to reap the benefit of alliances among equals. Each of these experiences has been etched into the collective memory of the Omanis, forming the mold from which their modern foreign policy would be cast. Friendships forged and lessons learned, all within the context of Oman's unique history and religious tradition, have shaped a country that values consultation over conflict, dialogue over dispute—positioning it as a potential, and welcome, source of moderation as it assumes an ever-increasing role on the world diplomatic stage.

Oman's historical relationships with countries such as Portugal and the United Kingdom have been discussed in previous chapters. Here I have chosen to highlight a relatively unknown but particularly amicable and enduring relationship: that between Oman and the United States. This chapter will briefly shed light on the history of interactions between these two strategic allies before focusing attention on the tenets of Oman's foreign policy under the leadership of Qaboos bin Said.

OMAN AND THE UNITED STATES

The friendship between the United States and Oman is as old as the United States itself. Since the birth of the American republic, Oman has stood as one of America's most trusted allies in the Middle East. After Morocco, Oman was the second country in the Arab world to establish diplomatic relations with the young republic. In the early nineteenth century, it became the first country in the region to send a political mission to the United States.

The unbroken history of cordial relations between the two countries can be traced to September 1790, when during the administration of President George Washington, the Boston ship *Rambler*, under the direction of Captain Robert Folger, became the first American merchant vessel to sail into the natural deepwater port in Oman's capital, Muscat. This would the first of many early interactions between the two maritime powers, with US merchant vessels continuing to sail into Muscat harbor carrying "exotic" products from the East Indies, such as tea, sugar, and spices.

Treaty of Amity and Commerce

During the reign of Said bin Sultan (1807–1856), Oman exercised unprecedented power, overseeing expansive domains from southern Arabia to the Horn of Africa, to the northern border of Portuguese-controlled Mozambique, and Zanzibar. As master of one of the most powerful naval fleets in Oman's history, the sultan and his government routinely received American shipmasters with great courtesy. Throughout the first half of the nineteenth century, Sultan Said was arguably the best-known, and widely admired, Arab ruler among the people of the United States.

A former US ambassador to the Middle East, the late Hermann Eilts, reflected on the significance of this early period of US-Omani relations, noting particularly its impact on cross-cultural perceptions:

> In a period when Americans were ill-informed about Arabs, and when their sparse contacts with Arabic-speaking peoples of North Africa were often contentious, Sultan Sa'id enjoyed an unrivaled reputation for forceful leadership, decisiveness, friendship, and commercial probity. . . . Rarely has an Arab leader, anywhere, made so positive an impression upon Americans.[1]

In the nineteenth century, Oman and its expansive domains in East Africa were major international hubs for trade and commerce. Edmund Roberts, an American merchant and diplomat, developed an amicable relationship with Sultan Said, first in 1828, while traveling to Zanzibar as a private citizen, and subsequently, as an official representative of the US government.[2] Roberts noted the distinct advantages Great Britain enjoyed over other countries in its commercial dealings with the sultan's realm. Negotiating on behalf of the United States, he pointed out that his government, unlike the British and the French, "had no territorial ambitions" abroad and was interested only in mutually beneficial commerce.

Apparently, Roberts's words were sufficiently persuasive, for on September 21, 1833, President Andrew Jackson and Sultan Said bin Sultan, representing the governments of the United States and Oman, respectively, signed a Treaty of Amity and Commerce. The first bilateral accord between the United States and a Persian Gulf state, it was preceded, among pacts with countries of the Arab world, only by a similar agreement signed with Morocco in 1787. The Treaty of Amity and Commerce was ratified by Congress on June 30, 1834.[3] In the following year, Roberts, having been awarded the designation of "special diplomatic agent," sailed to Muscat aboard the *Peacock* to exchange documents. Granting the young American republic the distinction of "most favored nation," the treaty extended to US merchants trading in Muscat and Zanzibar a variety of privileges that until then had been enjoyed only by British businessmen.[4] This was a significant economic achievement because it "implied the right to trade [with Zanzibar] in ivory and copal resin, the products most in demand by the merchants of New England."[5]

The ratification of the Treaty of Amity and Commerce was followed by a diplomatic "first": in 1837 Richard Palmer Waters of Salem, Massachusetts, arrived in Zanzibar to assume the new post of American consul, accredited to both Zanzibar and Muscat, the two centers of Omani rule. In addition, Sultan Said sent his personal envoy and representative, Ahmad bin Nu'man al-K'abi, to the United States to celebrate the friendship of the two countries. Carrying gifts for the new president, Martin Van Buren, Bin Nu'man began his journey in Muscat before proceeding to Zanzibar, where cargo was loaded aboard the tall-masted ship *Sultanah*, one of the newest and swiftest vessels of the Omani fleet. Navigating around the Cape of Good Hope and then across the turbulent waters of the Atlantic Ocean, the *Sultanah* stopped briefly at the island of Saint Helena before entering New York Harbor on April 30, 1840.

The first Arab diplomat dispatched to the United States, Ahmad bin Nu'man attracted considerable attention, generating favorable publicity. During his visits to both New York and Washington, his dignified demeanor, affable style, and quiet sense of humor endeared him to both local press and society. Several articles attesting to his celebrity survive in the archives of the *New York Daily News* and the now-defunct *New York Herald*. His portrait, painted by the celebrated American artist Edward Mooney, still stands among the murals of New York's City Hall. This early guest, coming from a land that for most Americans must have evoked images both exotic and mysterious, received honors rarely bestowed on any foreign representative before him.

The sultan's envoy brought a number of gifts to the US president, accompanied by the following note:[6]

His Excellency Martin Van Buren,
President of the United States of North America,
Washington

Muscat, December 25, 1839

Sir: I have the pleasure of sending to your Excellency, through friendship, vis:
2 good-bred Arab Nejd horses
1 string containing 150 pearls

> *2 separate large sized pearls*
> *1 carpet*
> *1 bottle of oil of roses*
> *4 cashmere shawls*
> *5 demijohns of rose-water*
> *Also 1 gold-mounted sword please to accept, with other mentioned articles.*
> *Hoping you will be pleased to accept the trifles from your friend,*
> *Syed Bin, Sultan*

This unprecedented gesture of foreign largesse extended to a US president caused quite a stir—as well as some confusion—sparking intense debate over the disposition of valuable gifts from the head of a foreign state. After much discussion, Congress agreed to accept them on the condition that they be received *by the US government* on the president's behalf.

While the two Arabian horses were sold in New York at auction for US$993.38 (the equivalent of about US$28,100 in 2014[7]), with the proceeds deposited into the National Treasury, the other gifts contributed to the earliest acquisitions of the new Smithsonian Institution, "an establishment for the increase and diffusion of knowledge among men," in Washington, DC. The exquisitely handwoven Persian silk carpet would eventually find its way to the "first ladies" exhibition of that institution's National Museum of American History, where until recently, mannequins were displayed on it, bedecked in the inaugural gowns worn by the wives of former and current presidents. Most of the diamonds presented on behalf of the "Imaum of Muscat" (not listed above but included in the inventory of gifts) were used in the making of the Smithsonian secretary's badge of office and the ceremonial mace. Other gems, in addition to the pearl necklace, are exhibited in the National Gem and Mineral Collection of the National Museum of Natural History.[8]

On July 31, 1840, with the *Sultanah* freshly refurbished at the Brooklyn Navy Yard, Ahmad bin Nu'man set sail for home, undoubtedly satisfied with his diplomatic triumph. He carried with him gifts for Sultan Said, from private American citizens as well as from President Van Buren, including mirrors and chandeliers, as well as intricately designed Colt firearms inscribed in Arabic, "From the President of the United States of America to the Imaum [*sic*] of Muscat."[9]

By any measure, the unprecedented mission of Ahmad bin Nu'man, the special representative of the Sultan of Oman to the United States, was a resounding diplomatic and public relations success. The welcome he received upon arriving in New York Harbor as the first Arab emissary to the United States was, in many ways, a harbinger of the strong alliance, both diplomatically and commercially, that has endured between the two countries for more than two centuries.

Diplomatic Representation in Oman

After the midpoint of the nineteenth century, the nature of US-Omani commercial relations was quite fluid. As bilateral trade declined, there was scant reason to justify the continued operation of the American consulate in Muscat, and so, for a time at least, its doors were closed. A combination of internal and external forces interrupted the status quo in relations between the two countries, although none suggested any degree of political discord.

The American Civil War precipitated large-scale commercial realignments worldwide. As cotton exports, the mainstay of the economy of the besieged Confederacy, were interrupted, they were supplanted by high-quality long-staple Egyptian cotton, which found eager markets abroad, particularly in the United Kingdom and India. The dynamics of maritime trade were further complicated by the 1869 opening of the Suez Canal and the advent of steamship navigation, both of which had a profound impact on international commerce.

Throughout this early period, as the United States refocused its attentions elsewhere, American interests in Oman were handled by American diplomats in other countries. In 1880 Louis Maguire, an Irish resident of Muscat who had represented a number of British and American interests in the sultanate, was selected as the new US consul. The reopening of this diplomatic office was greeted with great fanfare. After being received on July 22 by the new sultan, Turki bin Said (r. 1871–1888), son of the late sultan, Said bin Sultan, Maguire reported to Washington that "the Omanis had hoisted the American ensign over the Muscati forts and fired a 21-gun salute. All vessels in the Muscat harbor, Omani and foreign, had been decorated for the occasion and the populace of Muscat celebrated the day as a holiday."[10]

The practice of using non-American consuls to represent US interests in Oman continued until 1906. For a short time thereafter, American career officers served as consuls in Muscat until 1914, when due to the vagaries of the First World War, the United States chose to suspend its official presence in the sultanate.

As noted before, the relationship between the United States and Oman assumed a special, humanitarian dimension in the early decades of the twentieth century, as waves of American volunteers traveled to the sultanate to assist in improving education and healthcare standards among the people. Their efforts only served to strengthen the bonds of friendship and understanding between these two seemingly disparate societies.

In 1934, on the occasion of the centennial celebration of the Treaty of Amity and Commerce between the United States and Oman, Franklin Delano Roosevelt sent an envoy to Muscat to present a letter, on behalf of the American president, to the sultan of Oman, Said bin Taymur, inviting him to visit the United States. Arriving in Washington in 1938, the Omani head of state was officially welcomed by the secretary of state, Cordell Hull, given a tour of the United States, and feted as the guest of honor at a White House state dinner. During World War II, Sultan Said granted permission for US military planes bound for the Far East to access Royal Air Force (RAF) air facilities on Masirah Island and to refuel and service American aircraft in the southern city of Salalah, thus contributing significantly to the war's outcome.

In the 1950s, as prospects for significant oil discovery loomed in Oman, the United States proposed reestablishing a consulate in Muscat. Suggesting that the 1833 treaty should be updated, Sultan Said engaged in a lengthy series of negotiations with Walter Schwinn, the American consul general in Dhahran (Saudi Arabia). The new Treaty of Amity, Economic Relations, and Consular Rights, superseding the nineteenth-century agreement, was signed in Salalah on December 20, 1958. Within the next two years, the treaty was ratified by President Dwight D. Eisenhower and Sultan Said, reviving a long tradition of friendly relations between the two countries.

Sultan Qaboos and the United States

Although formal ties between the United States and Oman are longstanding, dating back to 1833, the importance of US-Omani relations has increased substantially since 1970. By all accounts, the United States is today Oman's key strategic ally.[11] Following his accession to power, Sultan Qaboos announced his determination to honor all previous agreements with the United States. In Washington, the State Department reaffirmed its own commitment to the same, adding a word of congratulations to the young leader.

The first US Embassy in Oman opened its doors in Muscat in July of 1972. William A. Stoltzfus Jr., then serving as the American ambassador to Kuwait, presented his credentials to Sultan Qaboos as a nonresident US ambassador. In the following year, the Embassy of Oman opened in Washington, DC, with Sayyid Faysal bin 'Ali Al Bu Said assigned to serve as ambassador. On July 17, 1974, William D. Wolle became the first resident US ambassador in Muscat.

Since the accession of Qaboos bin Said to the throne in 1970, Oman and the United States have cooperated in several joint ventures. From 1973 to 1983, American Peace Corps volunteers served the people of the sultanate, primarily in the fields of healthcare and education. In the early years of the renaissance and until 1992, teams from the US Federal Aviation Administration collaborated with Oman's Civil Aviation Department in the fields of aviation and technical cooperation. In another agreement, the bilateral Joint Commission for Economic and Technical Cooperation was established to provide US economic assistance to Oman. The Joint Commission remained in existence until the mid-1990s.

Talks on a bilateral Free Trade Agreement (FTA), another major milestone in the history of US-Omani relations, got under way in March 2005. Following the tireless efforts of Oman's formidable female ambassador in Washington, Hunaina Sultan al-Mughairy, the FTA was approved by Congress and signed on January 19, 2006. It went into effect in January 2009, making Oman the fourth Arab country in the entire Middle East and North Africa (MENA) region, after Jordan, Bahrain, and Morocco, to earn free-trade privileges.[12]

Sultan Qaboos has made two state visits to the United States: first in 1974 and again in 1983. In 1984 and 1986, George H. W. Bush, then the US vice president, traveled to Oman. The frequency of visits to the sultanate by US government officials has increased in recent years, with a brief visit by President Bill Clinton in March 2000, followed by trips by Vice President

Dick Cheney in 2002, 2005, and 2006. In May 2013, the US secretary of state, John Kerry, met with Sultan Qaboos in Muscat to discuss the sale to Oman of a US$2.1 billion missile system designed to coordinate the defense systems of the Gulf Cooperation Council (GCC) states in an effort to contain Iran.[13] Signaling the continued strength of US-Omani relations, Secretary Kerry traveled to Munich in January 2015 to visit Sultan Qaboos, who was staying in Germany for medical treatment. During that private meeting, the US emissary expressed his gratitude to the Omani head of state for the "longstanding and strong relationship" between the two countries.[14]

Current Areas of Bilateral Cooperation

At present, the focus of US-Omani bilateral cooperation is twofold. Following the attacks by agents of al-Qaeda in the United States on September 11, 2001, the international "war on terror" was launched. As an expanded global coalition was formed with the aim of combating terrorism on a variety of levels—legal, financial, and intelligence—the two allies formed a close partnership. The sultanate's impact on this effort has been invaluable. As an important strategic ally, Oman has been recognized as having been "proactive in its implementation of counterterrorism strategies and its cooperation with neighboring countries to prevent terrorists from moving freely throughout the Arabian Peninsula."[15]

The second area of US interest in Oman and the wider region is the protection of critical shipping lanes through the Strait of Hormuz, one of the world's most strategic chokepoints. Free and unfettered passage through this vital shipping lane is critical for the continued stability of the global economy. Military preparedness is but one essential piece of this equation. Oman's Royal Armed Forces, consisting of approximately seventy thousand troops, is one of the largest, best trained, and most professional military operations in the Gulf region. Its arsenal is continually being modernized and expanded.[16] As random acts of maritime piracy have intensified in recent years, particularly in the vicinity of the world's major chokepoints, including the Bab al-Mandab, separating Yemen from Somalia, Oman and the United States have joined forces to maintain security in the waters of the Gulf region, South Asia, and the Horn of Africa, combining their efforts and expertise to thwart these criminal acts.

FOREIGN POLICY UNDER SULTAN QABOOS

During the reign of Sultan Qaboos, Oman's diplomatic relations with the global community and, indeed, with its neighbors, have been inspired by the ruler's profound understanding of history, both his own and that of others. He has experienced life among other peoples and societies. He has traveled. He has seen the world. The amalgamation of these life experiences has given Qaboos bin Said a unique frame of reference that has enabled him to craft a selective and culturally authentic paradigm for national development. This he has done on both the domestic and international fronts.

The current sultan inherited a country that, while immeasurably rich in history and culture, had fallen into deep decline. As the third quarter of the twentieth century approached, the rest of the world was embracing modernization at a breathtaking pace; Oman, meanwhile, was isolated, impoverished, and underdeveloped. It lacked even the most basic modern infrastructure. In comparison with others, it seemed frozen in time.

In the meantime, all around this new young leader, a high-stakes poker game was rapidly unfolding among international players who were vying for regional hegemony. Although beset by formidable domestic challenges from within, Sultan Qaboos remained committed, from the beginning of his reign, to pursuing policies—both domestic and foreign—that would ensure the territorial integrity of Oman, guarantee the survival of the Al Bu Said dynasty, and transform his country into a modern, yet culturally authentic, state.[17]

Following a Path of Peace

The art of diplomacy, combined with independence, pragmatism, and moderation, has characterized Oman's foreign policy since 1970. As Sultan Qaboos explained on National Day in 1998, "Peace is the objective of the State. It is one of the principles of our internal and external policies. It is a strategic objective we endeavor to achieve for the sake of security, stability, development, and prosperity."[18]

The tenets of Qaboos's foreign policy are unambiguous: mutual respect for the national sovereignty of all states in the region, noninterference in the internal affairs of others, friendship with all, peaceful coexistence, and exchange of mutual interests. Sultan Qaboos's consistency on all of these levels has been impressive. "Pragmatic, independent, with a penchant for bold initiative and calculated risk taking, Oman's foreign policy has been extraordinarily successful in attaining the Sultanate's strategic, economic, military and security objectives."[19] Reflecting in 2006 on a policy that has been remarkably consistent for more than four decades, Oman's leader summarized his strategy for peaceful coexistence with the international community:

> Over the past decades the line we have followed in our foreign policy has . . . proven itself to be both sound and effective. We are committed to this path, which is based on a belief in fairness, justice, peace, security, tolerance and love. It calls for states to co-operate with one another in order to reinforce stability, promote growth and prosperity and deal with the causes of tension in international relations by finding just and permanent solutions to serious problems, thereby fostering peaceful coexistence between nations and generating well-being and prosperity for the whole of humanity.[20]

One particularly striking feature of Oman's foreign policy is that, to casual observers, it appears somewhat understated. Given the current political climate around the world, where hyperbole, acrimony, and thinly veiled threats appear to be the order of day, Oman's strategy for dealing with other countries might be characterized, by contrast, as "quiet" or "digni-fied," very much like the sultan himself (see figure 6.1 for a photograph of Qaboos bin Said in the fortieth year of his reign). This is likely a reflection of the Omani national temperament as well as its penchant for moderation and consistency, characteristics that typify the sultan's policies both at home and abroad.

Unencumbered by ideologies, embracing a laissez-faire attitude toward the internal affairs of other nations, and seeking peaceful alternatives to potentially flammable situations, both Qaboos bin Said and those close to him emphasize consistently the necessity for "mutual respect" as a pre-requisite for modern statecraft and bilateral diplomacy. "If you wish to be respected, you should respect others. You must try to understand the needs of the other side," asserted one Omani official. Paraphrasing a line attrib-uted to Abraham Lincoln, he said, "The best way to destroy an enemy is to make him into a friend."[21] Proud of their past and confident of their future, the Omanis, while never arrogant, are at peace with themselves, or, as one

Figure 6.1   Qaboos bin Said, sultan of Oman, in 2010

Photo by Salim al-Hashli. Courtesy of the Ministry of Information, Sultanate of Oman.

longtime "Omanophile" has observed, they are "comfortable in their own skin." They expect to deal with others as equals: "We owe nothing to anyone; either an equal relationship or none at all."[22]

On a regional level, Oman enjoys good relations with *all* countries of the Middle East, striving assiduously to maintain a policy of noninterference in the internal affairs of its neighbors—while expecting the same courtesy from others. This posture distinguishes the sultanate from other states in the region whose actions are frequently the focus of negative worldwide attention. Preferring to work behind the scenes, the leader of Oman is widely respected throughout the region as a wise elder statesman. As such, his counsel and wisdom are eagerly sought on a variety of issues, particularly when potentially combustible situations cry out for measured, sober judgment.

Although Oman's is a policy of noninterference, it is not a policy of isolationism. Sultan Qaboos considers Oman to be very much part of the world, "a world which, no-one doubts, thanks to the latest scientific advancements, has become smaller, like a village, . . . where no society can isolate itself without interacting and communicating with others, that is if that society seeks to achieve prosperity and welfare for its citizens."[23]

"Friend to all, enemy to none," aptly summarizes the policy of neutrality that underlies Oman's foreign policy. Preferring discussion to confrontation, Sultan Qaboos reminds his countrymen that it is "easy to demolish, but difficult to build," preferring the path of dialogue, including sitting face-to-face with adversaries in order to resolve differences. For Oman, military solutions are seen as a last resort and are appropriate, even then, only in the case of self-defense. "When countries go to war, there has been a failure in diplomacy," asserted a government adviser. "The enormous damage wrought by war may take generations to overcome." Echoes of the conventional Ibadhi emphasis on conciliation and peaceful resolution of disputes resound throughout Oman's vision of its relationship with the world, showing that here again tradition informs the present.

Of primary concern to Sultan Qaboos is, of course, the welfare of his people. As one analyst has observed, Oman's approach to foreign affairs serves that end: "Muscat turns on its head the old Middle East adage that 'the enemy of my enemy is my friend.' . . . The sultan realizes that making friends or avoiding making enemies is practical from a security vantage point. For Oman, 'the enemy (Iran) of my friend (the United States) may still be my friend.'"[24] In today's world, this is a policy that is honest, while, at the same time, almost disarming in its simplicity.

In 1970, when Qaboos bin Said acceded to the throne, only India and Great Britain had a diplomatic presence in Oman. Building upon these historic ties, Oman has expanded its diplomatic footprint, vis-à-vis the United States, the greater Middle East region, and the global community of nations. Eager to restore its place in the international arena, the sultanate joined both the League of Arab States and the United Nations in 1971. There is no question that Oman is back in the game.

Preserving Regional Stability

In 1970, as it emerged from a prolonged period of isolation, Oman set out to reclaim its historic legacy and to improve the well-being of its people while, at the same time, positioning itself as a good neighbor, bent on assuring peace and harmony in the region. Among the earliest priorities announced by the new sultan was the settlement of border disputes with Oman's neighbors in the Arabian Peninsula. This was achieved, over time, with characteristic style and political acumen. In this instance, as in so many others, the sultan of Oman distinguished himself as a patient and honest power broker. In the words of one observer, Qaboos bin Said has "managed to navigate the treacherous waters of Middle East politics with a quiet grace."[25]

Following the double-edged political tsunamis of 1979, the Iranian Revolution and the Soviet invasion of Afghanistan, concerns about regional stability in the Middle East and Central Asia escalated. Oman responded to these events and others by cooperating militarily with the United States and by calling for unity in the Arab world.

US-Omani Cooperation

Although Oman's foreign policy is firmly rooted in the principles of national sovereignty and independence, the sultanate has cooperated militarily with the United States in areas of perceived mutual interest. In one such instance, at the invitation of the United States, Oman signed the Facilities Access Agreement on April 21, 1980, granting American forces *provisional* access to its military facilities, airfields, and ports, including Thumrayt, Salalah, Mutrah, and Masirah Island, among others. In exchange, the sultanate received US$25 million in military credits and a US$250 million "facelift" for several military installations. Similar "access agreements" were renewed in 1985, 1990, 2000, and 2010.

Muscat's assent to the Facilities Access Agreement is an example of the long-term pragmatism that distinguishes Sultan Qaboos from other heads of state. Although it was an unpopular action, earning him the wrath of many in the Arab world at the time, "Oman refused to budge from its perceived long-term interests. Then, as now, it strove to delineate intrinsic interests and to persuade Washington to stand by its allies."[26]

Similarly, during the Gulf War of 1990–1991, when Iraq invaded and annexed Kuwait, US and British forces were permitted access to bases in Oman, while Omani ground troops were dispatched to protect Saudi Arabia from Iraqi aggression. In the words of a high-ranking American diplomat, Oman has been "a really good partner."

Promoting Arab Unity

The Islamic revolution in Iran in 1979 was a clarion call, in particular, for the Arab monarchies of the Persian Gulf. Shaken by regime change in Tehran and, in the following year, by the Iraq-Iran war, which would drag on for eight years at a massive cost in terms of lives and treasure, six countries of the region—Bahrain, Kuwait, Oman, Qatar, Saudi Arabia, and the United Arab Emirates (UAE)—met to reassess regional defense strategies. In 1981 these states, all monarchies, joined together to form the Gulf Cooperation Council (GCC), a subregional organization designed to ensure regional stability and to forge political and economic alliances at a time of unprecedented uncertainty.

In this context, Oman's pragmatic realpolitik, particularly vis-à-vis the Islamic Republic, and others, would prove highly useful in defusing tensions. Addressing the Arab Gulf States' Foreign Ministers' Conference in 1976, Sultan Qaboos made his position obvious: "The Sultanate of Oman clearly recognizes that it is important there should be mutual understanding so that agreement be reached on a formula for co-operation between the states of our region."[27]

Conversant in the complex history of both Oman and the greater Middle East, the longest-serving leader in the Arab world has frequently emphasized the need for regional unity, stressing the importance of reconciliation among the many states of the Arab *nation*. In 1978, on the occasion of Oman's eighth National Day, Sultan Qaboos spoke at length on this subject, warning of the dangers of inter-Arab bickering:

> The leaders of the Arab world must recognise that the Arab peoples cannot any longer afford to descend to the mutual recrimination and petty disputes which for far too long have been the cause of worsening relations between their states. How often in the past has the victory, when almost in our grasp, been dashed from our hands and has fallen to our enemies because of these attitudes and behaviours?[28]

As the Cold War dragged on throughout the decade that followed, the United States and its allies found themselves at a virtual standoff against the Union of Soviet Socialist Republics (USSR), as both sides jockeyed for position in the Middle East and elsewhere. Qaboos, with impressive pre-science, had warned of this danger a full year before the Soviet invasion of Afghanistan. Referring again to the discord among Arab nations, he asked, "Who gains by this discord between brother and brother? One has only to look around to find the answer. It is those who have made our Arab World the political and military battleground for their superpower ambitions, those whose clear intention it is to possess the mastery of the world."[29]

Ties with Egypt. Independence, which is at the root of Oman's foreign policy, has been borne out repeatedly, particularly in the context of some of the most intractable regional conflicts of our time. After Anwar Sadat and Menachem Begin signed the historic Camp David Accords in 1978, culminating in the Egyptian-Israeli peace treaty of 1979, Sultan Qaboos resisted the sweeping tide of Arab enmity against Cairo. When Egypt was scorned as a pariah, Oman was the only member of the Arab League, besides Sudan and Somalia, to maintain uninterrupted diplomatic relations with Cairo. Unafraid of acting independently, Sultan Qaboos did what he believed to be not only in the best interests of his own country but also in the best interests of the Arab nation. Eventually the tide would turn, and other Arab countries would follow Oman's lead, though perhaps not with the same objective:

> Throughout the 1980s, Sultan Qaboos remained unwavering in his support for Egypt and its peace treaty with Israel. The sultan's position eventually appeared to be vindicated. By the mid-1980s, the Arab League—even supported by Iraq, one of the radical "rejectionist" Arab states—was seeking to bring Egypt back into the Arab fold and create a united front against Iran.[30]

Years later, the ever-consistent Sultan Qaboos lauded the decision of the late King Hussein to restore ties with Cairo, characterizing the Jordanian monarch's action as an example of "wise statesmanship" and "an act of greatest significance to our collective aims," further calling on "all Arab leaders to throw their differences aside."[31]

Ties with Israel. Oman's position on self-determination for the Palestinian people is unassailable and fully consistent with that of its Arab and Muslim brethren. Yet, in the interest of regional—and world—peace, the government of Sultan Qaboos has proffered an olive branch to the Israelis on numerous occasions.

Following two major developments, the first after the 1993 Oslo Accords between the Palestine Liberation Organization and Israel calling for Palestinian autonomy, and in the following year, the Jordanian-Israeli rapprochement, Oman and Israel signed an agreement for the reciprocal opening of trade-representative offices in their respective capitals. In 1994, Oman was the first among the Gulf states to invite the Israeli prime minister, Yitzhak Rabin, to Muscat for meetings with the sultan. After Rabin's assassination, his successor, Shimon Peres, was invited to the Omani capital for the official opening of the Israel Trade Representative Office.[32]

In 1996, Oman and Israel established the Middle East Desalination Research Center (MEDRC) in Muscat, a multilateral organization dedicated to achieving peace and stability throughout the region by promoting water cooperation. Consistent with its long-term foreign policy strategy, Oman was instrumental in establishing this association and has chaired MEDRC since its founding.

With a focus on building bridges to peace through cooperative efforts designed to overcome water scarcity and provide fresh potable water, MEDRC provides advice and funds projects in many countries throughout the Middle East, with particular emphasis on the Palestinian territories, through the institution of the Palestinian Water Authority for Desalination and Water Reuse.[33]

Uncompromising Sovereignty. While Oman remains firmly committed to the goals of Arab unity, it is unswerving on questions of national sovereignty. This has been demonstrated on several occasions. In 2007 the sultanate announced, along with the UAE, that if the monetary union proposed by the GCC were to be approved, Oman would not join, affirming that the sultanate "was not willing to surrender its sovereignty on this contentious issue."[34] Similarly, during a regional security summit in December 2013, a proposal was put forward by Saudi Arabia to move the GCC toward a coalition similar to the model of the European Union. In a widely publicized announcement, Oman's representative at the summit, the minister responsible for foreign affairs,[35] stood alone, voicing his country's clear and unambiguous opposition to the notion, stating, "We are against a union. We will not prevent a union, but if it happens, we will not be part of it," adding that if the plan were to go through, "we would simply withdraw" from the GCC.[36]

In a subsequent interview with a high-level government official, the minister explained that the GCC partnership is predicated on the understanding that it proceeds only with issues on which all members are agreed. "If we do not agree," he stated, "we agree to disagree." When pressed further on the subject, he asserted that, as the region's oldest independent country, Oman considers national sovereignty to be a matter of honor. And, while the sultanate is prepared to *cooperate* with its Arab brothers, particularly in the areas of trade and commerce, the principle of noninterference in the internal affairs of other states in inviolable.[37] It goes without saying that the Omanis expect the same courtesy from others.

(Quietly) Mediating International Disputes

Oman's policy of neutrality and noninterference has enabled Sultan Qaboos to act as an important, if discreet, interlocutor among friends from across a broad spectrum. In recent history, his role as liaison has been effective, particularly in those instances involving friends of Oman whose relationship with each another is precarious at best. A factor that has contributed in no small part to his success is the relationship he has maintained with Iran.

Friendship with Iran

There is no doubt that among all the heads of state in the Gulf region, it is Sultan Qaboos bin Said who enjoys the best working relationship with the Islamic Republic of Iran. Given that the historical narratives of both Persia and Oman have intertwined, overlapped, and even, at times, been contentious, Qaboos's posture vis-à-vis the Islamic Republic is one of "positive-engagement strategy" rooted firmly in political reality. While acknowledged as both an idealist and a visionary, Qaboos bin Said is also a pragmatist. Iran is a close neighbor—and a *mighty* one—"neighbors in the past: neighbors in the future."

Omanis place an exceptionally high value on both friendship and loyalty. The sultan recalls vividly the fact that in the early, most critical years of his reign, Iran, under the leadership of the late shah Muhammad Reza Pahlavi, extended to Oman critical support as it fought to defeat the Marxist rebels in Dhofar. This prolonged and stubborn insurgency drained the nation's coffers at a time when massive capital infusions were urgently required elsewhere, to fund the construction of a modern infrastructure. Qaboos bin Said has never forgotten, nor will he likely forget, those who assisted him in his greatest hour of need.

The independence and perceived neutrality of Oman in the arena of regional and international affairs has earned the country and its leader the respect of neighbors, both near and far. While many of Oman's GCC friends view Iran as an "existential threat," voicing skepticism over any overtures toward the Islamic Republic, they understand and accept Oman's rationale, even applauding the sultan as a "defuser of tensions."[38] In a similar vein, the people and government of Iran hold the sultanate and, in particular, its leader, in high esteem, viewing Omanis as "different" from their Arab neighbors and regarding their head of state as a fair, impartial interlocutor. In the 1980s, during the bloody eight-year war between Iran and Iraq, Oman upheld a policy of neutrality between the warring Arab and Iranian states, maintaining diplomatic relations with both and actively endorsing United Nations Security Council resolutions calling for an end to the conflict. In the Middle East, such gestures are not soon forgotten.

Oman's uncanny ability to maintain a markedly distinct foreign policy from other Arab states, particularly with respect to its formidable neighbor across the Persian Gulf, was underscored in 2013 when the speaker of the Iranian parliament, Ali Larijani, visited Muscat. After meeting with Sultan Qaboos, Larijani could not have been more effusive in his praise:

> I am proud of the strong Iranian and Omani ties, which are brotherly and progressive. I have come here to talk about further expansion and strengthening of the relationship between the two countries. . . . His Majesty's balanced approach is what attracted us to his leadership. We laud his vision and strongly believe that he will continue to play a constructive role in the region.[39]

Hostage Releases, among Other Successes

At the same time that Oman has maintained cordial relations with Iran, it has cooperated with its longtime friend the United States as well as with other allies on many fronts. On more than one occasion, Sultan Qaboos has employed what he refers to as his "good ties" to Iran and others to help defuse potentially explosive situations, including acting as an effective intermediary to free foreign hostages.

Examples here include the successfully mediated release in 2007 of fifteen British naval personnel apprehended by Iran, as well as the release of three French nationals captured by al-Qaeda militants in Yemen in 2011. It was reported at the time that Oman acquiesced to a ransom of several million dollars.

In July 2009, three American hikers, Shane Bauer, Joshua Fattal, and Sarah Shourd, were detained on the Iraq-Iran border by Iran, where they were arrested and charged with espionage. Serving in a characteristic role as a discreet mediator between the United States and Iran, the government of Oman intervened. In September 2010, after Oman paid a reported ransom of US$500,000, the Omani government dispatched a private plane to Tehran to reunite Shourd with her family in Muscat.

One year later, Bauer's and Fattal's releases were similarly arranged, negotiated at a reported cost to Oman of US$500,000 each. Again, a royal plane was dispatched from Muscat for their transport out of Tehran. Following these sensitive negotiations, the US secretary of state, Hillary Clinton, traveled to the sultanate in October 2011 to express her nation's gratitude to Sultan Qaboos for his efforts on behalf of her fellow citizens. At that meeting, Sultan Qaboos referred to Clinton as "a lady I admire."[40]

Keeping the Oil Flowing

Oman's amicable relations with Iran, its relative neutrality, and its effective role as an interlocutor have placed it into an enviable position from which to defuse regional and international tensions surrounding the Strait of Hormuz, frequently a locus of contention as the chokepoint for 30 percent of all crude oil carried by sea. As the habitual bluster of hyperbole traverses the airwaves—with saber-rattling Iranians threatening to close the Strait of Hormuz, only to be met by Western politicians countering with bombastic, Armageddon-like scenarios of the consequences that will ensue—Sultan Qaboos, ever the voice of reason, urges all parties to put their differences "on hold," suggesting instead that "the United States and Iran should sit together and talk," while, at the same time, calmly declaring that "no one will block the Strait of Hormuz."[41]

Oman has direct influence over matters affecting the Strait of Hormuz because this "jugular of the world's economy"[42] is *shared* by Oman and Iran. Of additional importance is the fact that nearly all shipping (between 90 and 95 percent) that passes through the strait navigates through the deeper waters or "deep draft ports" that lie entirely within Omani, *not Iranian*, territorial waters.

Although Oman's foreign policy is marked by independence and neutrality, it is also pragmatic. In an attempt to circumvent potential problems with Iran, whose threats of unilateral action in the Strait of Hormuz could lead to serious economic repercussions internationally, Oman has engaged proactively, not only through diplomacy but also through the introduction of practical, long-term alternatives designed to guarantee that Gulf oil will reach its expectant customers abroad.

The massive US$1.5 billion port project at Duqm, located on the Arabian Sea approximately halfway between Muscat and Salalah, with its new dockyard facilities and ship maintenance services, has "the potential to become a major regional transport hub,"[43] enabling Oman to export its hydrocarbon resources without relying on the strait. This plan, which provides a practical alternative to passage through the Strait of Hormuz, demonstrates that while the government of Oman is committed to peace, striving to maintain its independence and neutrality, it is also proactive, seeking to ensure not only regional stability but also the preservation of its vital national interests. As Neubauer puts it,

By maintaining close ties with Iran, Oman is not only securing its own independence and prosperity, but it is also providing an important stabilizing factor in regard to the Strait of Hormuz and the region at large. In addition, the Duqm port illustrates the Sultanate's apparent objective to capitalize on its strategic location by establishing a business hub far removed from the volatile Strait. Between Iran tensions and Duqm's location, the port could help transform the country's economy as Oman faces dwindling reserves."[44]

Other GCC partners have considered similar courses of action, seeking to reduce their reliance on the Strait of Hormuz for the transshipment of oil. In the 1980s, Saudi Arabia constructed two major pipelines traversing the kingdom's giant landmass, from its Eastern Province on the Persian Gulf to the Red Sea on its western shores. In 2012, Abu Dhabi began construction of a 230-mile pipeline from the UAE to an offshore terminal between Musandam and the Batinah coast on the Sea of Oman, capable of carrying up to 1.5 million barrels a day to world markets.

Defusing a Nuclear Iran
As political campaigners and media pundits around the world appear ever poised to announce a preemptive strike against a nuclear Iran, the important, if discreet, role of Oman's leader as a circumspect arbiter must not be discounted. While the Kingdom of Saudi Arabia views Iran as an existential threat to the stability of the region, threatening to "cut off the head of the snake" with preemptive military strikes on Iranian nuclear sites, Sultan Qaboos has adopted a far more measured approach, seeking to strike a balance of power between Riyadh and Tehran. Determined to avoid further escalation of the seemingly intractable Sunni-Shi'a rivalry in the Middle East and to preserve some semblance of what remains of regional stability, the Omani leadership is resolute in its determination to steer clear of this high-stakes contest.[45] In the words of one seasoned Oman watcher, "Even if Tehran should develop a nuclear-weapons capability, Oman's pragmatism and less alarmist strategic calculation would likely trump US pressure to support, at least openly, military action against Iran."[46]

Oman's indispensable role as "honest broker" between Iran and the United States was amply, if discreetly, demonstrated in August 2013, in a move that has been described as "one of the biggest diplomatic developments in recent history."[47] Days after the accession to power of Hassan Rouhani as the new president of the Islamic Republic of Iran, Oman's Sultan Qaboos, "the only Gulf leader to maintain good relations with Tehran,"[48] flew to Iran as the first guest of the newly inaugurated official. As a candidate seeking to replace the former, vituperative "made-for-TV" president, Mahmoud Ahmadinejad, Rouhani broke ranks with his predecessor and advocated a new course of diplomacy, including improved ties with the West.

Although it was reported at the time that Qaboos's visit to Iran was focused primarily on "regional and international issues," as well as bilateral cooperation on economic and energy matters, Iranian media quoted diplomatic sources as saying that the sultanate was hoping to bolster its position as a mediator between Iran and the West.[49] According to the *Wall Street Journal*, a senior Iranian official said that the sultan "emphasized to Iran's leadership the White House's desire for direct talks."[50]

Days later, perhaps by coincidence (or perhaps not), the US president, Barack Obama, telephoned his Iranian counterpart in a move that was to signal a reversal of American diplomacy. Greeted by many as a long-overdue foreign policy milestone, this "olive branch," brokered, one can speculate, by a wise interlocutor, unleashed a predictable firestorm among hawks in both Washington and Tel Aviv. Within weeks, plans for the start of unprecedented, direct talks between Iran and the powerful P5+1 countries (including the five permanent members of the United Nations Security Council, namely the United States, Russia, China, the United Kingdom, and France, plus Germany) were announced. Expectations were that this diplomatic breakthrough would result in an accord curbing Iran's nuclear ambitions, including halting uranium enrichment; in return, the Iranians hoped that the international community would ease the sanctions that had crippled that country's economy for so long.

The media looked for news from Tehran, Washington, and assorted European capitals but managed to overlook one very significant fact. This diplomatic breakthrough, far from being sudden, was instead the result of several months of difficult, protracted, and secret deliberations between US representatives and their Iranian counterparts—in Muscat.

While the eyes of the world remained fixed on Geneva, scrutinizing every nuance surrounding negotiations between Western diplomats and their Iranian counterparts, the most interesting story, perhaps, was that through the intercession of Qaboos bin Said, "US diplomats [had] secretly huddled with a team of Iranian diplomats since 2011 to carry out bilateral talks aimed at securing an agreement to put the brakes on Iran's nuclear ambitions . . . in Muscat, far from the prying eyes of the international media."[51] And so it was: the government of Oman had brokered this deal, providing a venue on Omani soil so that sworn adversaries would be able to sort out the details of an agreement designed to dramatically ease international tensions.

This role of facilitator and interlocutor will prove to be invaluable as rhetoric continues to escalate in a region whose institutions, systems, and models are more fluid than ever before. As Oman pursues a *realistic* foreign policy, even distancing itself from its GCC neighbors with its program of "diplomacy and engagement" with Iran (and on a far more limited, if intermittent, basis with Israel), it is likely to find itself uniquely positioned to effect a peaceful resolution of some of the most contentious issues of the day.

The survival and continued prosperity of a relatively small, underpopulated state located in a region marred by glaring economic disparities, sectarian strife, and hegemonic aspirations would appear to be problematic. Nevertheless, with open eyes and long-term vision, the sultan of Oman has succeeded in containing both internal and external threats to national and regional security by investing in a strategy of "omnibalancing" or, as Marc O'Reilly has characterized it in this case, "Omanibalancing."[52] In the realm of foreign policy, this may include befriending traditional Arab enemies while simultaneously cementing longstanding relationships with its neighbors. This policy of prudent, measured balancing extends also to the incremental liberalization of social and political policies within the country, satisfying domestic aspirations while honoring tradition. Thus far, it has proven successful. And herein, until now at least, lies the "good news" story that is Oman today.

REFLECTIONS

Oman's relations with the rest of the world are best viewed through the prism of history, a history shaped by centuries of interaction with distant peoples and diverse cultures around the globe. The historic frame of reference from which the current leadership has fashioned its national policies is routed in its illustrious, yet often complicated, past. At the same time, the conduct of foreign affairs in Oman is also the product of a uniquely Omani ethos based, in large part, on a culture, including the Ibadhi tradition, which places a premium on consultation and peaceful settlement of disputes.

The story of the friendship between the United States and Oman adds an important, yet little-known, dimension to the contemporary narrative of US-Arab relations. This account will likely resonate with today's readers, illustrating as it does a period when US activity in at least one country in the Middle East was characterized largely by reciprocity, respect, and altruism—elements that endure to this day. From the founding of the American republic, the United States and Oman, both maritime powers with strong commercial interests worldwide, have maintained amicable relations. The persistent efforts of an American in 1833 led to a historic agreement with the sultanate allowing US merchants to engage in lucrative trade with Oman and East Africa. This bilateral milestone, at first commercial in nature, was followed by a diplomatic—and media—event, as the first emissary of an Arab ruler made his way to the United States, leaving in his wake a legacy of goodwill as well as material treasures that would be absorbed into America's national heritage.

As domestic and international events at midcentury altered the dynamics of international trade, commercial relations between the United States and Oman floundered, only to be revived in the 1880s with the opening of an American consulate in Muscat. For many decades thereafter, and until the accession to the throne of Qaboos bin Said in 1970, the focus of US involvement in Oman centered on the private initiative of volunteers who traveled to the sultanate to assist in the educational and healthcare needs of the population. Since 1970, US-Omani relations have deepened. Diplomatically, militarily, commercially, and culturally, ties between the two countries are at historic levels—a partnership based on mutual respect and national self-interests.

Oman's history of trusted friendships, combined with challenges to its independence, interference in its internal affairs, and the effects of being cut off from its Gulf region neighbors during the reign of Sultan Qaboos's father, have all contributed to the sultanate's unique relationship with its Middle Eastern neighbors as well as with the wider international community. Navigating through these exceedingly turbulent times, the Sultanate of Oman has fashioned a policy that is rooted in its own historical experience and religious tradition, a policy that also reflects a certain maturity of vision that is rooted in pragmatism. Characteristic of this policy are several inviolable principles, among which are the development and maintenance of good relations with Oman's neighbors, the preservation of national security through cooperation and peaceful dialogue, and the adoption of a pragmatic approach to bilateral relations, with an emphasis on geostrategic realities rather than fleeting ideologies.

Oman has worked to secure regional stability both by cooperating militarily with the United States and by promoting unity within the Arab nation, though Oman is unwilling to participate in any union that would pose a threat to its sovereignty. Oman has endeavored to remain a friend to everyone, an enemy to none, making it unique among its neighbors, as an increasingly important player in the high-stakes world of realpolitik. Admired for its independence, consistency, and moderation, the sultanate is increasingly being viewed as a venue for dialogue and reconciliation, a role for which it is eminently well suited. One reason for this is the close relationship Oman has maintained with the Islamic Republic of Iran. Sultan Qaboos's ability to work behind the scenes has enabled him to act as an effective intermediary in a variety of international disputes. His successes have included the release of hostages, the unfettered transport of essential hydrocarbons, and the facilitation of efforts to ease nuclear tensions.

The success of Oman's foreign policy is evident in the domestic arena as well. For more than four decades, this country has stood as an oasis of stability in the Middle East. This has enabled the government to pursue an ambitious program of development for its people, who currently enjoy one of the highest standards of living in the region. Omanis exude a sense of confidence and, though challenges lie ahead, a palpable sense of optimism permeates the air.

CHAPTER 7

CHALLENGES AND OPPORTUNITIES IN A
NEW CENTURY

Although the inventory of Oman's achievements is impressive by any standard, the sultanate, by virtue of geography, is part of a volatile world, where instability is currently the norm. As such, it is far from immune from the historic convulsions that have swept through the Middle East in recent years, undermining the status quo and toppling regimes like so many dominos.

Fortunately, a particularly striking feature of Qaboos bin Said's leadership style is his capacity for innovation. His entire career is testimony to this. As the person who has led Oman through, arguably, one of the most remarkable transformations of any country in modern history, he frequently *has had* to think "outside the box." This he has done quite effectively, and keeps on doing, as challenges continue to emerge.

As Oman's population continues to grow, the percentage of young people for whom tales of the increasingly distant, premodern era are mired in legend, is expanding. The expectations of many youthful, cosmopolitan Omanis today have escalated, particularly when measured against the lifestyles of their contemporaries in neighboring, far-wealthier, petrostates. Regional events in early 2011 provided the fodder for their perceived discontent. But the trajectory of Omani discontent was different than it was in other Middle Eastern states.

As other regimes have crumbled in the wake of the "Arab Spring," the government of Oman has listened and responded with reforms. As a growing contingent of young people have become restless, distracted in part by unrealistic expectations, Qaboos bin Said, in characteristic fashion, has emphasized the importance of their role in securing their "motherland's" future prosperity. When life in a modern, affluent society ironically has resulted in the kinds of health and safety problems that typically plague Western, industrialized nations, the Omani government has responded swiftly to promote public awareness and implement solutions. And, finally, when a few would seek to pervert Islam in order to justify a fanaticism that is antithetical to the faith, Sultan Qaboos has reminded his nation of its historic tradition of moderation and tolerance, reaffirming its commitment to dialogue and religious understanding.

THE "ARAB AWAKENING"

During the turbulent succession of events that sent the Middle East into a tailspin in 2011—a period known as the "Arab Spring," or the "Arab Awakening"—several governments were toppled in quick succession, first in Tunisia, followed by Egypt, then Libya, and, to a large extent, Yemen. While the status quo throughout the region was seriously undermined by months of violent protests and demands for regime change, the government of Oman weathered this regional tsunami wiser, but nonetheless intact. While popular protests, organized largely through text messaging and social media, spurred a number of social, economic, and political reforms, one Omani official, viewing these events through a longer, historical lens, insisted that their impact on the evolution of the state was limited. "We have had our Arab Awakening," he said. "Our awakening was in 1970."[1]

Challenge and Response

Young Omanis who first took to the streets in January 2011 failed to trigger the mass protests that shook the rest of the Arab world. Despite social-media chatter, strikes, and outbreaks in certain areas of the country, most notably in the port city of Sohar, where a local hypermarket[2] was set aflame, there was never any serious political challenge to the authority of Qaboos bin Said. Although they may have felt empowered by the *angst* of their brethren around the region, protestors did not demand the ouster of the head of state, petition for greater democratic reforms, or even denounce Israel. Rather, what brought citizens to the streets were economic issues, such as concerns about unemployment and personal debt and perceived corruption within the ranks of government. The following month, teachers rallied in a string of "Green Marches," protesting against higher pension contributions and demanding more frequent promotions. In a country where citizens are heavily subsidized, Omanis demanded larger allowances for water, electricity, and housing.[3]

Following the demonstrations of January and February, a petition was delivered to the Diwan of the Royal Court.[4] The petition, directed to the attention of the sultan, affirmed the citizens' loyalty to the head of state before presenting a list of popular grievances. Following that event, it is reported that Sultan Qaboos met with members of his trusted inner circle; with representatives of the elected parliamentary body, the *Majlis al-Shura*; and with a variety of citizens. In addition, he talked with trusted friends from abroad, including high-profile international leaders.

Sultan Qaboos took quick and decisive action, addressing citizens' concerns and effectively defusing a potentially destabilizing bombshell. After dispatching a ministerial representative to Sohar to hear the peoples' grievances, the ruler released six royal decrees over a period of several days, including specific promises of jobs and reforms.[5]

The results of the royal deliberations were swift, comprehensive, and far reaching. As part of a massive governmental reorganization, eight ministers, including some who had been specifically targeted by Omani citizens, were removed from office. In a highly symbolic, but also substantive, gesture, Sultan Qaboos chose many new ministers from the *Majlis al-Shura*, the *elected* lower house of the Omani parliament—public servants who had been, in fact, *preselected* by the voters. Chosen on the basis of their education, training, and merits, many of the new ministers held PhD degrees. Appointing *elected* officials to serve in ministerial posts introduced a new dynamic into the political landscape of the sultanate; the implications of this decision were significant.

In light of the venerable Omani tradition of *shura* (consultation), it is significant that Sultan Qaboos sent personal representatives to engage in direct consultation with the protestors to discuss their demands. This gesture was not lost on the citizens. "While some doubted that the messages [these representatives] brought came directly from the sultan, others appeared convinced. Despite these issues, the contact between the two sides was clearly important in facilitating understanding."[6] According to Worrall, "This active engagement, alongside the concessions and the overwhelming support for the sultan himself, marked the Oman Spring as rather different from uprisings elsewhere."[7]

Economic Reforms

Sweeping economic reforms quickly followed. In response to popular demand for greater employment opportunities, the government pledged to create 55,000 new jobs during the year 2012, with an additional 56,000 jobs promised for 2013.[8] The majority of the new employees would serve in the military or state security sectors. Unemployment benefits were raised to 150 Omani riyals (US$390) per month, and student stipends were increased.

In an apparent attempt to offset government spending, the state mandated a wage hike for Omanis employed in the private sector, hoping to attract more citizens to that sector. Effective as of July 2013, the minimum wage was increased by more than 60 percent to 325 Omani riyals (US$844) per month.[9] As part of the "Omanization" effort designed to decrease the country's dependence on foreign workers, national guidelines called for doubling the goal of Omani participation in the labor force—from the previous level of 15 percent to a new high of 30 percent. In February 2013, the *Shura* Council voted to restrict the number of foreign workers in Oman to 33 percent of country's total population, again in an effort "to create an employment balance."[10] Finally, focusing on the protection of consumers, a Customer Protection Authority was created to prevent price gouging, especially during religious feasts.

Political Initiatives

As the year 2011 continued to unfold, the dynamic nature of Oman's political landscape became ever-more apparent. Sultan Qaboos responded to the people's concerns by gradually liberalizing political and economic systems while, at the same time, attempting to maintain Oman's relatively high standard of living. The ruler announced a series of amendments to the Basic Law, Oman's constitution—the first since its publication in 1996. Although it has been reported that these changes had long been envisioned and discussed, their announcement came at an opportune time.

Under the sweeping new provisions of the amended Basic Law, the elected, lower house of the country's parliament, the *Majlis al-Shura*, would now exercise greatly enhanced powers, including the right to amend and approve laws proposed by the Council of Ministers, as well as the ability to propose legislation (see chapter 4). In an effort toward greater transparency, openness, and accountability, members of the *Majlis al-Shura* were also now granted unfettered access to any cabinet minister for the purpose of gathering information or posing questions.

Further, the head of state mandated that the Council of Ministers would meet each week to discuss the needs of the citizens, directing that body to send the reports of those deliberations to the ruler for his review. By order of the sultan, each ministry is now obliged to designate an individual whose function is to "serve the people," in an effort to eliminate favoritism, influence (*wasta*), and unnecessary delays.

With the expansion of the role, functions, and responsibilities of the State Audit Institution, citizens in Oman have the means through which to register complaints regarding perceived unfair practices, consumer violations, and corruption. In keeping with Sultan Qaboos's shift toward appointing technocrats, each department head within the ministry is required to hold at least a master's degree.

THE OMANI "YOUTH BULGE"

Finding ways to motive youth and respond to their concerns is a particularly important challenge in Oman. Fifty percent of the population is under the age of twenty-five. This is due to a number of factors, among which are Islamic cultural values that traditionally celebrate large families.[11] A relatively young marriage age for women is another customary practice in Oman, although this is changing gradually as more women pursue higher education and enter into the workforce. Modernization has also had a profound impact on family size and the current youth bulge. In the years following 1970, improvements in education, mobility, and employment opportunities, as well as massive public health initiatives that dramatically decreased infant and child mortality, contributed to a collective feeling of optimism resulting in accelerated birth rates.

Rising Expectations

Since the 2011 "Arab Awakening," young people throughout the Middle East have begun to display profound levels of frustration, even in countries like Oman that have managed to escape the disruption of regime change. Although polling data regularly cite Omanis as among the world's happiest people, the sultanate is not immune from the concerns that are endemic to the wider region.

Although they enjoy a standard of living that is enviable by any measure—particularly when compared with that of Omanis of less than half a century ago—Omani youth nonetheless share with their contemporaries elsewhere many of the same doubts and fears. Recent interviews strongly indicate that Omanis born after 1970—indeed, the vast majority, or 90 percent, of the total population—may not appreciate fully the Omani national narrative, including the extent to which their country has achieved modernity within the span of only two generations. Rather, like many young people the world over, young Omanis seem more concerned with their present circumstances, including growing personal debt, uncertain employment prospects, and the acquisition of high-end consumer goods. To a great extent, Oman's proximity to far more affluent Gulf Cooperation Council (GCC) states, where governmental largesse is truly extraordinary, has led its own young people to hold unrealistic expectations of what they can expect from their already exceedingly generous government.

From the earliest years of his reign, Sultan Qaboos has recognized the need to focus on youth and to prepare them for the challenges of remaining competitive in a dynamic, ever-expanding global economy. Through actions as well as speeches, he reaches out to them regularly. In 1976 he created a Ministry for Youth Affairs. Brimming with optimism, he called this gesture "testimony of our faith and pride in our young people and our determination that they shall be brought forward to play their full part."[12]

On the occasion of Oman's National Day celebration in 1982, only twelve years after initiating a national campaign for education, Sultan Qaboos addressed his countrymen again on the subject of youth. In this speech, the head of state singled out his young citizens for special attention, announcing plans to establish a national university (Sultan Qaboos University), construct a Sports City, and establish a Supreme Youth Council. He proclaimed 1983 as Omani Youth Year (only to be repeated in 1993)—"all this with the aim of focusing the role of our Youth and giving them every opportunity to play their part positively in all fields."[13]

Throughout the course of his reign, Oman's leader has alerted his young citizens to their responsibilities in a rapidly modernizing society. Putting them on notice, he has reminded them repeatedly that though much is given, much is expected in return. Celebrating the inauguration of the first Omani Youth Year in 1983, he spoke candidly, saying, "It is time for imagination, expectation, and hope, but, also young people must waste no time in getting down to the practical work of carrying out their national obligations."[14]

Throughout almost forty-five years on the throne, the ruler's attention to the children of the new Oman has not wavered. He addresses them frequently in honest, almost paternalistic tones. Using the bully pulpit to great, if gentle, effect, he alternately praises and admonishes them, urging young people to shoulder their responsibilities as they prepare themselves for an uncertain future. They must engage in "hard work" through dedication and focus, he advises, reminding them always of their "national obligations." On National Day in 1986, for example, the sultan affirmed the country's collective confidence in its young people while at the same time challenging them to live up to their potential: "We believe in the role of Omani youth in building the country. We call upon them to set a good example in adopting a responsible sense of duty and in seeking perfection in their work."[15]

As "motivator in chief," he urges those in the private sector to train, encourage, and employ young Omanis in their development plans and, at the same time, reminds Oman's youth, "the hope of the nation," of their equal responsibility in this endeavor:

> When we call upon you all to take care of our Youth's aspirations and ambitions, we also call with the same insistence upon our Youth to be aware of their responsibility for building our country. They must roll up their sleeves with the utmost energy to contribute positively towards our comprehensive development. They must be armed with patience and hope, determination and industry, and a spirit of sacrifice and unselfishness.[16]

Unemployment Anxiety

The combined issues of employment opportunity and economic security appear to be among the greatest concerns of Omani youth. In this they are not alone. According to a 2011 survey, 87 percent of young people in the GCC are impatient about their future, expressing deep concerns about job opportunities.[17]

The underlying problems are manifold. While the youth of the GCC countries enjoy exceptional advantages, including access to schooling at all levels, many university graduates soon discover that their elite education has not prepared them for the job market. In Oman, this shortage of qualified Omanis to fill specific employment needs has also been a roadblock in the national program of Omanization and, in particular, its objective of lessening the country's dependence on expatriate labor. With a seismic disconnect between education and productive skills, frustration is inevitable. Increasingly, the two ministries devoted to education[18] are addressing this issue, creating programs designed to make education more relevant to the developmental priorities of the country. As greater emphasis is placed on instruction that will meet specific employment needs, now and in the future—particularly in the areas of science, mathematics, information technology, and foreign languages—technical schools and vocational colleges are assuming an increasingly important role in the careers of young people.

There is also, of course, a cultural dimension to this problem; namely, the inclination for urban, middle-class people to disdain manual labor or "blue collar" professions, except at the managerial level. Sultan Qaboos has been very clear on this point, rarely missing an opportunity to emphasize the importance of seeking employment—in any field. On a "Meet the People" tour in 1995, for example, he explained, "There are some people who think that the jobs available are not suitable for them and refuse to accept them. Any who think they are above the work, whatever be the nature of such work, will not succeed in strengthening their economic situation."[19]

To the extent possible, the state has attempted to respond to the demand for greater employment opportunities by expanding the number of jobs in the public sector. As mentioned earlier, following the 2011 protests in Sohar, some 55,000 new government jobs were created, mostly in the security sector. Yet, because this is not a sustainable strategy, the state is aggressively seeking to reverse this tide, even encouraging its own employees to leave their government positions in order to join the private sector, preferably to start their own businesses.

To facilitate this process, a major national initiative is under way. During one of his periodic royal tours, this time to Bahla, in 2013, Sultan Qaboos announced the establishment of al-Rafd Fund, designed to encourage entrepreneurship by providing loans and financing for young entrepreneurs who either wish to create small or medium enterprises or plan to expand existing businesses. In creating this initiative, the government is targeting, among others, artisans, craftspeople, and local women.[20] Expressing optimism about the success of this program, Sultan Qaboos shared his hope that the fund would "bring prosperity to our sons and daughters."[21]

Starting from an initial capital base of 70 million Omani riyals (US$181 million), the fund, regulated by the newly established Public Authority for Small and Medium Enterprises, is expected to grow by 7 million Omani riyals (US$18 million) annually. Under this program, applicants may be eligible for loans of up to 100,000 Omani riyals (US$259,000)—twice the amount available under the Sanad program, a previous initiative charged by the sultan with a similar mission. Initial reports have been encouraging. By the end of 2014, al-Rafd Fund had financed 626 projects by distributing loans totaling more than 17 million Omani riyals (US$44 million).[22]

LIFESTYLE CHALLENGES IN AN AFFLUENT SOCIETY

A brief review of the mainstream media in twenty-first-century Oman reveals that among the major daily challenges faced by the population at large are those that are all too familiar to people in other affluent, industrialized societies—challenges that, in Oman, would have been inconceivable before 1970.

One of the most troubling of these patterns is the rate of high-speed traffic fatalities. As Oman has experienced remarkable development during the last four decades in terms of infrastructure development, economic growth,

and modernization, automobile usage and ownership has increased expo-
nentially. During one of his annual "Meet the People" tours in 2009, Sultan
Qaboos addressed the nation, urging his government and society to come
together to end the high incidence of injuries and deaths on Oman's roads.[23]
And although this national trend has been decreasing steadily in recent years,
Oman retains the distinction of ranking highest among the GCC states and
third highest in the eastern Mediterranean region in the number of fatalities
that occur on its roads every year.[24]

The causes of traffic accidents are complex and varied, including confusing highway configurations, erratic driver behavior, exceeding posted speed
limits, and precarious environmental conditions. Governmental action, combined with regular media coverage of this problem, has resulted in the introduction of a series of innovative measures designed to counteract this trend.

Increasing public awareness has proven to be an effective way to change
driver behavior. One of the most successful initiatives has been the establishment of the Traffic Safety Institute, whose primary mandate is to increase
public awareness of road safety through media campaigns.[25] Another group
that conducts road safety studies throughout the nation and publishes reports
of its findings is the Scientific Research Council.[26]

The first organization to take advantage of social media, Safety First,
Oman's leading road safety organization, is conducting a nationwide campaign to alert young people to the real-life consequences of reckless driving.
The campaign features a compelling video called "Tell Us Your Story," in
which a series of well-known Omanis, including national soccer team captain
'Ali al-Habsi and actor Saleh bin Zaal al-Farsi, take turns talking about someone they know who was killed or injured in a traffic accident.[27] First shown
during the Oman versus Australia World Cup Qualifier in June of 2012,
the video was then released through Facebook and Twitter. Commenting
on its success, Safety First founder and international rally champion Hamed
al-Wahaibi said,

> We have been overwhelmed by the number of people that have shown their
> support by viewing and sharing the video online. Social media's popularity has
> allowed us to spread the road safety message very quickly across Oman. It has
> been very touching to hear people's stories of loss from comments and emails
> we have been receiving. It has shown that this problem affects people from all
> walks of life.[28]

These efforts, and those of the Royal Oman Police (ROP) to toughen
penalties and increase enforcement, are working to reverse what was at one
time a rapidly rising trend. The most recent data from the ROP show that
90 percent of front-seat occupants wear seatbelts. There are stiff penalties
for driving under the influence, with the result that only 0.6 percent of traffic fatalities involve alcohol.[29] And in 2014, the ROP announced plans to
impose separate fines for each traffic violation, so that a motorist who com-
mits multiple violations—such as talking on a cellphone and speeding—would

receive multiple fines.[30] According to statistics released by Oman's Ministry of Information, the number of traffic accidents declined by 5 percent in 2013 compared with the previous year, while related injuries and deaths dropped by 7 percent and 20 percent, respectively.[31]

Modernization and increasing prosperity in Oman have also been accompanied by a sharp increase in a number of preventable health issues, such as diabetes, hypertension, coronary heart disease, obesity, and vitamin D deficiency, many of which correspond to physically inactive lifestyles. A major research study published in 2014 by researchers at Sultan Qaboos University cited a 2010 World Health Organization report indicating that the death rate in Oman from noncommunicable diseases—specifically those caused by lack of physical activity and poor eating habits—had soared to 83 percent. According to the report, Oman is not alone in this trend. "The rush toward . . . different kinds of new technologies in the Arab countries has had a negative impact on the patterns of social life and healthy lifestyle. People have become addicted to such means of amusement, abandoning all forms of sports and physical activities."[32]

To counter this trend, the government has implemented a program to promote healthy lifestyles. In schools, physical exercise is now a mandated part of the curricula. Public awareness campaigns about the benefits of physical exercise and better nutritional habits have been launched, while more fitness centers and sports facilities—particularly for women—are being introduced.

THE ROLE OF ISLAM IN MODERN OMAN

In the 1990s, as waves of radical religious fundamentalism swept through the Middle East, small sectors of Oman's young and vulnerable population seemed drawn to the appeals of fanatic Islamists, positing a potential, but short-lived, threat to national harmony and stability. It will be remembered that during his earlier years in Salalah, prior to assuming his role as sultan, Qaboos bin Said devoted himself to a rigorous course of study, immersing himself in Omani history, the Qur'an, and the teachings of Islam. This interlude prepared him both to preside over a modern state that would be at peace with its traditions and to successfully challenge any forces that would seek to undermine Islam. In this regard, his record can only be considered a success. For not only is cultural and religious diversity the accepted norm in Oman, but at the same time, the country is fast becoming a twenty-first-century center of interreligious dialogue and religious tolerance.

Affirmation of the Faith

During the period following World War II, the prevailing mood of the newly independent, developing countries in the Arab and Islamic Middle East and, indeed, in most of the modern—and modernizing—world was largely secular. But while others were eschewing tradition in favor of modernization,

Sultan Qaboos emphasized the importance of religion in Omani history and culture and, indeed, its relevance in his nation's development.

On November 18, 1977, on the occasion of Oman's seventh National Day, the sultan reminded his countrymen that along with academic and cultural education, "the standards and values bequeathed to us by our Holy Religion and our Arab traditions" must be maintained. Toward this end, he announced a review of the curricula in religious training institutions, ordering the inclusion of secular subjects "that will produce mature teachers of Islam, familiar with the ways of modern society and well-qualified to provide our people—and especially our young people—with the moral and spiritual guidance they must have."[33]

Oman and Islamists[34]

The potential for the religion of Islam to be perverted in the service of a violent political agenda was something that Qaboos bin Said had warned against long before the 2015 murders of the *Charlie Hebdo* journalists and six others in Paris or even the 2001 terrorist attacks in the United States. As early as 1971, only a year into his reign, Sultan Qaboos used the word "terrorism" (*irhab*) to describe "the communist gangs in the mountains of Dhofar" who were being abetted by the Marxist regime of the former People's Democratic Republic of Yemen. A decade later, he warned his countrymen of the danger that Islam could be used in the name of violence, saying, "We should . . . beware of those who distort the teachings of our Muslim religion to serve their own political purposes."[35]

Some two decades after Sultan Qaboos addressed this issue, and well after the protracted insurgency in Dhofar had been quashed, the specter of terrorism resurfaced in 1994, this time bringing with it a renewed sense of urgency, as Islamists within the sultanate's own community challenged the regime. Citing the Ibadhi penchant for moderation and peaceful resolution of conflict, the sultan of Oman warned that extremism, fanaticism, and factionalism in any form were contrary to the principles of tolerance inherent to Islam. Challenging extremists on theological grounds, Sultan Qaboos argued that those who would undermine the state in the name of the Qur'an were twisting the verses of that text to suit their own agendas.

Aware that the restlessness and alienation of Oman's youth had led to a stagnation leaving them vulnerable to Islamist appeals, Sultan Qaboos expressed sadness that this situation was "based on a lack of knowledge among the Muslim youth about the correct facts of their religion, [which] was exploited by some to perpetrate violence and propagate cases of difference that led to discord and hatred."[36] He urged Muslims to gain a better understanding of their faith as well as its true message, adding,

> In order that Muslims should not remain backward, while others advance, they
> are required by the Law of Islam to rectify this situation, and renew and revise
> their thinking so that they can apply the right solutions to modern problems

that are facing the Islamic community. Thus, they can show the world the reality of Islam, and its principles which are applicable to all times and places.[37]

To a large extent, Qaboos bin Said has been successful in neutralizing, at least within his own country, issues of extremism and religious fundamentalism, often citing Oman's Ibadhi tradition of moderation and tolerance along with Islam's general prescriptions for nonviolence and dialogue. At the opening of the Council of Oman's fifth term in 2011, he reiterated this principle by asserting, "The more thought becomes diverse, open and free of fanaticism, the more it becomes a correct and sound basis for the building of generations, the progress of nations and the advancement of societies."[38]

These efforts have been recognized by the United States Department of State in its annual *International Religious Freedom Report*. In 2012 the report hailed Oman's efforts to combat religious extremism, noting that the sultanate's message represents the spirit of "moderate and tolerant Islam."[39] The following year, the updated report again gave Oman high marks, citing religious freedom for non-Muslims and noting that members of other faith communities, including Christians, Buddhists, Sikhs, Baha'is, and Hindus, freely practice their traditions without restriction.[40]

A Dialogue of Differences

Looking ahead into this new century, it would appear that, in many ways, Oman is ideally positioned to serve as a venue for interreligious discourse across a broad field. On the one hand, this role is consistent with its history and culture; centuries of maritime activity to destinations around the globe have instilled in the collective psyche of the Omani people an unusual degree of respect toward people of widely varying traditions. This openness is further reinforced by the prevailing spirit of Ibadhism; with its emphasis on moderation and dialogue, it provides an ideal milieu for a "dialogue of differences."

This initiative is well under way, having been identified and seized upon by both Omanis and foreign visitors. In February 2014, the third annual Rapprochement and Human Harmony Week convened in Muscat at the Sultan Qaboos Higher Center for Culture and Science at the Sultan Qaboos Grand Mosque.

Organized under the auspices of the Office of the Adviser to His Majesty the Sultan for Cultural Affairs, this annual event brings together international scholars in an effort to promote a dialogue among diverse societies and to foster greater understanding. Its objective is "to ensure peaceful relations between cultures by developing cross-cultural efforts encouraging mutual respect."[41] Underscoring the importance of this effort, the secretary general of the Ministry of Foreign Affairs emphasized the urgency for dialogue in the world today: "In this century . . . we need to have harmony with each other by educating and understanding each other's cultures and societies."[42]

In spring of 2013, oceans away, Omanis themselves took their message on the road, as representatives of the sultanate's Ministry of *Awqaf* (charitable endowments) and Religious Affairs traveled to the United States for the first time to present an exhibition titled "Religious Tolerance: Islam in the Sultanate of Oman." Hosted by Salve Regina University in Newport, Rhode Island, the exhibition, which had visited more than two dozen cities in Europe, was intended "to acquaint the general public with the openness, tolerance, and religious acceptance found in Oman, where freedom of religion is guaranteed by the constitution, and the religious institutions of the Buddhists, Hindus, Catholics, Copts and other Christians are not only respected but supported by the state."[43]

In many respects, the designation of an annual "Interfaith Week" in Muscat, combined with Oman's efforts far beyond its shores, speaks to this country's determination to spread a message of understanding and inclusivity to all corners of the earth. This campaign—to recognize diversity and celebrate shared human values—is, in so many ways, another embodiment of the Omani cultural legacy, representing the latest manifestation of a unique modern paradigm in which the past continues to pave the way for the future.

REFLECTIONS

Since 1970, Qaboos bin Said, the longest-reigning leader in the Middle East, has transformed his beloved Oman, once ruefully dismissed as the "sick man of the Gulf," from an impoverished "hermit kingdom" to a culturally authentic, modern society whose international star continues to rise. When he assumed the throne on July 23 of that year, Oman lacked not only the most basic requirements of modern life, in terms of infrastructure and services, but also the political cohesion of a viable state. The changes that have taken place since then are nothing short of miraculous. By any measure, this is a "good news" story that, in many ways, is the stuff of lore.

The accomplishments of this wise and soft-spoken septuagenarian, whose country has achieved "a place at the table" of nations within less than two generations, are both impressive and staggering, particularly so from the perspective of those who have had the good fortune to observe the progress of this transformative renaissance since its earliest years. The legacy of Sultan Qaboos is characterized not only by the introduction of universal education and comprehensive health services amid a continually modernizing national infrastructure but also by an extraordinary degree of political acumen that has preserved Oman's sovereignty while simultaneously forging a foreign policy that distinguishes this relatively small country as an international intermediary of the highest caliber.

Internal modernization, dwindling oil reserves, regional instability, and a global revolution in technology have posed a new set of challenges—and opportunities—for this twenty-first-century country. The response of Qaboos bin Said to the "Arab Awakening" is particularly instructive. It demonstrates once again that Oman's sultan is the epitome of a "hands on" leader, one who is engaged in a continuing dialogue with his people and who responds with measures that promote domestic peace and stability—measures that, at the same time, are consistent with his vision of national growth.

The challenges that face Oman today are significant—particularly those that center around economic diversification, political transparency, privatization, and the meaningful employment of Oman's large youthful contingent. To address these concerns, the government has taken a series of bold initiatives, including encouraging the growth of new sectors, prioritizing educational objectives, guaranteeing citizen access to national leadership, and providing young people with the means to realize entrepreneurial dreams.

Reflecting upon the state of Omani society in the mid-twentieth century, it is somewhat ironic that, following the massive transformation of infrastructure, education, and healthcare in the sultanate, today's increasingly prosperous Omanis are making lifestyle choices—and experiencing consequences—that are closer to those found in Western, industrialized societies. As greater mobility, sedentary lifestyles, and the phenomenon of "fast-food" emporia take hold, the government again is taking bold measures to ensure the continued health and longevity of its population through the establishment of new state institutions as well as public awareness campaigns.

Omanis hold fast to Islam even while ensuring that members of other faith traditions are free to practice their own beliefs in the sultanate. Sultan Qaboos, a scholar of the faith, is an articulate spokesman for Islam and an unwavering foe of any who would seek to pervert the faith through acts of terror. In this respect, Oman continues to enjoy a rare measure of stability in the Middle East—and beyond—while serving as a stalwart ally in the global fight against terror. Taking this one step further is Oman's evolving role as a venue of interreligious dialogue, which surely places the sultanate on a level unmatched by any of its neighbors.

Undoubtedly the future will present both challenges and opportunities for the friendly and generous people I first encountered in this enchanting land more than forty years ago. History has demonstrated that they are up to the task. Blessed with a unique heritage, an enduring faith in God, and a strong sense of national cohesion, Oman has been reborn from virtual obscurity to a modern, yet culturally authentic, nation-state. It stands today poised to continue its journey while, at the same time, serving as an exemplar of moderation and inclusion in an increasingly divisive world.

Notes

Preface

1. The research project was titled "Beliefs and Practices Relating to Health, Nutrition and Child Bearing and Rearing in Nizwa and Sohar." For an account of the experiences of the young women who did the fieldwork in the two villages, see Nouhad Kanawati, Abla Kadi, Hind Masri, and Margaret Kapenga Shurdom, *Nizwa and Sohar 30 Years Ago: A Glimpse of the Past* (Lebanon: Chemaly & Chemaly, 2003).
2. Saniya Othman, *Tiflaki hatta al-Khamisah: dalil al-mar'ah al-'Arabiyah* [Your baby until the age of five: The Arabian woman's guide] (Beirut: Dar al-'Ilm, 1977).
3. CENTCOM, established in 1983, is a joint military command with responsibility for more than twenty countries in the "central" area of the globe, including several in the heartland of the Middle East, East Africa, and Central Asia.
4. See Linda Pappas Funsch, "The Stage Is Set," "U.S.-Omani Relations," "The People," "Governing," "Economy," "Women," "Oman Rediscovered," *Frederick News Post*, September 18–September 23, 2006, http://www.fredericknewspost .com/search/?t=article&s=start_time&sd=desc&d1=&q=funsch%2C+oman.

Introduction

1. This tradition, which will be explained in chapter 1, is said to have first taken hold in Oman, where it exists to this day. In addition, there are small communities of Muslims following the Ibadhi Islamic tradition in present-day Algeria, Tunisia, Libya, and East Africa.
2. Although Omani society is marked by religious diversity, particularly within the Islamic milieu, it should be noted that Omanis themselves stress the *unity* in this diversity, emphasizing the fact that Omani *nationality* overrides sectarian concerns.
3. The term "jihad," or "jihadism," as currently employed in the West, implying an Islamic "tenet" justifying wanton death and destruction, allegedly in the "name of God," is rejected by the majority of Muslims, who instead embrace the notion of jihad as a lifelong struggle or striving to live a good life and reject evil.

Chapter 1

1. John Henzell, "Madha Village's Pledge of Allegiance Changed the Map Forever," *The National*, January 27, 2012, http://www.thenational.ae/lifestyle/ madha-villages-pledge-of-allegiance-changed-the-map-forever.

2. Peter J. Ochs II, *Maverick Guide to Oman*, 2nd ed. (New York: Pelican, 2000), 81.

3. To gain a greater appreciation of the Indian Ocean in world history, see the "Indian Ocean in World History" website, an indispensable interactive resource featuring maps, documents, travelers' routes, goods, and technologies over the centuries. Developed in cooperation with the Sultan Qaboos Cultural Center, Washington, DC, it can be found at http://www.indianoceanhistory.org/.

4. The Omani "exclave" of Madha, also a part of the Musandam governorate, is another noncontiguous landmass located halfway between the Musandam peninsula and the rest of Oman.

5. "Chokepoints" are narrow channels along widely used global sea routes, some so narrow that restrictions are placed on the size of the vessel that can navigate through them.

6. US Energy Information Administration, *World Oil Transit Chokepoints*, updated November 10, 2014, http://www.eia.gov/beta/international/regions-topics .cfm?RegionTopicID=WOTC.

7. For a comprehensive, beautifully illustrated account of the history of seafaring in Oman, see *The Museum of the Frankincense Land: The Maritime Hall* ([Muscat]: Office of the Adviser to His Majesty the Sultan for Cultural Affairs, 2007).

8. Indonesia, the most populous Muslim nation in the world today, has Omani communities, "the forebears of which helped to spread Islam into the Far East" (Robert Kaplan, *Monsoon: The Indian Ocean and the Future of American Power* [New York: Random House, 2010], 26).

9. Vincent McBrierty and Mohammad al-Zubair, *Oman: Ancient Civilization, Modern Nation* (Dublin: Trinity College/Muscat: Bait Al Zubair Foundation, 2004), 19.

10. Kaplan, 25.

11. E. Harper Johnson, *Oman: A Pictorial Resuscitation* (Muscat: Ministry of Information, Sultanate of Oman, 1997), 58.

12. Kaplan, 53.

13. Sigurd Neubauer, "Oman: Advancing Modern Diplomacy, Celebrating Historic Shipbuilding Traditions," *Foreign Policy Journal*, March 16, 2013, http://www .foreignpolicyjournal.com/2013/03/16/oman-advancing-modern-diplomacy -celebrating-historic-shipbuilding-traditions/.

14. Kaplan, 53. Although da Gama was largely successful in achieving his goals, which focused on bringing the lands and people of the East under Portugal's control, it is cruelly ironic that, over time, Ahmad bin Majid's role in assisting the Portuguese would usher in an era of unwelcome aggression on Oman's shores as well as on the coasts of other countries.

15. The music of Oman is similarly infused with a heavy, rhythmic, and percussive beat, distinctly African in sound and mood, particularly in the use of drums.

16. B. Nicolini cites G. F. Hourani, *Arab Seafaring* (Princeton, NJ: Princeton University Press, 1951; rev. ed., 1995), in stating that "'dow' is a Swahili name, not used by the Arabs but adopted by English writers in the incorrect form of 'dhow'" (xix).

17. Some writers surmise that the identical nomenclature of the Omani and Lebanese ports suggests that either the Phoenicians or the Omanis were aware of the other and their respective maritime pursuits, explaining, perhaps, why the Omanis named their most renowned easternmost harbor after Lebanon's of the same appellation.

18. For a complete account of this fascinating adventure, see Tim Severin, *The Sindbad Voyage* (New York: Little Brown and Company, 1998); also, John Lawton, "The Sindbad Voyage," *Saudi Aramco World*, September/October, 1981, http://www.saudiaramcoworld.com/issue/198105/the.sindbad.voyage.htm.

19. Robert Jackson, "Sailing through Time: Jewel of Muscat," *Saudi Aramco World*, May/June 2012, http://www.saudiaramcoworld.com/issue/201203/sailing.through.time.jewel.of.muscat.htm.

20. In Singapore's capital city, visitors can stroll down "Muscat Street," restored and renovated in 2012, to glimpse murals of journeys made by Omani dhows to Asia centuries ago. See Elham Pourmohammadi, "Omani Landscape in Singapore Lane," *Times of Oman*, July 14, 2014, http://www.timesofoman.com/News/36652/Article-Omani-landscape-in-Singapore-lane.

21. Also known as *Boswellia carteri* or *Boswellia undulato crenata*.

22. Rhea Talley Stewart, "A Dam at Marib," *Saudi Aramco World*, March/April 1978, http://www.saudiaramcoworld.com/issue/197802/a.dam.at.marib.htm.

23. Kaplan, 23.

24. Esther Sternberg, *Healing Places: The Science of Place and Well-Being* (Cambridge, MA: Belknap Press of Harvard University Press, 2009), 86.

25. Kaplan, 23.

26. For a comprehensive, illustrated account of the legacy of frankincense in Oman, including descriptions of relevant archeological sites, see *The Museum of the Frankincense Land: The History Hall* ([Muscat]: Office of the Adviser to His Majesty the Sultan for Cultural Affairs, 2007).

27. Kaplan, 23.

28. Marco Polo, *The Travels of Marco Polo* (New York: Grosset & Dunlap, n.d.), 300.

29. Ibid., 301.

30. Samuel Lee, trans. and ed., *The Travels of Ibn Battuta in the Near East, Asia & Africa, 1325–1354* (Mineola, NY: Dover, 2004).

31. The Land of Frankincense in Dhofar was the third Omani site to be included in the World Heritage list, following the Bahla Fort (1987) and the archaeological sites of Bat, al-Khutm, and al-'Ayn (1988). The *aflaj* irrigation systems were added to the UNESCO World Heritage list in 2006.

32. J. N. Wilford, "On the Trail from the Sky: Roads Point to a Lost City," *New York Times*, February 5, 1992, http://www.nytimes.com/1992/02/05/world/on-the-trail-from-the-sky-roads-point-to-a-lost-city.html.

33. *The Museum of the Frankincense Land: The History Hall*, 108.

34. McBrierty and al-Zubair, 12.

35. Stewart.

36. Isam al-Rawas, in *Oman in Early Islamic History* (Reading: Ithaca Press, 2000), 28, referring to another Arabic source.

37. National Centre for Statistics and Information, Sultanate of Oman, http://www.ncsi.gov.om/.

38. See chapter 5 for governmental initiatives to reduce the country's dependence on guest workers through the strategy of Omanization.

39. The work of Donald and Eloise Bosch in Oman will be discussed in greater detail in chapter 4.

40. Donald Bosch and Eloise Bosch, *The Doctor and the Teacher* (Muscat: Apex, 2000), 41.

41. al-Rawas, 35–36.

42. For insights on the Prophet Muhammad's selection of 'Amr ibn al-'As to represent Islam in Oman, see al-Rawas, 39.

43. Here, I am indebted to al-Rawas, 39–40, for his references to several Arabic sources.

44. Mir Zohair Husain (*Global Islamic Politics* [New York: HarperCollins, 1995], 208) suggests that Ibadhism is "a branch of Shi'a Islam."

45. The title *shaykh*, ordinarily applied to the chief of a tribe, is also used as an honorific title for respected male elders. See John Duke Anthony, *Historical and Cultural Dictionary of the Sultanate of Oman and Emirates of Eastern Arabia* (Metuchen, NJ: Scarecrow Press, 1976), 103.

46. Robert Geran Landen explains that "while in most Muslim countries the title 'sayyid' signifies that its holder is a descendant of the Prophet Muhammad, in Oman it means only that the possessor is a member of the . . . [royal] Al Bu Said family, a lineage with no blood ties to the family of Muhammad" (*Oman Since 1856: Disruptive Modernization in a Traditional Arab Society* [Princeton, NJ: Princeton University Press, 1967], 59, n. 22).

47. Valerie Hoffman, "Ibadi Islam: An Introduction," April 1, 2001, http://islam .uga.edu/ibadis.html.

48. Jeremy Jones, *Negotiating Change: The New Politics of the Middle East* (New York: I. B. Tauris, 2007), 159.

49. The applicability of these principles to Oman's modern foreign policy will be explored at greater length in chapter 6.

50. For a comprehensive overview of Ibadhi theology, including its distinctive teachings and literary traditions, see Valerie J. Hoffmy, *The Essentials of Ibadhi Islam* (Syracuse, NY: Syracuse University Press, 2012).

51. E. Harper Johnson (*Oman: A Pictorial Resuscitation*) visited the Great Mosque of Xi'an, or Qing Shen Si, one of the largest mosques in China's Shaanxi province, dating from 742 CE, Tang dynasty.

52. Samuel M. Zwemer, "Notes on Oman," *National Geographic*, January 1911, 89–98.

53. Ray F. Skinner, *Christians in Oman* (Morden, Surrey: Tower Press, 1996).

54. Throughout the discussion of the prevailing religious ethos in Oman, readers will note, perhaps, the author's limited use of the term "tolerance." Although this term is widely employed in the context of interfaith dialogue and behavior, it has limited utility here because of its negative connotation of reluctant sufferance.

55. "Abrahamic" religions—Judaism, Christianity, and Islam—are bound by their avowed monotheism, espoused first by the prophet Abraham and espoused throughout the following centuries by a long line of prophets, including Jesus, and ending with the revelations received by the "seal of the Prophet" Muhammad (570–632 CE).

56. See chapter 7 for more information on Oman's role in interfaith dialogue.

57. Kaplan, 42.

58. Fredrik Barth, *Sohar: Culture and Society in an Omani Town* (Baltimore, MD: Johns Hopkins University Press, 1983).

59. From McBrierty and al-Zubair, 24, citing X. B. Billecocq, *Oman: Vingt-cinq siècles de récits de voyage: Twenty-five centuries of travel writing* (Paris: Relations Internationales & Culture, 1994), 127.

60. Robert Alston and Stuart Laing, *Unshook till the End of Time: A History of Relations between Britain & Oman 1650–1970* (London: Gilgamesh Publishing, 2012), 12.

61. Bayard Taylor, ed., *Travels in Arabia*, rev. by Thomas Stevens (New York: C. Scribner's Sons, 1893), 41.

62. Ibid., 42.

63. "The institution of the *majlis* is testimony that a degree of democracy exists within the traditional social norms of the communities of Eastern Arabia" (Anthony, 59).

64. Chapter 4 will show how the *shura* concept, which was revered in traditional society, was not only preserved but also enhanced in the political narrative of modern Oman.

65. A *wali* is the equivalent of a provincial governor of a designated district (*wilayah*) in Oman, a tradition going back hundreds of years. Appointed by the ruler, he confers with local *shaykhs* to mediate problems, assess community needs, and assume responsibility for local administration. When required, the *wali* acts as liaison between the central government and his constituents.

66. Philip Hitti, *History of the Arabs* (New York: St. Martin's, 1967), 27.

67. This has become a curious irony of history, considering that, while fashioning the clandestine Sykes-Picot Agreement in 1916, Britain and France excluded this area from their projected post–World War I territorial conquests in the Middle East—a mere twenty-two years before the discovery of vast oil reserves in Eastern Arabia.

68. For an introduction to the tradition of preparing the *shuwa*, see "Omani Shuwa—Eid November 6–7, 2011," YouTube video, 3:33, posted by Antonio Andrade, February 27, 2011, https://www.youtube.com/watch?v=s-p1DDzUCAU.

69. *The Museum of the Frankincense Land: The History Hall*, 57.

70. "Dried Up Aflaj and the Cost of Damage," *Oman Daily Observer*, April 15, 2014, http://main.omanobserver.om/dried-up-aflaj-and-the-cost-of-damage/.

71. Jeremy Jones and Nicholas Ridout, *Oman: Culture and Diplomacy* (Edinburgh: Edinburgh University Press, 2012), 56.

72. Ibid., 57.

CHAPTER 2

1. Traditionally, Omanis whose surnames begin with "Ba" or "Bin" are often descended from the Hadramuti people of what is present-day Yemen.

2. Isam al-Rawas, *Oman in Early Islamic History* (Reading: Ithaca Press, 2000), 29.

3. Vincent McBrierty and Mohammad al-Zubair, *Oman: Ancient Civilization, Modern Nation* (Dublin: Trinity College/Muscat: Bait Al Zubair Foundation, 2004), 17.

4. Robert Kaplan, *Monsoon: The Indian Ocean and the Future of American Power* (New York: Random House, 2010), 49.

5. McBrierty and al-Zubair, 22.

6. Joseph A. Kechichian, *Oman and the World: The Emergence of an Independent Foreign Policy* (Santa Monica, CA: Rand, 1995), 122.

7. Donald Hawley, *Oman*, rev. ed. (London: Stacey International, 2005), 42.

8. Sultan bin Mohammad al-Qasimi, *Deep-Seated Malice*, trans. Gavin Watterson & Basil Hatem (London: Saqi Books, 2006), 36–37.

9. Sultan's Armed Forces Museum, Bayt al-Falaj, Muscat, Oman.

10. McBrierty and al-Zubair, 23.

11. Kechichian, 122.

12. Arabic names reveal a person's relationship with immediate family members as well as his or her ancestry. While customs and usages vary widely in the

Arabic-speaking world, the following naming practices are common. *Ibn* or *bin* (the form used most commonly in Oman) translates as "son of"; in the case of females, the form is *bint*. An individual's given name is followed by the name of his or her father. When further information is provided, such as the tribal or family affiliation, the name is indicated by *al* ("of the") followed by the identity of the tribe or family. Thus, *Nasr bin Murshid al-Ya'rubi* identifies the individual as Nasr (given name), the son of Murshid, of the Ya'rubid tribe.

13. "Imam" is a term laden with many meanings. According to John Duke Anthony, it "originally signified the individual who lead the prayers of Islam and only later acquired the meaning of a religious leader who also headed the Islamic state. During the classical Ibadi Imamate in Eastern Arabia, the Imam was the religious leader of the community . . . as well as the commander-in-chief of the Ibadi army and the head of state. . . . [Eventually] its religious attributes were overshadowed by its secular functions. The [latest] Ibadi dynasty, the Al Bu Said, [have] dropped the title of imam and have ruled as secular leaders only" (*Historical and Cultural Dictionary of the Sultanate of Oman and Emirates of Eastern Arabia* [Metuchen, NJ: Scarecrow Press, 1976], 45).

14. It is common practice to identify a ruler by his or her first, or given name, often preceded by the title, such as, in the case of Oman, *Imam*, *Sultan*, or *Sayyid*.

15. In this case, as well as in some subsequent cases, "Sultan" is a *given name*, popular in eastern Arabia, and is not meant to suggest a title. Traditionally, Omani rulers were known by the title of *Sayyid*. As a title, "sultan" has been in use only since the nineteenth century; it was originally applied to Sayyid Said, who ruled over the apogee of Omani maritime power. By the end of the century, the title "sultan" had gained general acceptance (see Anthony, 107).

16. Kechichian, 121.

17. Ibid., 23.

18. In 1729 the Portuguese attempted but failed to recapture Zanzibar and Muscat, shattering any hope of ever returning to the Arabian Gulf and the Indian Ocean. See Peter Vine and Paula Casey-Vine, eds. *Oman in History* (London: Immel Publishing, 1995), 397–398.

19. Sultan's Armed Forces Museum.

20. Ibid.

21. After holding Gwadar for two hundred years, Oman relinquished its sovereignty to Pakistan in 1958, at a cost of UK£3 million (Kechichian, 229).

22. McBrierty and al-Zubair, 24.

23. Vine and Casey-Vine, 397.

24. See "Indian Ocean in World History" (Sultan Qaboos Cultural Center, Washington, DC, accessed November 23, 2014, www.indianoceanhistory.org), an interactive website focusing on the history, culture, and heritage of the Indian Ocean region.

25. Beatrice Nicolini, *The First Sultan of Zanzibar: Scrambling for Power and Trade in the Nineteenth-Century Indian Ocean* (Princeton, NJ: Markus Wiener Publishers, 2012), xiv.

26. Vine and Casey-Vine, 413.

27. Ibid., 399.

28. Ibid., 404.

29. Ibid., 404.

30. Ibid., 406.

31. Robert Geran Landen, *Oman Since 1856: Disruptive Modernization in a Traditional Arab Society* (Princeton, NJ: Princeton University Press, 1967), 57.

32. Uzi Rabi, *The Emergence of States in a Tribal Society: Oman under Sa'id bin Taymur, 1932–1970* (Brighton, UK: Sussex Academic Press, 2006), 26.

33. Sultan's Armed Forces Museum.

34. The United Arab Emirates, established in 1971, is a federation of seven principalities, including Abu Dhabi, Ajman, Dubai, Ra's al-Khaymah, Sharjah, al-Fujayrah, and Umm al-Qaywayn.

35. *Oman 2012–2013* ([Muscat]: Ministry of Information, Sultanate of Oman, 2012), 40–41. The choice of Oman as a commercial destination was not limited to European powers. In the eighteenth century, US merchant ships were drawn to Oman, such as the *Rambler*, which arrived in Muscat in 1790.

36. "Muscat and Oman," a political designation first applied to this historic land in the eighteenth century, was formally recognized by the Treaty of Seeb in 1920; it reflected a de facto division within the country, with imams ruling over the interior, largely tribal populations, and the sultans of Muscat controlling the coastal regions; it lasted until 1954 when "Oman" was reunited by Sultan Said bin Taymur (Carol J. Riphenburg, *Oman: Political Development in a Changing World* [Westport, CT: Praeger Press, 1998], 40–41).

37. Here, as well, "Sultan" is a *given name* rather that a title for a head of state.

38. "An Agreement Entered into by the Imam of the State of Oman with Captain John Malcolm Bahadoor, Envoy from the Right Honourable the Governor General, Dated the 21st of Shaban 1213 Hegira, or 18th January 1800," *A Collection of Treaties, Engagements, and Sunnuds, Relating to India and Neighbouring Countries*, accessed January 12, 2015, http://archive.org/stream/ collectionoftrea07aitcuoft/collectionoftrea07aitcuoft_djvu.txt.

39. The Wahhabis, referring to themselves as Muwahhidun, are adherents of a fundamentalist variation of Islam, popularized by Muhammad bin 'Abd al-Wahhab, an eighteenth-century religious scholar in central Arabia. This form of Islam is the state religion in the kingdom of Saudi Arabia today and prevails among several tribes in Oman, Qatar, and the United Arab Emirates.

40. Sources differ with respect to the exact year of Said bin Sultan's ascension to power.

41. Nicolini, citing an account written by James Silk Buckingham, a journalist working for the British East India Company. Buckingham, she reports, met with the sultan between 1817 and 1818 and was "clearly overwhelmed and seduced by the personality and charisma" of the prince, whom he described as "one of the principal Sovereigns of the East" (99–100).

42. Kechichian, 31.

43. "The word 'Zanzibar' is of Persian or Arabic origin. The Persians derive the name from Zangh Bar, meaning 'the Negro Coast.' On the other hand the Arabs deduce the name from the Arabic Zayn Z'al Barr, meaning 'Fair is this land'" (Farouk Abdullah al-Barwani, "People and Culture," *Zanzinet Forum*, accessed January 13, 2015, http://www.zanzinet.org/zanzibar/people/people.html).

44. Nicolini, xviii, n. 11.

45. McBrierty and al-Zubair, 30.

46. Beginning with the accession of Said bin Sultan and continuing to this day, each Al Bu Saidi monarch has taken the secular title of "sultan," replacing "imam," with its religious or spiritual connotations.

47. Vine and Casey-Vine, 432.

48. Jeremy Jones and Nicholas Ridout, *Oman: Culture and Diplomacy* (Edinburgh: Edinburgh University Press, 2012), 131.

49. Ibid., 130–131.

50. Ibid., 131.

51. Kaplan, n. 38.

52. The term "Zanzibari" refers to an Omani living in a region extending from Somalia in the north to Mozambique in the south, including the islands of Zanzibar and Lamu, and extending inland as far as Rwanda.

53. Robert W. Harms, Bernard K. Freamon, and David W. Blight, eds., *Indian Ocean Slavery in the Age of Abolition* (New Haven, CT: Yale University Press, 2013), n.p.

54. Landen, 71.

55. Ibid., 71.

56. Kechichian, 243.

57. Landen, 200.

58. Kechichian, 126.

59. It is important to note, though, that despite the perceived degree of British involvement in Oman's affairs, Oman was the only country—whether shaykhdom or emirate—in the Gulf region to remain free of *direct* British control.

60. W. D. Peyton, *Old Oman* (London: Stacey International, 1983), 12.

61. The prohibition of smoking might be viewed as "enlightened" by today's health norms, but it was a serious departure from the customs and culture of the mid-twentieth century.

62. Pauline Searle, *Dawn over Oman*, 3rd ed. (London: Allen & Unwin, 1979), 4.

63. Personal interview with a high-ranking Omani official, December 2013.

64. Sergey Plekhanov, *A Reformer on the Throne: Sultan Qaboos bin Said Al Said* (London: Trident Press, 2004), 23.

65. Robert Alston and Stuart Laing, *Unshook till the End of Time: A History of Relations between Britain & Oman 1650–1970* (London: Gilgamesh Publishing, 2012), 198.

66. Calvin H. Allen and W. Lynn Rigsbee, *Oman under Qaboos: From Coup to Constitution, 1970–1996* (London: Frank Cass Publishers, 2000), 3.

67. Ibid.

68. Landen, 404–405.

69. Ibid., 408.

70. Alston and Laing, 199.

71. Ibid., 189.

72. Landen, 409.

73. J. E. Peterson, *Oman in the Twentieth Century: Political Foundations of an Emerging State* (New York: Barnes & Noble, 1978), 182–184.

74. W. D. Peyton's *Old Oman* provides a wonderful yet balanced description of pre-Renaissance Oman; see especially p. 11.

75. Searle, 20.

76. Matein Khalid, "Oman: Diplomacy and Economics in the Arabian Gulf," *Khaleej Times*, October 10, 2007, http://www.khaleejtimes.com/Display Article New .asp?xfile=data/opinion/2007/October/opinion_October34.xml& section=opinion&col=.

77. Personal interview with an eyewitness in Muscat, 2013.

78. Personal interview with David Bosch, Muscat, December 2013.

79. Christopher Dickey, "The Slow Luxury of Oman," *Newsweek*, May 7, 2007, http://www.newsweek.com/slow-luxury-oman-101441.

80. Allen and Rigsbee, 26.

CHAPTER 3

1. In the interest of clarity regarding nomenclature, Sultan Qaboos is a member of both the *al-Said* family, a dynasty that has ruled Oman since 1744 (and in which power remains centralized), and the larger *Al Bu Said* tribe, which contains several branches whose members use the surname *al-Busaidi*. The *al-Said* family, the pool from which the head of state is chosen, is reported to be small, with fewer than a hundred male members ("Family Tree of Sultan Qaboos," *The Sultanate of Oman*, http://www.sultanaatoman.nl/id27.htm).

2. Sergey Plekhanov, *A Reformer of the Throne: Sultan Qaboos bin Said Al Said* (London: Trident Press, 2004), 10–11.

3. Ibid., 23.

4. Pauline Searle, *Dawn over Oman*, 3rd ed. (London: Allen & Unwin, 1979), 22.

5. Plekhanov, 85.

6. Ibid., 22.

7. Alan Clark, *Diaries* (London: Weidenfeld & Nicholson, 1993).

8. Here it should be pointed out that in the 1960s, freedom of movement was a challenge for everyone in Oman. With only 10 kilometers (6 miles) of paved road, all within the city limits of Muscat and neighboring Mutrah, mobility was severely restricted. For those residing in distant Salalah, some 870 kilometers (540 miles) from the capital, life was simple and opportunities for public engagement were limited.

9. Anne Joyce, "Interview with Sultan Qaboos bin Said Al Said," *Middle East Policy* 3, no. 4 (April 1995): 1.

10. Personal interview with a senior Omani government official, Muscat, October 2012.

11. Robert Alston and Stuart Laing, *Unshook till the End of Time: A History of Relations between Britain & Oman 1650–1970* (London: Gilgamesh Publishing, 2012), 259.

12. Qabus bin Said, *The Royal Speeches of his Majesty Sultan Qaboos bin Said, 1970–2010* ([Muscat]: Ministry of Information, Sultanate of Oman, 2010), 5 (hereafter, *Royal Speeches*).

13. *Royal Speeches*, 377.

14. E. Harper Johnson, *Oman: A Pictorial Resuscitation* (Muscat: Ministry of Information, Sultanate of Oman, 1997), 26.

15. Robert Geran Landen, *Oman Since 1856* (Princeton, NJ: Princeton University Press, 1967), hardly mentions Qaboos, referring only once to the "heir apparent" on the last page after extensively celebrating the achievements of Sultan Said.

16. Donald Bosch and Eloise Bosch, *The Doctor and the Teacher* (Muscat: Apex, 2000), 61.

17. Searle, 55.

18. According to John Duke Anthony, a "*khanjar* is a dagger carried in a silver sheath with a distinctive 45-degree angle. The *khanjar* is carried by nearly all of the tribesmen of Oman" (*Historical and Cultural Dictionary of the Sultanate of Oman and Emirates of Eastern Arabia* [Metuchen, NJ: Scarecrow Press, 1976], 54).

19. Citizenship is so immutable in Oman that it wasn't even forfeited by those who fought against the government in the Dhofar rebellion. In October of 2013, Abdel Aziz Abdul Rahman al-Qadi, reputedly the last of the Communist rebels to have fought in the Dhofari war of the 1960s and 1970s, returned from exile to Oman, at which time Sultan Qaboos restored Omani citizenship to al-Qadi and his family.
20. Plekhanov, 254.
21. *BTI 2012—Oman Country Report* (Gütersloh: Bertelsmann Stiftung, 2012), 17.
22. Joseph A. Kechichian, "A Vision of Oman: State of the Sultanate, Speeches by Qaboos bin Said, 1970–2006," *Middle East Policy* 15, no. 3 (2008): 122.
23. Joyce, 1.
24. J. E. Peterson, *Oman in the Twentieth Century: Political Foundations of an Emerging State* (New York: Barnes & Noble, 1978), 189.
25. Ibid., 194.
26. Established in the 1950s, the Sultan's Armed Forces today includes the Royal Army, the Navy, and other defense forces of the Sultanate of Oman.
27. *Royal Speeches*, 40–41.
28. The birthday of the sultan, called "National Day," is celebrated each year in Oman as a national holiday.
29. *Royal Speeches*, 42.
30. Ibid., 62.
31. Peterson, 96.
32. Ibid., 192, referencing the *Financial Times* (London), January 14, 1977.
33. In a 2013 personal interview, a palace insider told me, "His Majesty has always valued his friendship with the people of Iran; if the people of Iran decide to change their government, that is their business. We do not interfere in the internal affairs of other countries."
34. Plekhanov, 54.
35. Carol J. Riphenburg, *Oman: Political Development in a Changing World* (Westport, CT: Praeger Press, 1998), 91–92.
36. Ibid., 92.
37. *Royal Speeches*, 313.
38. Riphenburg, 92.
39. Apropos of this discussion, it might be instructive to point out that *ijtihad* (interpretation of *shari'ah* law and sacred texts) is encouraged within the Ibadhi tradition.
40. Kechichian, 112.
41. *Royal Speeches*, 369.
42. Robert D. Kaplan, *Monsoon: The Indian Ocean and the Future of American Power* (New York: Random House, 2010), 40.
43. Personal interview with a former US ambassador to Oman, Washington, DC, November 1, 2013.
44. This highly anticipated event, to which my husband and I were invited in 2007, features male and female riders of the Royal Cavalry and Royal Household Troops as well as the Royal Guard. In addition, the program highlights students and equestrians from across the country, performing with precision and grace.
45. *The Rilm* [International Repertory of Music Literature] *Blog*, "The Sultan's Bagpipes," June 24, 2013, http://bibliolore.org/2013/06/24/the-sultans-bagpipes/.

46. In this context, a "tattoo" is a traditional British military exercise consisting of highly staged outdoor performances featuring bagpipes and regimental bands.
47. For a vivid eyewitness account of one such event, see Anne Rasmussen, "AKR in Oman #5: The Sultan's Tattoo," *William and Mary Blogs*, December 9, 2010, http://blogs.wm.edu/2010/12/09/akr-in-oman-5-the-sultan%E2%80%99s -tattoo/.
48. During a visit to the governorate of Dhofar in 2007, my husband and I enjoyed a worship service in Salalah in a fairly modest church building. Filling that sacred space was the power of glorious organ music, the result of one such royal gift, adding immeasurable beauty to the experience.
49. "Muscat Royal Opera House and Royal Oman Symphony Orchestra," *Gulf Art Guide*, accessed November 13, 2014, http://gulfartguide.com/muscat/ muscat-opera-house-oman-symphony-orchestra/#sthash.Eaqsetrd.dpuf.
50. Ibid.
51. *Royal Speeches*, 5.
52. Ibid., 14.
53. Ibid., 13.
54. Ibid., 296.
55. Ibid., 295.
56. Joyce, 1.
57. Johnson, 26.
58. *Royal Speeches*, 5.
59. For a detailed discussion of the history and fabrication of Omani crafts and clothing, see Neil Richardson and Marcia Dorr, *The Craft Heritage of Oman* (London: Motivate Publishing, 2004).
60. Christine Drake, *The Sultanate of Oman* (Seattle, WA: Market House Book Company, 2004), 75.
61. Spud Hilton, "Oman Holiday: Formerly Sealed-Off Sultanate Offers Real Arabian Treasures," *SFGate*, March 30, 2008, http://www.sfgate.com/travel/ article/Oman-Holiday-Formerly-sealed-off-sultanate-3220408.php.
62. Attributed to the economist Herman Franssen, at the fortieth-anniversary celebration of the reign of Sultan Qaboos bin Said, "Oman 2010: 40 Years—Building the Future," conference sponsored by the Sultan Qaboos Cultural Center and the Elliott School of International Affairs at George Washington University, Washington, DC, September 30, 2010.

CHAPTER 4

1. Qabus bin Said, *The Royal Speeches of His Majesty Sultan Qaboos bin Said, 1970–2010* ([Muscat]: Ministry of Information, Sultanate of Oman, 2010), 17 (hereafter, *Royal Speeches*).
2. "Renaissance" (*al-nahda*) is the term most frequently used by Omanis to describe the transformation of their country from the dark ages to modernity since the ascension to power of Qaboos bin Said in 1970.
3. Ibrahim B. Syed, "The Pleasures of Seeking Knowledge," *Islamicity.com*, November 4, 2009, http://www.islamicity.com/articles/Articles.asp?ref=IC0601-2883.
4. Donald Bosch and Eloise Bosch, *The Doctor and the Teacher* (Muscat: Apex, 2000), 34.
5. The historical account that follows is borrowed, in large part, from recollections of Donald and Eloise Bosch, in their invaluable memoir *The Doctor and the Teacher*.

6. Bosch and Bosch, 33.

7. Ibid.

8. The Basic Statute of the State, Ministry of Legal Affairs, Royal Decree 96/101, 1996, Amended by Royal Decree 2011/99, Art. 13, accessed January 14, 2015, http://www.mola.gov.om/eng/basicstatute.aspx (hereafter, Basic Statute).

9. *Oman 2013–2014* ([Muscat]: Ministry of Information, Sultanate of Oman, 2013), 186.

10. "School Vision," *British School Muscat*, accessed January 10, 2015, http://www.britishschoolmuscat.com/vision.php.

11. *Times of Oman*, November 9, 2003.

12. British School Muscat, *Fortieth Anniversary Newsletter*, March 2013, http://www.britishschoolmuscat.com/docs/40th-anniversary/2nd-edition-2.pdf.

13. The International Baccalaureate (IB) Foundation, founded in 1968, offers highly respected programs of rigorous international education that "develop the intellectual, personal, emotional and social skills needed to live, learn and work in a rapidly globalizing world" (http://www.ibo.org).

14. *Higher Education Admission Statistics for the Academic Year 2011/2012* ([Muscat]: Ministry of Higher Education, Sultanate of Oman), 62.

15. Ibid., 36. This figure includes the College of Applied Sciences, the Institutes of Health, Nursing, and Pharmacy, the technical colleges, the Institute of Shari'a Sciences, and Sultan Qaboos University.

16. *Oman 2013–2014*, 190.

17. Ibid., 188.

18. Ibid., 189.

19. Ibid., 191–192.

20. Qaboos bin Said, quoted in Sergey Plekhanov, *A Reformer on the Throne: Sultan Qaboos bin Said Al Said* (London: Trident Press, 2004), 238.

21. *Oman 2014–2015* ([Muscat]: Ministry of Information, Sultanate of Oman, 2014), 180.

22. *Royal Speeches*, 248. Following the announcement in May 2012 that SQU would establish a Department of Political Sciences, the name of the College of Commerce and Economics was changed to the College of Economics and Political Sciences (*Oman 2012–2013* [Muscat: Ministry of Information, Sultanate of Oman, 2012], 183).

23. *Royal Speeches*, 407.

24. *Oman 2013–2014*, 188.

25. *BTI 2014—Oman Country Report* (Gütersloh: Bertelsmann Stiftung, 2014), 14. The Human Development Index is an internationally recognized ranking of countries based on development factors.

26. *Oman 2013–2014*, 182.

27. *Analysis of Oman's 2014 Budget*, KPMG in Oman, January 2, 2014. http://www.kpmg.com/Global/en/IssuesAndInsights/ArticlesPublications/mesa-tax-update/Documents/oman-jan-2014.pdf.

28. "Oman's Education Budget Clocks $3.38 Billion in 2013," *Times of Oman*, July 5, 2014, http://www.timesofoman.com/News/36221/Article-Oman%E2%80%99s-education-budget-clocks-$3%2038-billion-in-2013.

29. Donald A. Luidens, "Legacies of the Mission to Arabia," *Perspectives: A Journal of Reformed Thought* (March/April 2013), http://perspectivesjournal.org/blog/2013/03/01/legacies-of-the-mission-to-arabia/.

30. According to Donald Bosch, "Forty years later this resulted in the construction of Oman's first large surgical hospital, the American Mission Hospital (initially

called the 'Charles H. Knox Memorial Hospital') in Mutrah" (Donald T. Bosch, *The American Mission Hospitals in Oman: 1893–1974; 81 Years* [Mutrah: Mazoon Printing Press, 2001], 9).

31. Ibid., 10.
32. Ibid., 21.
33. Bosch and Bosch, 5–6.
34. Timothy S. Harrison, "Memories of an American Missionary Family in the Persian Gulf," *Joint Archives Quarterly* 18, no. 3 (Fall 2008): 4.
35. In 1930, while traveling by ship to the United States, Harrison's first wife, Regina Rabbe Harrison, was lost at sea. Married to Paul Harrison for fourteen years, she left behind her husband and three children, including Timothy, who became a physician and visited Oman frequently as a visiting professor of surgery. See Donald T. Bosch, 47.
36. Harrison, 4–5.
37. Donald T. Bosch, 51.
38. Wendell Philips, *Qataban and Sheba: Exploring the Ancient Kingdoms on the Biblical Spice Routes of Arabia* (New York: Harcourt, Brace, 1955), 330.
39. Pauline Searle, *Dawn over Oman*, 3rd ed. (London: Allen & Unwin, 1979), 61. Pauline Searle, whose husband worked for Petroleum Development Oman, lived in Oman for nine years, covering the Dhofari rebellion as a journalist for Reuters.
40. The American Mission Hospital was also known as the Charles H. Knox Memorial Hospital and later as al-Rahma Hospital.
41. Donald T. Bosch, 86.
42. Bosch and Bosch, 20.
43. Searle, 62.
44. Donald T. Bosch, 104.
45. Bosch and Bosch, 61.
46. Searle, 61.
47. Donald and Eloise Bosch coauthored their first book, *Seashells of Oman*, in 1982. This was followed by *Seashells of Southern Arabia* in 1989.
48. Donald Bosch died in 2012 at the age of ninety-five. Eloise Bosch, his wife of seventy years, continues to live in the home they shared in Muscat overlooking the Sea of Oman.
49. Bosch and Bosch, 19.
50. *Oman 2014–2015*, 183.
51. Ibid., 184.
52. Andy Sambidge, "Oman Announces $1bn Medical City Project," *Arabian Business*, September 30, 2011, http://www.arabianbusiness.com/oman-announces -1bn-medical-city-project-422927.html.
53. "Oman Medical City Is Taking Its First Step in 2016," *Middle East North Africa Financial Network*, September 22, 2013, http://www.menafn.com/ 1093701325/Oman-Medical-City-is-taking-its-first-step-in-2016?src=MOEN.
54. "International Medical City in Salalah to Boost GCC Medical Tourism," *PR Newswire*, July 17, 2013, http://www.prnewswire.com/news-releases/international -medical-city-in-salalah-to-boost-gcc-medical-tourism-215814121.html.
55. World Health Organization, *Country Cooperation Strategy for WHO and Oman 2010–2015* (Cairo: WHO Regional Office for the Eastern Mediterranean, 2010), 7.
56. *BTI 2014—Oman Country Report*, 2.
57. In 1970, 118 of every 1,000 live newborns died within their first year; by 2011 that number had dropped to 9.5. In 1970, 181 of every 1,000 live newborns

died before the age of five; by 2011 that number had dropped to 11.9 (*Oman 2013–2014*, 197–198).

58. World Health Organization, 20.

59. *Royal Speeches*, 326.

60. The seminal work on this subject is Edward W. Said, *Orientalism* (New York: Random House, 1978). Also, see Suha Sabbagh's, introduction, "The Debate on Arab Women," in her *Arab Women: Between Defiance and Restraint* (New York: Olive Branch Press, 1996).

61. Salma M. al-Lamki, "The Development of Human Resources in the Sultanate of Oman: Omanization and the Role of Women" (paper presented at the Sultan Qaboos Cultural Center, Washington, DC, June 22, 2006), 7.

62. Nouriya Siddani, *Tarih al-mar'ah al-'umaniyyah* (Kuwait: Matabi dar-assiyasah, 1984).

63. Basic Statute, Art. 17.

64. *Women in Oman* ([Muscat]: Ministry of Foreign Affairs, Sultanate of Oman, 2010).

65. *Mahr* represents an Islamic prescription that holds the groom's family responsible to present a gift to the future bride prior to marriage. Called "bride wealth" by anthropologists, this practice is the reverse of the "dowry" concept that was widely observed, until recently, in many Western societies. *Mahr* represents a measure of economic security for the woman because the gift, whether jewelry, land, or other disposable property, continues to belong exclusively to her, for her own personal use, after the wedding. In 2011 the government of Oman announced the creation of a "marriage fund" providing loans to enable persons of limited financial means to marry (Rafiq A. Tschannen, "Oman: Majlis Approves Marriage Fund Panel Proposals," *Muslim Times*, May 29, 2011, http://www.themuslimtimes.org/2011/05/religion/oman-majlis-approves-marriage-fund-panel-proposals).

66. *Oman 2014–2015*, 192.

67. Sunil K. Vaidya, "Oman 'Regional Pioneer for Women's Rights,'" *gulfnews.com*, March 9, 2008, http://gulfnews.com/news/gulf/oman/oman-regional-pioneer-for-women-s-rights-1.90692.

68. Carol J. Riphenburg, *Oman: Political Development in a Changing World*, (Westport, CT: Praeger Press, 1998), 177.

69. Ibid.

70. Stuart W. Holliday, "Oman at the Crossroads: The Development of Popular Participation in Government," *Middle East Insight* 12, no. 1 (November/December 1995): 71.

71. Jeremy Jones, *Negotiating Change: The New Politics of the Middle East* (New York: I. B. Tauris, 2007), 159.

72. Ibid., 160.

73. *Oman 2012–2013*, 144.

74. *Royal Speeches*, 121.

75. Ibid.

76. Aflah H. S. al-Rawahy, "Islamic Concept of Al-Shura and the Omani Model," (lecture, Virginia & Washington, DC, September 2000), 32.

77. *Royal Speeches*, 255.

78. Traditionally, Oman was governed through a *wilayat* (pl.), or "provincial," system, with each *wilayah* (sing.), administered by a *wali* (governor), who functioned as the provincial administrator and protector of law and order. *Walis* serve

as liaisons among the various tribes and between the people and the national authorities.

79. *Royal Speeches*, 255–256.

80. *Oman 2013–2014*, 66.

81. There are sixty-one *wilayat* (districts) in Oman. Each *wilayah* (sing.) is entitled to at least one representative in the *Majlis al-Shura*; those with populations of more than thirty thousand are represented by two members.

82. Mrudu Naik, "Will Women Make It to the Majlis Al Shura This Time?" *Times of Oman*, October 12, 2011, 1.

83. Saleh al-Shaibany, "Disappointing Result for Women," *Times of Oman*, October 17, 2011, 1.

84. *Oman 2012–13*, 63.

85. *Oman 2012–13*, 53.

86. Ibid., 116–117.

87. Interview with high-ranking Omani government employee, April 2015.

88. The title "sayyidah" is the feminine form of "sayyid" (lord), indicating royal rank. Nawwal bint Tariq was the first cousin of Qaboos bin Said, the daughter of his father's brother, Tariq, who served briefly as prime minister of Oman in the 1970s.

89. The inclusion of the representatives of the *Dawla* and *Shura* Councils, as well as the chairman of the Supreme Court, was introduced in the amended provisions to the Basic Law of 2011.

90. Basic Statute, Art. 6.

91. Robert Kaplan, *Monsoon: The Indian Ocean and the Future of American Power* (New York: Random House, 2010), 42.

92. Ibid., 41.

93. Jan Morris, "The Changing Face of an Old Friend," *Financial Times*, November 5, 2005, http://www.ft.com/intl/cms/s/0/241ba1a8-4da2-11da-ba44-0000779e2340.html.

94. Kaplan, 40.

CHAPTER 5

1. *BTI 2014—Oman Country Report* (Gütersloh: Bertelsmann Stiftung, 2014), 14.

2. *Oman 2012–2013* ([Muscat]: Ministry of Information, Sultanate of Oman, 2012), 236.

3. Ivan Kushnir, *Gross Domestic Product (GDP) in Oman*, http://kushnirs.org/macroeconomics/gdp/gdp_oman.html#change; "GDP per Capita (Current US$)," *World Bank*, accessed January 6, 2015, http://data.worldbank.org/indicator/NY.GDP.PCAP.CD.

4. Based on data released by the Ministry of National Economy in 2013, oil and gas revenues accounted for almost 84 percent of total government revenues, or slightly more than 40 percent of Oman's Gross Domestic Product; *Oman 2013–2014* ([Muscat]: Ministry of Information, 2013), 250.

5. International Monetary Fund (IMF) estimates put Oman's GDP growth at 6 percent, on average, during the first decade of the twenty-first century. See Graeme Buckley and Gary Rynhart, *The Sultanate of Oman, The Enabling Environment for Sustainable Enterprises: An "EESE" Assessment*, Employment Report No. 14 (Geneva: International Labour Office, 2011), 14.

6. Lois M. Critchfield, *Oman Emerges: An American Company in an Ancient Kingdom* (Vista, CA: Selwa Press, 2010), 6.

7. US Energy Information Center, *Oman*, updated December 5, 2014, http://www.eia.gov/countries/cab.cfm?fips=MU.

8. *Petroleum Development Oman*, http://www.pdo.co.om/.

9. 2013 figures from the Oman Ministry of Oil and Gas.

10. Average daily oil production rose from 885,000 barrels in 2011 to 918,000 barrels in 2012, while revenues from 2011 to 2012 increased by almost 34 percent; *Oman 2013–2014* ([Muscat]: Ministry of Information, 2013), 250–251.

11. US Central Intelligence Agency, "Oman," *The World Factbook*, updated June 22, 2014, https://www.cia.gov/library/publications/the-world-factbook/geos/mu.html.

12. Ibid.

13. Daniel Wagner and Giorgio Cafiero, "Oman Has Its Cake and Eats It Too—for Now," *Real Clear World*, July 29, 2013, accessed December 8, 2014, http://www.realclearworld.com/articles/2013/07/29/oman_has_its_cake_and_eats_it_too_--_for_now_105348.html.

14. "More Than Half of GCC Population Under Age 25," *Arab News*, July 17, 2012, http://www.arabnews.com/saudi-arabia/more-half-gcc-population-under-age-25.

15. US Central Intelligence Agency.

16. Buckley and Rynhart, 51.

17. Hydrocarbon extraction is largely a mechanized, non-labor-intensive undertaking that does not satisfy large-scale demands for employment.

18. Qabus bin Said, *The Royal Speeches of his Majesty Sultan Qaboos bin Said, 1970–2010* ([Muscat]: Ministry of Information, Sultanate of Oman, 2010), 240 (hereafter, *Royal Speeches*).

19. "Oman's Population Passes Landmark Figure," *Times of Oman*, April 23, 2014, http://www.timesofoman.com/News/32830/Article-Oman%E2%80%99s-population-passes-landmark-figure.

20. Herman Franssen, Remarks at "Oman 2010: 40 Years—Building the Future," Conference sponsored by the Sultan Qaboos Cultural Center and the Elliott School of International Affairs at George Washington University, Washington, DC, September 30, 2010.

21. Christopher Kelly, "Oman: Doing Localisation Right," *ArabianOilandGas.com*, June 1, 2014, http://www.arabianoilandgas.com/article-12539-oman-doing-localisation-right/2/.

22. Faizul Haque, "Power, Water Sector Targets Total Omanisation by 2019," *Times of Oman*, September 16, 2014, http://www.timesofoman.com/News/39942/Article-Power-water-sector-targets-total-Omanisation-by-2019.

23. *Royal Speeches*, 199.

24. Ibid., 335.

25. Ibid., 487.

26. *BTI 2014—Oman Country Report*, 20; Saleh al-Shaibany, "Oman Raises Minimum Wage to Avert Future Protests," *Al Arabiya News*, February 9, 2013, http://www.alarabiya.net/articles/2013/02/09/265333.html.

27. "Oman Inflation Rate: 2005–2014," *Trading Economics*, accessed December 8, 2014, http://www.tradingeconomics.com/oman/inflation-cpi.

28. "Inflation in Oman Lowest in GCC," *Times of Oman*, July 12, 2014, http://www.timesofoman.com/news/36538/Article-Inflation-in-Oman-lowest-in-the-GCC.

29. The inflation rate in Oman is reported by the National Center for Statistics Information–Oman. From 2005 to 2014, Oman's inflation rate averaged 4.8 percent, ranging from a high of 14.5 percent in June 2008 to a low of 0.3 percent in October 2013 ("Oman Inflation Rate: 2005–2014").

30. *Oman 2014–2015* ([Muscat]: Ministry of Information, Sultanate of Oman, 2014), 244.

31. Buckley and Rynhart.

32. Greta Holtz, "Reaping Benefits of US-Oman Trade Pact," Special to the *Times of Oman*, December 1, 2013, http://www.timesofoman.com/News/Article-26421.aspx.

33. Greta C. Holtz, "Building on the FTA," *Oman: A Nation on the Move, 1970–2013* (Muscat: United Press and Publishing, 2013), 32, accessed January 15, 2015, http://www.readwhere.com/read/190213/A-Nation-on-the-Move/Oman-A-Nation-On-The-Move-1970-2013#page/32/2; US Embassy in the Sultanate of Oman, "US-Oman FTA: A Win for Bilateral Trade," *Times of Oman*, July 4, 2013, http://www.timesofoman.com/Columns/1220/Article-US-Oman-FTA-A-win-for-bilateral-trade.

34. *Oman 2014–2015*, 246.

35. "Arable land (% of land area) in Oman," *Trading Economics*, accessed January 11, 2015, http://ieconomics.com/arable-land--oman.

36. Faisal Mohammed Naim, "How 'Bout a Date? Oman's Most Favorite Fruit," *Times of Oman*, July 11, 2014, http://www.timesofoman.com/news/36492/Article-How-%E2%80%99bout-a-Date?-Omans-most-favourite-fruit.

37. The principle behind a "recharge dam" is that by stopping water and retaining it behind a manmade structure, available water will be forced into existing aquifers, increasing the supply in existing wells and/or, in the case of Oman, within the *falaj* system. The remaining aboveground water resulting from this construction is beneficial for wildlife and, in particular, endangered species.

38. "Overview on Desalinated Water in the Sultanate of Oman," Oman Power and Water Procurement Co. (SAOC), accessed December 8, 2014, http://www.medrc.org/home/research/Overview.pdf.

39. A. E. James, "Water Desalination Capacity in Oman Set for 66% Jump," *Times of Oman*, March 1, 2014, http://www.timesofoman.com/News/Article-30479.aspx.

40. *Oman 2012–2013*, 258.

41. Ibid., 276.

42. *Royal Speeches*, 192 (National Day, November 18, 1987).

43. *Oman 2012–2013*, 261.

44. Ibid., 296.

45. *Oman 2014–2015*, 302.

46. *Oman 2013–2014*, 302–303.

47. Robert Kaplan, *Monsoon: The Indian Ocean and the Future of American Power* (New York: Random House, 2010), 46.

48. Conrad Prabhu, "US Firm Wins Duqm City Master-Plan Contract," *Oman Daily Observer*, October 17, 2011, 21.

49. "Emerging Oman," *Times of Oman*, July 23, 2013, http://www.timesofoman .com/News/Article-20243.aspx.

50. Ibid.

51. US Central Intelligence Agency.

52. A. E. James, "Full Steam Ahead for Oman Railway," *Times of Oman*, February 6, 2014, http://www.timesofoman.com/News/Article-29401.aspx.

53. Pico Iyer, "Arabian Heights," *Financial Times*, September 21, 2012, http://www.ft.com/cms/s/2/307fbe88-fd9b-11e1-8fc3-00144feabdc0.html.

54. *Airport History—Muscat Airport*, Oman Airports Management Company, accessed December 11, 2014, https://www.omanairports.co.om/Page.aspx ?MID=38&PGID=21.

55. "Muscat International Airport, Oman," *Airport-technology.com*, accessed January 12, 2015, http://www.airport-technology.com/projects/muscat-airport/.

56. James, 306; *2013 ACI World Airport Traffic Report* (Airports Council International, 2013).

57. *Oman 2013–2014*, 306–307.

58. US Energy Information Administration; "Electricity Production (kWh)," *World Bank*, accessed December 15, 2014, http://data.worldbank.org /indicator/EG.ELC.PROD.KH?order=wbapi_data_value_2011+wbapi_data _value&sort=desc.

59. A. E. James, "Oman to Set Up Four New Solar Power Pilot Projects," *Times of Oman*, May 20, 2015, http://www.timesofoman.com/News/51972/Article -Oman-to-set-up-four-new-solar-power-pilot-projects.

60. US Central Intelligence Agency.

61. "World Development Indicators: The Information Society," Table 5.12, *World Bank*, http://wdi.worldbank.org/table/5.12.

62. *Vision of Humanity*, Institute for Economics and Peace, accessed January 17, 2015, http://www.visionofhumanity.org/#page/indexes/global-peace-index/ 2011/MRT,OMN/OVER.

63. *Oman 2014 Crime and Safety Report*, United States Department of State Bureau of Diplomatic Security, Overseas Security Advisory Council, February 20, 2014, https://www.osac.gov/pages/ContentReportDetails.aspx?cid=15191.

64. The sites include Nizwa Falaj Daris, the largest example of Oman's ancient irrigation system; the Land of Frankincense, a group of archaeological sites in the governorate of Dhofar; the cluster of Bronze Age archaeological sites at Bat, al-Khutm, and al-'Ayn; and the Bahla Fort.

65. Iyer.

66. Spud Hilton, "Oman Holiday: Formerly Sealed-Off Sultanate Offers Real Arabian Treasures," *SFGate*, March 30, 2008, http://www.sfgate.com/travel/ article/Oman-Holiday-Formerly-sealed-off-sultanate-3220408.php.

67. Essa bin Mohammed al-Zedjali, "Tangible Facts Behind Choice of Muscat as Arab Tourism Capital," *Times of Oman*, October 18, 2011, http://www .gulfinthemedia.com/index.php?m=opinions&id=577331&lim=&lang=en&tbl post=2011_10.

68. Sarah Khan, "20. Oman," in "52 Places to Go in 2015," *New York Times*, updated May 29, 2015, http://www.nytimes.com/interactive/2015/01/11/ travel/52-places-to-go-in-2015.html?_r=0.

69. "The original links courses, which are mostly found in the U.K., were situated in the thin strip of sand, grass and dunes that lay between the sea and agricultural land. The courses 'linked' them together. Links style courses will have undulating

fairways, sand dunes, deep bunkers and few (if any) trees" ("What Are the Different Types of Golf Courses," *Golflink*, accessed January 16, 2015, http://www .golflink.com/list_427_what-different-types-golf-courses.html).

70. Hilton.

71. *Royal Speeches*, 107–108 (November 18, 1980).

72. Frank Coles, "Making Waves," *Business Traveler Middle East*, March/April 2006, 23.

73. *Royal Speeches*, 280 (Speech in Brazil on the occasion of the United Nations Conference on Environment and Protection, June 2, 1992).

74. *Royal Speeches*, 168 (National Day Address, 1985).

75. *Royal Speeches*, 274 (December 21, 1991).

76. *Omani Sites on the World Heritage List*, Office of the Adviser to His Majesty the Sultan for Cultural Affairs, accessed December 14, 2014, http://omanwhs.gov .om/.

77. J. E. Peterson, *Oman's Insurgencies: The Sultanate's Struggle for Supremacy* (London: Saqi Books, 2008).

78. *Oman 2012–2013*, 269.

79. Peter Vine and Paula Casey-Vine, eds. *Oman in History* (London: Immel Publishing, 1995), 413.

80. For descriptions of petroglyphs in other regions of Oman, Pauline Searle references Keith Preston, "An Introduction to the Anthropomorphic Content of the Rock Art of Jebel Akhdar," *Journal of Oman Studies* 2 (1976): 17–38.

81. Walter Dinteman, *Forts of Oman* (Dubai: Motivate Publishing, 1993), 124.

82. "Preface," *The Sultan Qaboos Grand Mosque* (Muscat: Apex Publishing, 2001). The poignancy of this affirmation is inescapable, coming as it did only four months before the tragic events of September 11, 2001, set in motion a global firestorm against a perceived "monolithic Islam" at the center of an ominous civilizational clash.

83. Ibid., 45.

84. Kaplan, 70.

85. *Royal Speeches*, 108.

86. Ibid., 286.

87. Ibid., 185.

88. *Oman 2013–2014*, 59.

CHAPTER 6

1. Hermann F. Eilts, *A Friendship Two Centuries Old: The United States and the Sultanate of Oman* (Washington, DC: Sultan Qaboos Cultural Center, Middle East Institute, 1990, 4.

2. Edmund Roberts (1784–1836) was designated "first merchant consul" and "special agent" of the United States (1832–34), commissioned to negotiate treaties with Siam, Muscat, and Cochin, China.

3. This document was superseded by the Treaty of Amity, Economic Relations, and Consular Rights, signed at Salalah (Dhofar) on December 20, 1958.

4. See Beatrice Nicolini, *The First Sultan of Zanzibar: Scrambling for Power and Trade in the Nineteenth-Century Indian Ocean* (Princeton, NJ: Markus Wiener Publishers, 2012), 141; *Treaty of Amity and Commerce: The United States and Muscat, 21 September, 1933. U.S. Treaty Series*, n. 247, reproduced in J. C.

Hurewitz, *Diplomacy in the Near and Middle East: A Documentary Record, 1535–1956*, vol. 1 (Princeton, NJ: Van Nostrand, 1956), 108.

5. Nicolini, 141. In the eighteenth and nineteenth centuries, *gum copal*, a tree resin, was a valuable ingredient in the production of high-quality wood varnish, used in the manufacture of furniture, horse carriages, and later, train carriages. See Ralph Mayer, *The Artist's Handbook of Materials and Techniques* (New York: Viking, 1976) 194–96.

6. Cited in E. Harper Johnson, *Oman, A Pictorial Resuscitation* (Muscat: Ministry of Information, Sultanate of Oman, 1997), 116.

7. Samuel H. Williamson, "Seven Ways to Compute the Relative Value of a U.S. Dollar Amount, 1774 to Present," *MeasuringWorth*, 2015, http://www .measuringworth.com/ppowerus/.

8. Accession 18815, Department of Anthropology, National Museum of Natural History, Smithsonian Institution, Washington, DC. The link between the Sultanate of Oman and the Smithsonian Institution is deep. In 2005 the Smithsonian's thirty-ninth Folklife Festival, celebrated annually on the National Mall in Washington, DC, featured Oman, the only Arab country ever to have been so honored at this prestigious venue.

9. Johnson, 120.

10. Eilts, 16–17.

11. Jeremy Jones and Nicholas Ridout, *Oman, Culture and Diplomacy* (Edinburgh: Edinburgh University Press, 2012), 211.

12. According to the Office of the United States Trade Representative, "The United States–Oman FTA . . . builds on existing FTAs to promote economic reform and openness. Implementation of the obligations contained in the comprehensive agreement will generate export opportunities for U.S. goods and services providers, solidify Oman's trade and investment liberalization, and strengthen intellectual property rights protection and enforcement" ("Oman Free Trade Agreement," Free Trade Agreements, Office of the United States Trade Representative, accessed January 17, 2015, http://www.ustr.gov/trade-agreements/ free-trade-agreements/oman-fta).

13. Daniel Wagner and Giorgio Cafiero, "Oman Has Its Cake and Eats It Too—for Now," *Real Clear World*, July 29, 2013, accessed December 8, 2014, http:// www.realclearworld.com/articles/2013/07/29/oman_has_its_cake_and_eats _it_too_--_for_now_105348.html.

14. "Kerry Meets Ailing Oman Sultan in Germany," *Agence France Presse*, January 11, 2015, http://www.france24.com/en/20150110-kerry-meets-ailing-oman -sultan-germany/.

15. Kenneth Katzman, "Oman: Reform, Security, and U.S. Policy," *Congressional Research Service*, March 4, 2008, 2.

16. The various branches that comprise the Sultan's Armed Forces are the Royal Army, Royal Air Force, Royal Navy, Royal Guard, and Royal Oman Police.

17. It is interesting to ponder what role Qaboos's extensive interlude of study and reflection in Salalah as a young man in his twenties might have played in shaping his vision for the country's future.

18. Qabus bin Said, *The Royal Speeches of his Majesty Sultan Qaboos bin Said, 1970–2010* ([Muscat]: Ministry of Information, Sultanate of Oman, 2010), 395 (hereafter, *Royal Speeches*).

19. Matein Khalid, "Oman: Diplomacy and Economics in the Arabian Gulf," *Khaleej Times*, October 10, 2007, http://www.khaleejtimes.com/DisplayArticleNew

.asp?xfile=data/opinion/2007/October/opinion_October34.xml&section=opinion&col=.

20. *Royal Speeches*, 488.
21. Personal interview with an Omani government official, February 2014. In response to a woman who asked him why he used sympathetic language in his speeches when he described Southern rebels, Lincoln is reported to have said, "Do I not destroy my enemies when I make them my friends?" In 1837 the same words were also attributed to the Holy Roman Emperor Sigismund of Luxemburg (1368–1437) by Joseph Belcher and Jost Elfers in *The Family Magazine* (London: Thomas Ward and Co., 1837), 123.
22. Personal off-the-record interview with a close advisor to Sultan Qaboos bin Said.
23. *Royal Speeches*, 467.
24. Jeffrey A. Lefebvre, "Oman's Foreign Policy in the Twenty-First Century," *Journal of the Middle East Policy Council* 17, no. 1 (Spring 2010), http://mepc.org/journal/middle-east-policy-archives/omans-foreign-policy-twenty-first-century?print.
25. Hanna Kozlowska, "Who Is the Shadowy Sultan That Shepherded the Nuclear Deal with Iran?" *Foreign Policy*, November 26, 2013, http://foreignpolicy.com/2013/11/26/who-is-the-shadowy-sultan-that-shepherded-the-nuclear-deal-with-iran/.
26. Joseph A. Kechichian, *Oman and the World: The Emergence of an Independent Foreign Policy* (Santa Monica, CA: Rand, 1995), 158.
27. *Royal Speeches*, 71–72.
28. Ibid., 92.
29. Ibid.
30. Lefebvre. Lefebvre explains that the Arab change of heart was precipitated by Arab fears of Iran's success following a 1982 offensive deep into Iraqi territory during the eight-year war between the two countries.
31. *Royal Speeches*, 144.
32. In the year 2000, in the wake of public demonstrations stemming from the second Palestinian *intifada*, Oman closed the Israeli trade office in Muscat and the Omani trade office in Israel.
33. From the mission statement, Middle East Desalination Research Center, http://www.medrc.org/.
34. Ebby Chacko George, "Oman Not to Join GCC Monetary Union," *Oman Daily Observer*, January 8, 2007.
35. This title contains the words "responsible for" because Sultan Qaboos is in actuality the minister of foreign affairs for Oman.
36. "Oman against Gulf States Union," *Oman Daily Observer*, December 8, 2013.
37. Personal interview with a high-ranking Omani official, December 2013.
38. Personal interview with a US diplomat, November 2013.
39. "Iran Hails Its Strong Ties with Sultanate," *Times of Oman*, December 7, 2013, 1.
40. Judith Miller, "The View from the Gulf: America's Quiet Go-Between Speaks," Interview with Sultan Qaboos bin Said, January 31, 2012, *Fox News*, http://www.foxnews.com/world/2012/01/31/view-from-gulf-americas-quiet-go-between-speaks/.
41. Ibid.
42. According to the US Energy Information Administration, approximately seventeen million barrels per day were shipped through the Strait of Hormuz in 2013. See US Energy Information Administration, *World Oil Transit Chokepoints*,

last modified November 10, 2014, http://www.eia.gov/beta/international/regions-topics.cfm?RegionTopicID=WOTC.

43. Sigurd Neubauer, "Oman's Neutral Approach to Maritime Security," *Middle East Institute*, June 18, 2013, http://www.mei.edu/content/omans-neutral-approach-maritime-security.

44. Ibid.

45. Wagner and Cafiero.

46. Lefebvre.

47. Kozlowska.

48. "Oman's Sultan Qaboos in Tehran for Energy, Economy Talks," *Agence France-Presse*, August 25, 2013, http://www.globalpost.com/dispatch/news/afp/130825/omans-sultan-qaboos-tehran-energy-economy-talks.

49. Ibid.

50. Jay Solomon and Carol E. Lee, "U.S.-Iran Thaw Grew from Years of Behind-the-Scenes Talks," *Wall Street Journal*, November 7, 2013, http://www.wsj.com/articles/SB10001424052702303309504579181710805094376.

51. Kozlowska.

52. Marc J. O'Reilly, "*Omanibalancing*: Oman Confronts an Uncertain Future," *Middle East Journal* 52, no. 1 (Winter 1992): 70–84.

Chapter 7

1. Personal interview with high-level Omani governmental official, December 2013.

2. A hypermarket is a combination grocery store and department store, similar to a Wal-Mart Supercenter in the United States.

3. James Worrall, "Oman: The 'Forgotten' Corner of the Arab Spring," *Middle East Policy* 19, no. 3 (Fall 2012), http://www.mepc.org/journal/middle-east-policy-archives/oman-forgotten-corner-arab-spring?print.

4. Not to be confused with the sultan's cabinet or the Council of Oman, the Diwan of the Royal Court is an advisory council that also serves as a liaison between the sultan and the people. The Diwan "has slowly become a kind of super-ministry above all the other Cabinet departments" (Marc Valeri, *Oman: Politics and Society in the Qaboos State* [New York: Oxford University Press, 2013], 180).

5. This scenario underscores the efficacy of the "top-down" ruling style of the newer generation of leaders in the Gulf region, which enables reforms to be initiated from above. Although disparaged in Western, industrialized societies, this form of decision making serves to accelerate the implementation of national projects and reforms, unencumbered by the delays, logjams, and stalemates implicit in many Western, "democratic" legislative systems. It is important to add that the venerable tradition of *shura* (consultation) is a fundamental element in all such decisions. See Jeremy Jones, *Negotiating Change: The New Politics of the Middle East* (New York: I. B. Tauris, 2007).

6. Worrall, 6/14. In reference to this, Worrall cites Shaddad al-Musalmy, "Salalah Protesters Face Dilemma Over Call to End Protests," *Muscat Daily*, April 2, 2011, http://www.muscatdaily.com/Archive/Stories-Files/Salalah-protesters-face-dilemma-over-call-to-end-protests.

7. Worrall.

8. Saleh al-Shaibany, "Oman Raises Minimum Wage to Avert Future Protests," *Al Arabiya News*, February 9, 2013, http://www.alarabiya.net/articles/2013/02/09/265333.html.

9. Ibid.

10. Ibid.

11. Hoda Rashad, Magued Osman, and Farzaneh Roudi-Fahimi, *Marriage in the Arab World* (Washington, DC: Population Reference Bureau, 2005), http://www.prb.org/pdf05/marriageinarabworld_eng.pdf.

12. Qabus bin Said, *The Royal Speeches of his Majesty Sultan Qaboos bin Said, 1970–2010* ([Muscat]: Ministry of Information, Sultanate of Oman, 2010), 68 (hereafter, *Royal Speeches*).

13. *Royal Speeches*, 128.

14. Ibid., 140. This excerpt is taken from Sultan Qaboos's address to the nation on November 18, 1983, inaugurating a year dedicated to Omani youth.

15. Ibid., 185.

16. Ibid., 300.

17. Mona al-Munajjed and Karim Sabbagh, *Youth in GCC Countries: Meeting the Challenge* (Booz and Co., 2011), 27.

18. Oman has a Ministry of Education as well as a Ministry of Higher Education, both currently headed by women.

19. *Royal Speeches*, 332.

20. *Oman 2013–2014* ([Muscat]: Ministry of Information, Sultanate of Oman, 2013), 268.

21. Ibid., 59.

22. "Al Rafd Fund Board Reviews Financing Procedures," *Oman Daily Observer*, December 3, 2014, http://www.gulfinthemedia.com/index.php?m=economics&id=728369&lim=&lang=en&tblpost=2014_12.

23. See "Qaboos bin Said Condemns Reckless, High-Speed Driving," YouTube video, 5:56, posted by Salim and Salimah, Safe and Sound, May 9, 2010, https://www.youtube.com/watch?v=ArHvTT4oyro.

24. Siham Gaber Farag, Ibrahim H. Hashim, Saad A. El-Hamrawy, "Analysis and Assessment of Accident Characteristics: Case Study of Dhofar Governorate, Sultanate of Oman," *International Journal of Traffic and Transportation Engineering* 3, no. 4 (2014): 189, http://article.sapub.org/10.5923.j.ijtte.20140304.03.html; *Global Status Report on Road Safety, Time for Action* (Geneva: World Health Organization, 2009).

25. Hamed bin Hashel al-Qareeni, "Traffic Safety Institute Systematic Knowledge to Enhance Road Safety," Sultanate of Oman, Royal Oman Police, April 26, 2015, http://www.rop.gov.om/english/articledetails.asp?articleid=24.

26. "Road Safety Research Program," *The Research Council*, March 30, 2013, https://home.trc.gov.om/tabid/314/language/en-US/Default.aspx.

27. "Safety First: Tell Us Your Story (English Subtitles)," Google+ video, 1:53, from the nationwide campaign by Safety First, posted by Hassan al-Shouli, June 10, 2012, https://plus.google.com/+HassanAlShouli/posts/bcMZ3AvDR98.

28. "Road Safety Campaign Goes Online," *Times of Oman*, June 16, 2012, http://www.thefreelibrary.com/Road+safety+campaign+goes+online+conversation+with+Omani+youth.-a0293263220.

29. *Global Status Report on Road Safety 2013: Supporting a Decade of Action* (Geneva: World Health Organization, 2013), 173.

30. Fahad al-Ghadani, "Multiple Fines on Drivers to Help Curb Indiscipline in Oman," *Times of Oman*, October 18, 2014, http://www.timesofoman.com/News/41431/Article-Multiple-fines-on-drivers-to-help-curb-indiscipline-in-Oman.

31. *Oman, 2014–2015* ([Muscat]: Ministry of Information, Sultanate of Oman, 2014), 161.

32. "Looming Danger: Public Health is Endangered by Our Lifestyles and Eating Habits," *Tawasul* [Academic bulletin published by Deanship of Research/ Sultan Qaboos University in cooperation with Oman News Agency, Muscat] no. 11 (February 2014): 12.

33. *Royal Speeches*, 78.

34. For a comprehensive analysis of the meaning of "Islamism," including its many manifestations throughout history as well as its applicability in the twenty-first century, see Mehdi Mozaffari, "What is Islamism? History and Definition of a Concept," *Totalitarian Movement and Political Religions* 8, no. 1 (March 2007): 17–33.

35. *Royal Speeches*, 129.

36. Ibid., 313.

37. Ibid.

38. *Oman 2013–2014*, 97–98.

39. Ibid., 96–97.

40. *International Religious Freedom Report for 2013*, United States Department of State, Bureau of Democracy, Human Rights, and Labor, http://www.state.gov/documents/organization/222519.pdf.

41. "Oman to Go Ahead in Promoting Religious Tolerance, Foreign Ties," *Oman Daily Observer*, February 5, 2014, 4.

42. Ibid.

43. George Popp, "Letter of Introduction," *Religious Tolerance: Islam in the Sultanate of Oman*, http://www.islam-in-oman.com/en/organization/introduction-tolerance-oman/.

Bibliography

2013 ACI World Airport Traffic Report. [Montreal:] Airports Council International, 2013.

Agence France Presse. "Kerry Meets Ailing Oman Sultan in Germany." January 11, 2015. http://www.france24.com/en/20150110-kerry-meets-ailing-oman-sultan -germany/.

———. "Oman's Sultan Qaboos in Tehran for Energy, Economy Talks." August 25, 2013. http://www.globalpost.com/dispatch/news/afp/130825/om ans-sultan -qaboos-tehran-energy-economy-talks.

"Agriculture in the Sultanate of Oman." *Nizwa.net.* http://www.nizwa.net/agr/ agriculture.html.

"An Agreement Entered into by the Imam of the State of Oman with Captain John Malcolm Bahadoor, Envoy from the Right Honourable the Governor General, Dated the 21st of Shaban 1213 Hegira, or 18th January 1800." *A Collection of Treaties, Engagements, and Sunnuds, Relating to India and Neigh- bouring Countries.* http://archive.org/stream/collectionoftrea07aitcuoft/ collectionoftrea07aitcuoft_djvu.txt.

Ahmed, Leila. *Women and Gender in Islam.* New Haven, CT: Yale University Press, 1992.

Airport History—Muscat Airport. Oman Airports Management Company. Accessed December 11, 2014. https://www.omanairports.co.om/Page.aspx?MID=38& PGID=21.

Allen, Calvin H., and W. Lynn Rigsbee. *Oman under Qaboos: From Coup to Constitu- tion, 1970–1996.* London: Frank Cass Publishers, 2000.

Allen, Rory Patrick. *Oman under Arabian Skies.* Cambridge: Vanguard Press, 2010.

Alston, Robert, and Stuart Laing. *Unshook till the End of Time: A History of Relations between Britain & Oman 1650–1970.* London: Gilgamesh Publishing, 2012.

Analysis of Oman's 2014 Budget. KPMG in Oman, January 2, 2014. http://www .kpmg.com/Global/en/IssuesAndInsights/ArticlesPublications/mesa-tax -update/Documents/oman-jan-2014.pdf.

Anthony, John Duke. *Historical and Cultural Dictionary of the Sultanate of Oman and the Emirates of Eastern Arabia.* With contributions from John Peterson and Donald Sean Abelson. Metuchen, NJ: Scarecrow Press, 1976.

Arab Media Outlook: 2011–2015. Dubai: Dubai Press Club, 2012.

"Arable land (% of land area) in Oman," *Trading Economics,* accessed January 11, 2015, http://ieconomics.com/arable-land--oman.

Arab News. "More Than Half of GCC Population under Age 25." July 17, 2012. http://www.arabnews.com/saudi-arabia/more-half-gcc-populations-under-age-25.

Barrault, Michèle. *Regards, Oman.* Translated by Nadia Fairbrother. [France]: Edi- tions Michel Hetier, 2010.

Barth, Fredrik. *Sohar: Culture and Society in an Omani Town.* Baltimore, MD: Johns Hopkins University Press, 1983.

al-Barwani, Farouk Abdullah. "People and Culture." *Zanzinet Forum.* Accessed January 13, 2015, http://www.zanzinet.org/zanzibar/people/people.html.

Beauty Has an Address—Oman. Sultanate of Oman Tourism Website. Accessed January 17, 2015. http://www.omantourism.gov.om/wps/portal/mot/tourism/oman/home.

Bertelsmann Stiftung. *BTI 2012—Oman Country Report.* Gütersloh: Bertelsmann Stiftung, 2012.

———. *BTI 2014—Oman Country Report.* Gütersloh: Bertelsmann Stiftung, 2014.

Billecocq, X. B. *Oman: Vingt-cinq siècles de récits de voyage: Twenty-five centuries of travel writing.* Paris: Relations Internationales & Culture, 1994.

Bosch, Donald, and Eloise Bosch. *The Doctor and the Teacher.* Muscat: Apex, 2000.

Bosch, Donald T. *The American Mission Hospitals in Oman: 1893–1974; 81 Years.* Mutrah: Mazoon Printing Press, 2001.

———. *Collectible Eastern Arabian Seashells.* Muscat: Mazoon Printing, n.d.

Bouji, Anne. *This is Oman.* Rev. ed. Muscat: Al Roya Press, 2011.

Buckley, Graeme, and Gary Rynhart. *The Sultanate of Oman, the Enabling Environment for Sustainable Enterprises: An "EESE" Assessment.* Employment Report No. 14. Geneva: International Labour Office, 2011.

al-Busaidi, Mubarek. "Life in the Renaissance." Speech delivered at Sultan Qaboos Cultural Center. Washington, DC, June 29, 2006.

Clapp, Nicholas. *The Road to Ubar: Finding the Atlantis of the Sands.* 1998. London: Souvenir Press, 2000.

Clark, Alan. *Diaries.* London: Weidenfeld & Nicholson, 1993.

Coles, Frank. "Making Waves." *Business Traveler Middle East,* March/April 2006.

Critchfield, Lois M. *Oman Emerges: An American Company in an Ancient Kingdom.* Vista, CA: Selwa Press, 2010.

Dickey, Christopher. "The Slow Luxury of Oman." *Newsweek,* May 7, 2007. http://www.newsweek.com/slow-luxury-oman-101441.

Damluji, Salma Samar. *The Architecture of Oman.* Reading, UK: Garnet Publishing, 1998.

Dinteman, Walter. *Forts of Oman.* Dubai: Motivate Publishing, 1993.

Drake, Christine. *The Sultanate of Oman.* Seattle, WA: Market House Book Company, 2004.

Dresch, Paul, and James P. Piscatori. *Monarchies and Nations: Globalisation and Identity in the Arab States of the Gulf.* London: I. B. Tauris, 2005.

Eakin, Hugh. "In the Heart of Mysterious Oman." *New York Review of Books,* August 14, 2014.

Education in Oman: The Drive for Quality. Ministry of Education, Sultanate of Oman, and the World Bank, 2013. http://www-wds.worldbank.org/external/default/WDSContentServer/WDSP/IB/2013/03/04/000356161_20130304124223/Rendered/PDF/757190ESW0v20W0ector0Report0English.pdf.

Eickelman, Christine. *Women and Community in Oman.* New York: New York University Press, 1984.

Eickelman, Dale F., and James Piscatori. *Muslim Politics.* 2nd ed. Princeton, NJ: Princeton University Press, 2004.

Eilts, Hermann F. *A Friendship Two Centuries Old: The United States and the Sultanate of Oman.* Washington DC: Sultan Qaboos Cultural Center, Middle East Institute, 1990.

"Electricity Production (kWh)." *World Bank.* Accessed December 15, 2014. http://data.worldbank.org/indicator/EG.ELC.PROD.KH?order=wbapi_data_value_2011+wbapi_data_value&sort=desc.

Farag, Siham Gaber, Ibrahim H. Hashim, and Saad A. El-Hamrawy. "Analysis and Assessment of Accident Characteristics: Case Study of Dhofar Governorate, Sultanate of Oman." *International Journal of Traffic and Transportation Engineering* 3, no. 4 (2014): 189–198.

Fiennes, Ranulph. *Atlantis of the Sands: The Search for the Lost City of Ubar.* London: Bloomsbury, 1992.

Franssen, Herman. Remarks at "Oman 2010: 40 Years—Building the Future." Conference sponsored by the Sultan Qaboos Cultural Center and the Elliott School of International Affairs at George Washington University. Washington, DC, September 30, 2010.

Friedman, Uri. "Oman: The World's Hostage Negotiator." Passport. *Foreign Policy*, November 14, 2011. http://foreignpolicy.com/2011/11/14/oman-the-worlds-hostage-negotiator/.

Funsch, Linda Pappas. "Building a New Oman: The Hijab Factor." Speech presented at the Sultan Qaboos Cultural Center, Washington, DC, July 12, 2006 and June 24, 2008.

———. "The Convergence of Tradition and Modernization: Sultanate of Oman." Speech presented at the World Affairs Council, Washington, DC, June 26, 2007.

———. "Economy." *Frederick News-Post*, September 21, 2006. http://www.fredericknewspost.com/economy/article_134b2050-f0ac-11e2-a993-0019bb30f31a.html.

———. "Governing a Sultanate." *Frederick News-Post*, September 20, 2006. http://www.fredericknewspost.com/governing-a-sultanate/article_ed876f54-f0ab-11e2-a91b-0019bb30f31a.html.

———. "Legacy of US-Omani Bilateral Relations." Paper presented at the symposium *Oman in the Twenty-First Century*, Washington, DC, December 3, 2014.

———. "Oman Rediscovered." *Frederick News-Post* , September 23, 2006. http://www.fredericknewspost.com/oman-rediscovered/article_64de4a82-f0ac-11e2-8a77-0019bb30f31a.html.

———. "Oman's Unique Journey toward Modernization." Speech presented at the World Bank, Washington, DC, March 31, 2008.

———. "On the World's Stage." *Frederick News-Post*, December 18, 2011.

———. "Overview of Oman." Speech presented at the Sultan Qaboos Cultural Center, Washington, DC, June 12, 2008.

———. "The People of Oman." *Frederick News-Post*, September 19, 2006. http://www.fredericknewspost.com/the-people-of-oman/article_c04d75c4-f0ab-11e2-aeb4-0019bb30f31a.html.

———. "The Role of Women in Development in Oman." Presentations on panel discussions at the National Council on US-Arab Relations, Washington, DC, February 2012, February 2013, and February 2014.

———. "The Stage Is Set." *Frederick News-Post*, September 18, 2006. http://www.fredericknewspost.com/the-stage-is-set/article_0e0219c0-f0aa-11e2-a7a1-0019bb30f31a.html.

———. "U.S.-Omani Relations." *Frederick News-Post*, September 19, 2006. http://www.fredericknewspost.com/u-s--omani-relations/article_7c82379a-f0aa-11e2-9960-0019bb30f31a.html.

————. "Women and Economic Development in the Sultanate of Oman." Speech presented at the Center for Contemporary Arab Studies, Georgetown University, February 2009.

————. "Women in the New Oman." *Frederick News-Post*, September 22, 2006. http://www.fredericknewspost.com/women-in-the-new-oman/article_3ed2c6a6 -f0ac-11e2-b2ff-0019bb30f31a.html.

Gavin, James. "Why this Non-OPEC Gulf Country is Outpacing its GCC Neighbors' Economies." *Al Bawaba*, November 3, 2013. http://www.albawaba.com/ business/oman-economy-530933.

George, Ebby Chacko. "Oman Not to Join GCC Monetary Union." *Oman Daily Observer*, January 8, 2007.

al-Ghadani, Fahad. "Multiple Fines on Drivers to Help Curb Indiscipline in Oman." *Times of Oman*, October 18, 2014. http://www.timesofoman.com/News/ 41431/Article-Multiple-fines-on-drivers-to-help-curb-indiscipline-in-Oman.

Ghubash, Hussein. *Oman—The Islamic Democratic Tradition*. Hoboken: Taylor and Francis, 2014.

Haque, Faizul. "Power, Water Sector Targets Total Omanisation by 2019." *Times of Oman*, September 16, 2014. http://www.timesofoman.com/News/39942/ Article-Power-water-sector-targets-total-Omanisation-by-2019.

Harms, Robert W., Bernard K. Freamon, and David W. Blight, eds. *Indian Ocean Slavery in the Age of Abolition*. New Haven, CT: Yale University Press, 2013.

Harrison, Timothy S. "Memories of an American Missionary Family in the Persian Gulf." *Joint Archives Quarterly* 18, no. 3 (Fall 2008): 1–9.

Hatem, M. Abdel-Kader. *Land of the Arabs* New York: Longman Group, 1977.

Hawley, Donald. *Oman*. Rev. ed. London: Stacey International, 2005.

Hawley, Ruth. *Silver: The Traditional Art of Oman*. London: Stacey International, 2005.

Henzell, John. "Madha Village's Pledge of Allegiance Changed the Map Forever." *The National*, January 27, 2012. http://www.thenational.ae/lifestyle/ madha-villages-pledge-of-allegiance-changed-the-map-forever.

Highet, Juliet. *Frankincense: Oman's Gift to the World*. New York: Prestel Publishing, 2006.

Hill, Ann, and Daryl Hill. *The Sultanate of Oman: A Heritage*. London: Longman, 1977.

Hilton, Spud. "Oman Holiday: Formerly Sealed-Off Sultanate Offers Real Arabian Treasures." *SFGate*, March 30, 2008. http://www.sfgate.com/travel/article/ Oman-Holiday-Formerly-sealed-off-sultanate-3220408.php.

Hitti, Philip. *History of the Arabs*. New York: St. Martin's Press, 1967.

Hoch, Christopher. "The Strait of Hormuz: Potential for Conflict." *ICE Case Studies*. http://www1.american.edu/ted/ice/HORMUZ.htm.

Hoffman, Valerie J. *The Essentials of Ibadhi Islam*. Syracuse, NY: Syracuse University Press, 2012.

————. "Ibadi Islam: An Introduction." April 1, 2001. http://islam.uga.edu/ ibadis.html.

Holliday, Stuart W. "Oman at the Crossroads: The Development of Popular Participation in Government." *Middle East Insight* 12, no. 1 (November/December 1995): 69–71.

Holsbergen, Tonny. *Faces of Oman*. London: Motivate Publishing, 2006.

Holtz, Greta. C. "Building on the FTA." In *Oman: A Nation on the Move, 1970–2013*, 32. Muscat: United Press and Publishing, 2013. Accessed January 15, 2015.

http://www.readwhere.com/read/190213/A-Nation-on-the-Move/Oman-A-Nation-On-The-Move-1970-2013#page/32/2.

———. "Reaping Benefits of US-Oman Trade Pact." Special to the *Times of Oman*, December 1, 2013. http://www.timesofoman.com/News/Article-26421.aspx.

Hourani, G. F. *Arab Seafaring*. Rev. ed. Princeton, NJ: Princeton University Press, 1995.

Howk, Jason Criss. "Lions in the Path of Stability and Security: Oman's Response to Pressing Issues in the Middle East." Master's thesis, Naval Postgraduate School, 2008. OCLC (301318065).

Huntington, Samuel P. "The Clash of Civilizations?" *Foreign Affairs* 72, no. 3 (1993): 22–49.

Hurewitz, J. C. *Diplomacy in the Near and Middle East: A Documentary Record, 1535–1956*. Princeton, NJ: Van Nostrand, 1956.

Husain, Mir Zohair. *Global Islamic Politics*. New York: HarperCollins, 1995.

"Indian Ocean in World History." Sultan Qaboos Cultural Center. Accessed November 23, 2014. www.indianoceanhistory.org.

International Religious Freedom Report for 2013. United States Department of State, Bureau of Democracy, Human Rights, and Labor. http://www.state.gov/documents/organization/222519.pdf.

Iyer, Pico. "Arabian Heights." *Financial Times*, September 21, 2012. http://www.ft.com/cms/s/2/307fbe88-fd9b-11e1-8fc3-00144feabdc0.html.

Jackson, Robert. "Sailing through Time: Jewel of Muscat." *Saudi Aramco World*, May/June 2012. http://www.saudiaramcoworld.com/issue/201203/sailing.through.time.jewel.of.muscat.htm.

Jahn, Hanka, and Alessandro Gugolz. "Healthcare in the Sultanate of Oman." *Lex Arabiae*, January 2010. http://lexarabiae.meyer-reumann.com/blog/2010-2/healthcare-in-the-sultanate-of-oman/.

James, A. E. "Full Steam Ahead for Oman Railway." *Times of Oman*, February 6, 2014. http://www.timesofoman.com/News/Article-29401.aspx.

———. "Oman to Set Up Four New Solar Power Pilot Projects." *Times of Oman*, May 20, 2015. http://www.timesofoman.com/News/51972/Article-Oman-to-set-up-four-new-solar-power-pilot-projects.

———. "Water Desalination Capacity in Oman Set for 66% Jump." *Times of Oman*, March 1, 2014. http://www.timesofoman.com/News/30479/Article-Water-desalination-capacity-in-Oman-set-for-66-jump.

Johnson, E. Harper. *Oman: A Pictorial Resuscitation*. Muscat: Ministry of Information, Sultanate of Oman, 1997.

Jones, Jeremy. *Negotiating Change: The New Politics of the Middle East*. New York: I. B. Tauris, 2007.

Jones, Jeremy, and Nicholas Ridout. "Democratic Development in Oman." *Middle East Journal* 59, no. 3 (Summer 2005): 376–392.

———. *Oman: Culture and Diplomacy*. Edinburgh: Edinburgh University Press, 2012.

Joyce, Anne. "Interview with Sultan Qaboos bin Said Al Said." *Middle East Policy* 3, no. 4 (April 1995): 1–6.

Kanawati, Nouhad, Abla Kadi, Hind Masri, and Margaret Kapenga Shurdom. *Nizwa and Sohar 30 Years Ago: A Glimpse of the Past*. Lebanon: Chemaly & Chemaly, 2003.

Kapiszewski, Andrzej, Abdulrahman Al-Salimi, and Andrzej Pikulski. *Modern Oman: Studies on Politics, Economy, Environment and Culture of the Sultanate*. Krakow: Ksiegarnia Akademicka, 2006.

Kaplan, Robert. "The Indian Ocean World Order." *Real Clear World*, April 10, 2014, http://www.realclearworld.com/articles/2014/04/10/the_indian_ocean_world_order.html.

———. *Monsoon: The Indian Ocean and the Future of American Power*. New York: Random House, 2010.

Katz, Mark N. "In Oman's War-Torn Dhofar Region . . . Today Only 39 Rebels Remain." *Christian Science Monitor*, January 18, 1983. http://www.csmonitor.com/1983/0118/011848.html.

Katzman, Kenneth. "Oman: Reform, Security, and U.S. Policy." Congressional Research Service. December 27, 2013. http://www.fas.org/sgp/crs/mideast/RS21534.pdf.

———. "Oman: Reform, Security, and U.S. Policy." Congressional Research Service. March 4, 2008.

Kay, Shirley. *Enchanting Oman*. 1988. Dubai: Motivate Publishing, 2001.

Kechichian, Joseph A. *Oman and the World: The Emergence of an Independent Foreign Policy*. Santa Monica, CA: Rand, 1995.

———. *Political Participation and Stability in the Sultanate of Oman*. 2nd ed. Dubai: Gulf Research Center, 2006.

———. "A Vision of Oman: State of the Sultanate, Speeches by Qaboos bin Said, 1970–2006." *Middle East Policy* 15, no. 3 (2008): 112–133.

Kelly, Christopher. "Oman: Doing Localisation Right." *ArabianOilandGas.com*, June 1, 2014. http://www.arabianoilandgas.com/article-12539-oman-doing-localisation-right/2/.

Khalid, Matein. "Oman: Diplomacy and Economics in the Arabian Gulf." *Khaleej Times*, October 10, 2007. http://www.khaleejtimes.com/Display ArticleNew.asp?xfile=data/opinion/2007/October/opinion_October34.xml&section=opinion&col=.

Khan, Jemima. "Oman, Oh Boy." *Vanity Fair on Travel*, April 2012.

Khan, Sarah. "20. Oman." In "52 Places to Go in 2015." *New York Times*. Updated May 29, 2015. http://www.nytimes.com/interactive/2015/01/11/travel/52-places-to-go-in-2015.html?_r=0.

Knight, Sam. "Exclusive First Look: Hotel in Dramatic Location Opens in Oman." *Financial Times*, April 18, 2014. http://www.ft.com/cms/s/2/d2e126ce-c3bc-11e3-a8e0-00144feabdc0.html.

Kozlowska, Hanna. "Who Is the Shadowy Sultan That Shepherded the Nuclear Deal with Iran?" *Foreign Policy*, November 26, 2013. http://foreignpolicy.com/2013/11/26/who-is-the-shadowy-sultan-that-shepherded-the-nuclear-deal-with-iran/.

Kushnir, Ivan. *Gross Domestic Product (GDP) in Oman*. http://kushnirs.org/macroeconomics/gdp/gdp_oman.html#change.

al-Lamki, Salma M. "The Development of Human Resources in the Sultanate of Oman: Omanization and the Role of Women." Paper presented at the Sultan Qaboos Cultural Center, Washington, DC, June 22, 2006.

Landen, Robert Geran. *Oman Since 1856: Disruptive Modernization in a Traditional Arab Society*. Princeton, NJ: Princeton University Press, 1967.

Lawton, John. "The Sindbad Voyage." *Saudi Aramco World*, September/October 1981. http://www.saudiaramcoworld.com/issue/198105/the.sindbad.voyage.htm.

Lee, Samuel, trans. and ed. *The Travels of Ibn Battuta in the Near East, Asia & Africa, 1325–1354*. Mineola, NY: Dover, 2004.

Lefebvre, Jeffrey A. "Oman's Foreign Policy in the Twenty-First Century." *Journal of the Middle East Policy Council* 17, no. 1 (Spring 2010): 99–114. http://

mepc.org/journal/middle-east-policy-archives/omans-foreign-policy-twenty
-first-century?print.

Levenson, Jay, ed. *Encompassing the Globe: Portugal and the World in the 16th and 17th Centuries.* Washington, DC: Arthur M. Sackler Gallery, 2007.

Limbert, Mandana E. *In the Time of Oil: Piety, Memory and Social Life in an Omani Town.* Stanford, CA: Stanford University Press, 2010.

"Looming Danger: Public Health is Endangered by Our Lifestyles and Eating Habits." *Tawasul* [Academic bulletin published by Deanship of Research/ Sultan Qaboos University in cooperation with Oman News Agency, Muscat] no. 11 (February 2014): 12–14.

Luidens, Donald A. "Legacies of the Mission to Arabia." *Perspectives: A Journal of Reformed Thought* (March/April 2013). http://perspectivesjournal.org/blog/2013/03/01/legacies-of-the-mission-to-arabia/.

Lunde, Paul. "The Indian Ocean and Global Trade." Special issue of *Saudi Aramco World* 56, no. 4 (July/August 2005).

Maamiry, Ahmed Hamoud. *Oman and Ibadhism.* New Delhi: Lancers Books, 1980.

Mayer, Ralph. *The Artist's Handbook of Materials and Techniques.* New York: Viking, 1976.

McBrierty, Vincent, and Mohammad al-Zubair. *Oman: Ancient Civilization, Modern Nation.* Dublin: Trinity College/Muscat: Bait Al Zubair Foundation, 2004.

Middle East Desalinization Research Center, http://www.medrc.org/.

Miller, Judith. "Creating Modern Oman: An Interview with Sultan Qaboos." *Foreign Affairs* 76, no. 3 (May/June 1997): 13–18.

———. "The View from the Gulf: America's Quiet Go-Between Speaks." *Fox News.* Interview with Sultan Qaboos bin Sa'id, January 31, 2012. http://www.foxnews.com/world/2012/01/31/view-from-gulf-americas-quiet-go-between-speaks/.

Morris, Jan. "The Changing Face of an Old Friend." *Financial Times,* November 5, 2005. http://www.ft.com/intl/cms/s/0/241ba1a8-4da2-11da-ba44-0000779e2340.html.

———. *Sultan in Oman.* 1957. London: Eland, 2008.

Morris, Miranda, and Pauline Shelton. *Oman Adorned: A Portrait in Silver.* London: Apex Publishing, 1997.

Mozaffari, Mehdi. "What is Islamism? History and Definition of a Concept." *Totalitarian Movement and Political Religions* 8, no. 1 (March 2007): 17–33.

al-Munajjed, Mona, and Karim Sabbagh. *Youth in GCC Countries: Meeting the Challenge.* Booz and Co., 2011.

al-Musalmy, Shaddad. "Salalah Protesters Face Dilemma over Call to End Protests." *Muscat Daily,* April 2, 2011. http://www.muscatdaily.com/Archive/Stories-Files/Salalah-protesters-face-dilemma-over-call-to-end-protests.

"Muscat International Airport, Oman." *Airport-technology.com.* Accessed January 12, 2015. http://www.airport-technology.com/projects/muscat-airport/.

"Muscat Royal Opera House and Royal Oman Symphony Orchestra." *Gulf Art Guide.* Accessed November 13, 2014. http://gulfartguide.com/muscat/muscat-opera-house-oman-symphony-orchestra/#sthash.Eaqsetrd.dpuf.

Naik, Mrudu. "Will Women Make It to the Majlis Al Shura This Time?" *Times of Oman,* October 12, 2011.

Naim, Faisal Mohammed. "How 'Bout a Date? Oman's Most Favorite Fruit." *Times of Oman,* July 11, 2014. http://www.timesofoman.com/news/36492/Article-How-%E2%80%99bout-a-Date?-Omans-most-favourite-fruit.

Neubauer, Sigurd. "Oman: Advancing Modern Diplomacy, Celebrating Historic Shipbuilding Traditions." *Foreign Policy Journal,* March 16, 2013. http://www

.foreignpolicyjournal.com/2013/03/16/oman-advancing-modern-diplomacy
-celebrating-historic-shipbuilding-traditions/.

———. "Oman's Neutral Approach to Maritime Security." *Middle East Institute*,
June 18, 2013. http://www.mei.edu/content/omans-neutral-approach-maritime
-security.

Nicolini, Beatrice. *The First Sultan of Zanzibar: Scrambling for Power and Trade in
the Nineteenth-Century Indian Ocean.* Princeton, NJ: Markus Wiener Publishers,
2012.

Ochs, Peter J., II. *Maverick Guide to Oman.* 2nd ed. New York: Pelican, 2000.

Olson, Charles J. *Voices of Oman: A Different Mid-East Story, an Oral History of the
Oman Renaissance.* London: Stacey International, 2011.

"Oman 2010: 40 Years—Building the Future." Conference sponsored by the Sultan
Qaboos Cultural Center and the Elliott School of International Affairs at George
Washington University. Washington, DC, September 30, 2010.

Oman 2014 Crime and Safety Report. United States Department of State Bureau of
Diplomatic Security, Overseas Security Advisory Council (OSAC). February 20,
2014. https://www.osac.gov/pages/ContentReportDetails.aspx?cid=15191.

Oman: A Nation on the Move, 1970–2013. Muscat: United Press and Publishing,
2013.

"Oman 'An Irresistible Glow of Religious Pluralism.'" Hartford (CT) Seminary.
Accessed January 15, 2015. http://www.hartsem.edu/2013/01/oman-irresistible
-glow-religious-pluralism/.

Oman Daily Observer. "Al Rafd Fund Board Reviews Financing Procedures." December 3, 2014. http://www.gulfinthemedia.com/index.php?m=economics&id=72
8369&lim=&lang=en&tblpost=2014_12.

———. "Dried Up Aflaj and the Cost of Damage." April 15, 2014. http://main
.omanobserver.om/dried-up-aflaj-and-the-cost-of-damage/.

———. "Oman against Gulf States Union." December 8, 2013.

"Oman Free Trade Agreement." Free Trade Agreements. Office of the United
States Trade Representative. Accessed January 17, 2015. http://www.ustr.gov/
trade-agreements/free-trade-agreements/oman-fta.

The Omani Costumes. Muscat: Oman Women's Association, 2003.

"Oman in Interreligious Dialogue." Religious Tolerance: Islam in the Sultanate of
Oman. http://www.islam-in-oman.com/en/related/.

"Oman Inflation Rate: 2005–2014." *Trading Economics.* Accessed December 8,
2014. http://www.tradingeconomics.com/oman/inflation-cpi.

"Omani Shuwa—Eid November 6–7, 2011." YouTube video, 3:33. Posted by Antonio
Andrade, February 27, 2011. https://www.youtube.com/watch?v=s-p1DDz
UCAU.

Omani Sites on the World Heritage List. Office of the Adviser to His Majesty the
Sultan for Cultural Affairs. Accessed December 14, 2014. http://omanwhs.gov
.om/.

"Oman Medical City Is Taking Its First Step in 2016." *Middle East North Africa
Financial Network,* September 22, 2013. http://www.menafn.com/1093701
325/Oman-Medical-City-is-taking-its-first-step-in-2016?src=MOEN.

Oman: People and Heritage. Ruwi: Oman Daily Observer/ Oman Newspaper House,
1994.

"Oman to Go Ahead in Promoting Religious Tolerance, Foreign Ties" *Oman
Observer,* February 4, 2014.

O'Reilly, Marc J. "*Omanibalancing*: Oman Confronts an Uncertain Future." *Middle
East Journal* 52, no. 1 (Winter 1998): 70–84.

Othman, Saniya. *Tiflaki hatta al-Khamisah: dalil al-mar'ah al-'Arabiyah* [Your baby until the age of five: The Arabian woman's guide]. Beirut: Dar al-'Ilm, 1977.

"Overview on Desalinated Water in the Sultanate of Oman." Oman Power and Water Procurement Co. (SAOC). Accessed December 8, 2014. http://www.medrc .org/home/research/Overview.pdf.

Owtram, Francis. *A Modern History of Oman: Formation of the State since 1920.* London: I. B. Tauris, 2004.

Pereira, Shaly, and Jaya Ramesh. "Amouage—The Pride of Oman," *Mangalorean,* May 16, 2007. http://www.mangalorean.com/browsearticles.php?arttype=Feat ure&articleid=1012.

Peterson, J. E. "Oman Faces the Twenty-First Century." In *Political Change in the Arab Gulf States: Stuck in Transition,* edited by Mary Ann Tétreault, Andrzej Kapiszewski, and Gwenn Okruhlik, 99–118. London: Lynne Reinner Publishers, 2011.

———. *Oman in the Twentieth Century: Political Foundations of an Emerging State.* New York: Barnes & Noble, 1978.

———. "Oman's Diverse Society: Northern Oman" *Middle East Journal* 58, no. 1 (Winter 2004): 32–51.

———. *Oman's Insurgencies: The Sultanate's Struggle for Supremacy.* London: Saqi Books, 2008.

———. "Oman: Three and a Half Decades of Change and Development," *Middle East Policy* 11, no. 2 (Summer 2004): 125–137.

Petroleum Development Oman website. http://www.pdo.co.om/Pages/Home .aspx.

Peyton, W. D. *Old Oman.* London: Stacey International, 1983.

Phillips, Wendell. *Qataban and Sheba: Exploring the Ancient Kingdoms on the Biblical Spice Routes of Arabia.* New York: Harcourt, Brace, 1955.

Plekhanov, Sergey. *A Reformer on the Throne: Sultan Qaboos bin Said Al Said.* London: Trident Press, 2004.

Polo, Marco. *The Travels of Marco Polo.* New York: Grosset & Dunlap, n.d.

Popp, George. "Letter of Introduction" *Religious Tolerance: Islam in the Sultanate of Oman.* http://www.islam-in-oman.com/en/organization/introduction-tolerance -oman/.

Pourmohammadi, Elham. "Omani Landscape in Singapore Lane." *Times of Oman,* July 14, 2014, http://www.timesofoman.com/News/36652/Article-Omani -landscape-in-Singapore-lane.

Prabhu, Conrad. "US Firm Wins Duqm City Master-Plan Contract." *Oman Daily Observer,* October 17, 2011, 21.

Preston, Keith. "An Introduction to the Anthropomorphic Content of the Rock Art of Jebel Akhdar." *Journal of Oman Studies* 2 (1976): 17–38.

"Qaboos bin Said Condemns Reckless, High-Speed Driving." YouTube video, 5:56. Posted by Salim and Salimah, Safe and Sound, May 9, 2010. https://www .youtube.com/watch?v=ArHvTT4oyro.

Qabus bin Said. *The Royal Speeches of his Majesty Sultan Qaboos bin Said, 1970–2010.* [Muscat]: Ministry of Information, Sultanate of Oman, 2010.

al-Qareeni, Hamed bin Hashel. "Traffic Safety Institute Systematic Knowledge to Enhance Road Safety." Sultanate of Oman, Royal Oman Police, April 26, 2015. http://www.rop.gov.om/english/articledetails.asp?articleid=24.

al-Qasimi, Sultan bin Mohammad. *Deep-Seated Malice.* Translated by Gavin Watterson & Basil Hatem. London: Saqi Books, 2006.

Rabi, Uzi. *The Emergence of States in a Tribal Society: Oman under Sa'id bin Taymur, 1932–1970.* Brighton, UK: Sussex Academic Press, 2006.

Rajab, Jehan S. *Silver Jewelry of Oman.* Kuwait: Tareq Rajab Museum, 1997.

Range, Peter Ross. "Oman." *National Geographic,* May 1995, 112–138.

Rashad, Hoda, Magued Osman, and Farzaneh Roudi-Fahimi. *Marriage in the Arab World.* Washington, DC: Population Reference Bureau, 2005. http://www.prb .org/pdf05/marriageinarabworld_eng.pdf.

al-Rawahy, Aflah H. S. "Islamic Concept of Al-Shura and the Omani Model." Lecture presented in Virginia and Washington, DC, September 2000.

al-Rawas, Isam. *Oman in Early Islamic History.* Reading: Ithaca Press, 2000.

Richardson, Neil, and Marcia Dorr. *The Craft Heritage of Oman.* 2 vols. London: Motivate Publishing, 2004.

The Rilm [International Repertory of Music Literature] *Blog.* "The Sultan's Bagpipes," June 24, 2013, http://bibliolore.org/2013/06/24/the-sultans-bagpipes/.

Riphenburg, Carol J. *Oman: Political Development in a Changing World.* Westport, CT: Praeger Press, 1998.

"Road Safety Research Program." *The Research Council,* March 30, 2013. https:// home.trc.gov.om/tabid/314/language/en-US/Default.aspx.

Ruete, Emilie [née Sayyida, princess of Zanzibar and Oman]. *Memoirs of An Arabian Princess from Zanzibar.* New York: Markus Weiner, 1989.

Sabbagh, Suha. *Arab Women: Between Defiance and Restraint.* New York: Olive Branch Press, 1996.

Said, Edward W. *Orientalism.* New York: Random House, 1978.

———. "The Clash of Ignorance." *The Nation,* October 22, 2001.

Sambidge, Andy. "Oman Announces $1bn Medical City Project." *Arabian Business,* September 30, 2011. http://www.arabianbusiness.com/oman-announces-1bn -medical-city-project-422927.html.

al-Sarmi, Abdullah bin Mohammed. "From One University to 54 Higher Education Institutions: The Experience of Oman in Higher Education." *QS Showcase,* February 11, 2014. http://qsshowcase.com/main/from-one-university-to-54-higher -education-institutions-the-experience-of-oman-in-higher-education/.

Searle, Pauline. *Dawn over Oman.* 3rd ed. London: Allen & Unwin, 1979.

Severin, Tim. *The Sindbad Voyage.* New York: Little Brown and Company, 1998.

al-Shaibany, Saleh. "Disappointing Result for Women." *Times of Oman,* October 17, 2011.

———. "Oman Raises Minimum Wage to Avert Future Protests." *Al Arabiya News,* February 9, 2013. http://www.alarabiya.net/articles/2013/02/09/265333 .html.

Shaw-Smith, Peter. "Oman Affirms Schedule for Salalah and Muscat." *IHS Airport 360,* June 8, 2014. http://www.ihsairport360.com/article/4275/oman-affirms -schedule-for-salalah-and-muscat.

Siddani, Nouriya. *Tarih al-mar'ah al-'umaniyyah.* Kuwait: Matabi dar-assiyasah, 1984.

Skinner, Ray F. *Christians in Oman.* Morden, Surrey: Tower Press, 1996.

Solomon, Jay, and Carol E. Lee, "U.S.-Iran Thaw Grew from Years of Behind-the-Scenes Talks." *Wall Street Journal,* November 7, 2013. http://www.wsj.com/ articles/SB10001424052702303309504579181710805094376.

Sternberg, Esther. *Healing Places: The Science of Place and Well-Being.* Cambridge, MA: Belknap Press of Harvard University Press, 2009.

Stewart, Rhea Talley. "A Dam at Marib." *Saudi Aramco World*, March/April 1978. http://www.saudiaramcoworld.com/issue/197802/a.dam.at.marib.htm.

Sultanate of Oman. The Basic Statute of the State. Ministry of Legal Affairs. Royal Decree 96/101, 1996; Amended by Royal Decree 2011/99. Accessed January 14, 2015. http://www.mola.gov.om/eng/basicstatute.aspx.

———. "Family Tree of Sultan Qaboos," *The Sultanate of Oman*, http://www.sultanaatoman.nl/id27.htm.

———. *Higher Education Admission Statistics for the Academic Year 2011/2012*. [Muscat]: Ministry of Higher Education, Sultanate of Oman, 2012.

———. *Inclusive Education in the Sultanate of Oman*. [Muscat]: Ministry of Education, Sultanate of Oman, 2008. http://www.ibe.unesco.org/National_Reports/ICE_2008/oman_NR08.pdf.

———. *The Museum of the Frankincense Land: The History Hall*. [Muscat]: Office of the Adviser to His Majesty the Sultan for Cultural Affairs, Sultanate of Oman, 2007.

———. *The Museum of the Frankincense Land: The Maritime Hall*. [Muscat]: Office of the Adviser to His Majesty the Sultan for Cultural Affairs, Sultanate of Oman, 2007.

———. *National Report on Quality Education in Oman*. [Muscat]: Ministry of Education, Sultanate of Oman, 2004. http://www.ibe.unesco.org/International/ICE47/English/Natreps/reports/oman_part_1.pdf.

———. *Oman 2012–2013*. [Muscat]: Ministry of Information, Sultanate of Oman, 2012.

———. *Oman 2013–2014*. [Muscat]: Ministry of Information, Sultanate of Oman, 2013.

———. *Oman 2014–2015*. [Muscat]: Ministry of Information, Sultanate of Oman, 2014.

———. *Oman, A Seafaring Nation*. 3rd ed. [Muscat]: Ministry of Heritage and Culture, Sultanate of Oman, 2005.

———. *Women in Oman*. [Muscat]: Ministry of Foreign Affairs, Sultanate of Oman, 2010.

Sultanate of Oman. National Centre for Statistics and Information. Last modified December 2014. http://www.ncsi.gov.om/NCSI_website/N_statistics.aspx.

The Sultan Qaboos Grand Mosque. Muscat: Apex Publishing, 2001.

Takriti, Abdel Razzaq. *Monsoon Revolution: Republicans, Sultans, and Empires in Oman, 1965–1976*. New York: Oxford University Press, 2013.

Taylor, Bayard, ed. *Travels in Arabia*. Revised by Thomas Stevens. New York: C. Scribner's Sons, 1893.

Thesiger, Wilfred. *Arabian Sands*. New ed. Dubai: Motivate Publishing, 2010.

Times of Oman. "Al Rafd Fund Provides OMR14m Loan." June 6, 2014. http://www.timesofoman.com/News/34900/Article-Al-Rafd-Fund-provides-OMR14m-loan.

———. "Emerging Oman." July 23, 2013. http://www.timesofoman.com/News/Article-20243.aspx.

———. "Inflation in Oman Lowest in the GCC." July 12, 2014. http://www.timesofoman.com/news/36538/Article-Inflation-in-Oman-lowest-in-the-GCC.

———. "Iran Hails Its Strong Ties with Sultanate." December 7, 2013.

———. "Oman's Education Budget Clocks $3.38 Billion in 2013." July 5, 2014. http://www.timesofoman.com/News/36221/Article-Oman%E2%80%99s-education-budget-clocks-$3%2038-billion-in-2013.

———. "Oman's Population Passes Landmark Figure." April 23, 2014. http://www
.timesofoman.com/News/32830/Article-Oman%E2%80%99s-population
-passes-landmark-figure.

———. "Road Safety Campaign Goes Online." June 16, 2012. http://www.the
freelibrary.com/Road+safety+campaign+goes+online+conversation+with+Omani
+youth.-a0293263220

Townsend, John. *Oman: The Making of a Modern State*. London: Croon Helm,
1977.

"The Traditional Aflaj Irrigation System." *Nizwa.net*. Accessed January 10, 2015.
http://www.nizwa.net/agr/falaj/.

Trebay, Guy. "Story of Oman." *Travel and Leisure*, March 2007.

Tschannen, Rafiq A. "Oman: Majlis Approves Marriage Fund Panel Proposals." *Muslim Times*, May 29, 2011. http://www.themuslimtimes.org/2011/05/religion/
oman-majlis-approves-marriage-fund-panel-proposals.

US Central Intelligence Agency. "Oman." *The World Factbook*. Last modified June
22, 2014. https://www.cia.gov/library/publications/the-world-factbook/geos
/mu.html.

US Embassy in the Sultanate of Oman, "US-Oman FTA: A Win for Bilateral Trade,"
Times of Oman, July 4, 2013, http://www.timesofoman.com/Columns/1220/
Article-US-Oman-FTA-A-win-for-bilateral-trade.

US Energy Information Administration. *Oman*. Country Analysis Brief. Last modified December 5, 2014. http://www.eia.gov/countries/cab.cfm?fips=MU.

———. "Strait of Hormuz is Chokepoint for 20% of World's Oil." *Today in Energy*.
September 5, 2012. http://www.eia.gov/todayinenergy/detail.cfm?id=7830.

———. *World Oil Transit Chokepoints*. Last modified November 10, 2014. http://
www.eia.gov/beta/international/regions-topics.cfm?RegionTopicID=WOTC.

Vaidya, Sunil K. "Oman 'Regional Pioneer for Women's Rights.'" *gulfnews.com*,
March 9, 2008. http://gulfnews.com/news/gulf/oman/oman-regional-pioneer
-for-women-s-rights-1.90692.

Valeri, Marc. *Oman: Politics and Society in the Qaboos State*. New York: Oxford University Press, 2013.

Vine, Peter, and Paula Casey-Vine, eds. *Oman in History*. London: Immel Publishing, 1995.

Vision of Humanity, Institute for Economics and Peace, accessed January 17, 2015,
http://www.visionofhumanity.org/#page/indexes/global-peace-index/2011/
MRT,OMN/OVER.

Wagner, Daniel, and Giorgio Cafiero. "Oman Has Its Cake and Eats It Too—for
Now." *Real Clear World*, July 29, 2013. http://www.realclearworld.com/artic
les/2013/07/29/oman_has_its_cake_and_eats_it_too_--_for_now_105348
.html.

The Week. "Stress on Peace at Interfaith Week." February 6, 2014. http://www
.theweek.co.om/disCon.aspx?Cval=7646.

West, Ben. "Avoiding the 'Al-Bling' Environment." *Financial Times*, August 11, 2007.
http://www.ft.com/intl/cms/s/0/698f287a-47a3-11dc-9096-0000779fd2ac
.html#axzz3OvDkNu7b.

Wikan, Unni. *Behind the Veil in Arabia: Women in Oman*. Chicago: University of
Chicago Press, 2001.

Wilford, J. N. "On the Trail from the Sky: Roads Point to a Lost City." *New York
Times*, February 5, 1992. http://www.nytimes.com/1992/02/05/world/on
-the-trail-from-the-sky-roads-point-to-a-lost-city.html.

Wilkinson, John C. *Ibadhism: Origin and Early Development in Oman.* New York: Oxford University Press, 2010.

———. *The Imamate Tradition of Oman.* Cambridge, UK: Cambridge University Press, 2009.

William and Mary Blogs. "AKR in Oman #5: The Sultan's Tattoo." Blog entry by Anne Rasmussen, December 9, 2010, http://blogs.wm.edu/2010/12/09/akr -in-oman-5-the-sultan%E2%80%99s-tattoo/.

"World Development Indicators: The Information Society." Table 5.12. *World Bank.* http://wdi.worldbank.org/table/5.12.

World Health Organization. *Country Cooperation Strategy for WHO and Oman 2010–2015.* Cairo: WHO Regional Office for the Eastern Mediterranean, 2010.

———. *Global Status Report on Road Safety 2013: Supporting a Decade of Action* (Geneva: World Health Organization, 2013), 173.

Worrall, James. "Oman: The 'Forgotten' Corner of the Arab Spring." *Middle East Policy* 19, no. 3 (Fall 2012): 98–115.

———. *Statebuilding and Counterinsurgency in Oman: Political, Military and Diplomatic Relations at the end of Empire.* London: I. B. Tauris, 2014.

Zarins, Juris. *The Land of Incense: Archaeological Work in the Governorate of Dhofar, Sultanate of Oman, 1990–1995.* [Muscat]: Sultan Qaboos University, 2001.

al-Zedjali, Essa bin Mohammed. "Tangible Facts Behind Choice of Muscat as Arab Tourism Capital." *Times of Oman,* October 18, 2011. http://www .gulfinthemedia.com/index.php?m=opinions&id=577331&lim=&lang=en&tblp ost=2011_10.

Zwemer, Samuel M. "Notes on Oman." *National Geographic,* January 1911, 89–98.

INDEX